NH

Quest for a
Sustainable
Society

Pergamon Titles of Related Interest

Barney   THE GLOBAL 2000 REPORT TO THE PRESIDENT OF THE
          U.S.
Botkin/Elmandjra/Malitza   NO LIMITS TO LEARNING
Cleveland   THE MANAGEMENT OF SUSTAINABLE GROWTH
Feld   A VOICE CRYING IN THE WILDERNESS: Essays on the
          Problems of Science and World Affairs
Hill/Utterback   TECHNOLOGICAL INNOVATIONS FOR A DYNAMIC
          ECONOMY
Laszlo   THE INNER LIMITS OF MANKIND
Slappey   THE FUTURE OF BUSINESS — ANNUAL REVIEW 1980/81

Related Journals*

CONSERVATION AND RECYCLING
ENVIRONMENT INTERNATIONAL
THE ENVIRONMENTAL PROFESSIONAL
FUTURICS
GEOFORUM
HABITAT INTERNATIONAL
LONG RANGE PLANNING
UNDERGROUND SPACE
URBAN SYSTEMS

*Free specimen copies available upon request.

PERGAMON POLICY STUDIES ON BUSINESS AND ECONOMICS

Quest for a Sustainable Society

Edited by
James C. Coomer

Published in cooperation with
The Woodlands Conference

Pergamon Press
NEW YORK • OXFORD • TORONTO • SYDNEY • PARIS • FRANKFURT

Pergamon Press Offices:

U.S.A.   Pergamon Press Inc., Maxwell House, Fairview Park,
              Elmsford, New York 10523, U.S.A.

U.K.   Pergamon Press Ltd., Headington Hill Hall,
              Oxford OX3 0BW, England

CANADA   Pergamon Press Canada, Ltd., Suite 104, 150 Consumers Road,
              Willowdale, Ontario M2J 1P9, Canada

AUSTRALIA   Pergamon Press (Aust.) Pty. Ltd., P.O. Box 544,
              Potts Point, NSW 2011, Australia

FRANCE   Pergamon Press SARL, 24 rue des Ecoles,
              75240 Paris, Cedex 05, France

FEDERAL REPUBLIC   Pergamon Press GmbH, Hammerweg 6, Postfach 1305,
OF GERMANY   6242 Kronberg/Taunus, Federal Republic of Germany

Library of Congress Cataloging in Publication Data

Woodlands Conference on Growth Policy, 3d, 1979.
  Quest for a sustainable society.

  (Pergamon policy studies on business and economics)
  Selection of papers from the conference held
Oct. 28-31.
  1. Economic development—Congresses. 2. Stagnation
(Economics)—Congresses. I. Coomer, James C.,
1939-   . II. Title. III. Series.
HD73.W66 1979a   338.9   80-24158
ISBN 0-08-027168-5

Printed in the United States of America

For Jane and Alice.

Daily reminders that quality is better than quantity.

Contents

FOREWORD: The Woodlands Conferences on Growth
             Policy   ix

CHAPTER

1   Introduction: The Nature of the Quest
             for a Sustainable Society   1
             James C. Coomer

PART 1: THE ENVIRONMENT OF THE SUSTAINABLE
          SOCIETY

2   Diversity and the Steady State   13
             Paul R. Ehrlich

3   Social, Environmental, and Economic
             Implications of Widespread Conversion
             to Biomass-based Fuels   32
             Arthur A. Few, Jr.

4   Some Implications of Low Economic Growth
             Rates for the Development of Science
             and Technology in the United Kingdom 53
             Michael Gibbons

5   Science, Technology, and the Emerging
             Postindustrial Society   70
             Tom Stonier

PART 2:   QUALITATIVE COMPONENTS OF SUSTAINABLE
          SOCIETIES

   6   New Metaphors, Myths, and Values for a
                 Steady-State Future   89
                 Robert L. Chianese

   7   The Issue Is Human Quality: In Praise
                 of Children   103
                 James Garbarino

   8   Feeding the Transitional Society   124
                 Anne H. Ehrlich

PART 3:   INSTITUTIONAL MODIFICATIONS FOR A
          SUSTAINABLE SOCIETY

   9   World Politics and Sustainable Growth:
                 A Structural Model of the World
                 System   145
                 George Modelski

  10   Business Organizations in the Sustainable
                 Society   164
                 Dillard B. Tinsley

  11   Ecosystem Education: A Strategy for
                 Social Change   183
                 Edward T. Clark, Jr.
                 W. John Coletta

PART 4:   CONSEQUENCES OF SUSTAINABLE GROWTH:
          TWO CASE STUDIES

  12   Nature's Technology   211
                 David Hopcraft

  13   Lessons from the Coastline of America:
                 Management Strategies for a
                 Sustainable Society   225
                 Kathryn Cousins

Index   245

About the Editor   255

About the Contributors   257

NA

Foreword

In 1974 George P. Mitchell, President and Chairman of the Board of Mitchell Energy & Development Corp., resolved to set in motion a ten-year process to encourage the rethinking of growth policy, by sponsoring five biennial conferences and, with his wife Cynthia, offer the Mitchell Prize "to those individuals demonstrating the highest degree of creativity in designing workable strategies to achieve sustainable societies."

The first such Conference, in 1975, was the product of the quite sudden concern, in the early 1970s, about the physical limits to growth. The question posed was: ". . . how might a modern society be organized to provide a good life for its citizens without requiring ever-increasing population growth, energy resource use, and physical output?"(1) In the autumn of 1977, the Second Woodlands Conference, still viewed as a part of a continuing effort to define a "steady-state society," focused on alternatives to growth.

Meanwhile, academic researchers, business analysts, and government planners - in both industrial and developing countries - were asking hard questions not only about the consequences of indiscriminate economic growth, but also about a "no-growth" philosophy based on the prospective exhaustion of nonrenewable resources. By this time, renewable "bioresources" and expandable "information resources," added to new estimates of the future availabilities of even the nonrenewable resources, made some continuing economic growth possible - and the fairer distribution of wealth and income made it clearly necessary.

The United States and, indeed, other industrial societies seemed already to be in transition toward a new concept of growth policy that would be neither indiscriminate material growth (measured by GNP) nor "no-growth" (also measured by GNP). Public attention, therefore, shifted toward the more complex and integrative questions of purpose and human needs - "Growth for what?" "Growth for whom?" - and toward the apparent incapacity of social institutions to cope with the complexities of affluence, inflation, and fairness.

In planning the Third Woodlands Conference, responsibility for management was placed in the hands of the University of Houston. David Gottlieb, sociologist and dean of social sciences, became its chief administrator and James C. Coomer, political scientist and professor in the Future Studies program at the University's Clear Lake campus served as executive officer for the Woodlands Conference.

The original sponsors (Mitchell Energy and Development Corporation and the University of Houston) then brought into consultation and cosponsorship John and Magda McHale, whose Center for Integrative Studies had been moved to the University of Houston, and the Aspen Institute for Humanistic Studies, whose Program in International Affairs had been collaborating with the McHales in a series of studies on basic human needs, supply potential, and the dynamics of development.

The Third Conference, held at The Woodlands (near Houston) from October 28 to 31, 1979, was the culmination of an eighteen-month process that generated ten commissioned Mitchell Award papers, nine winning open-competition Mitchell Prize papers, and eight advance workshops. These included consultations in Europe, Japan, and Mexico; meetings in Houston of experts on bioresources, work and education, information and communications, the economics of the future and the future of economics; and a summer workshop on "The Limits to Government," held in Aspen, Colorado. In 1978 and 1979, this was certainly the nation's broadest, deepest, and most exciting nongovernmental inquiry on growth policy.

The present volume(2) brings together the nine prize-winning papers from the 1979 Mitchell Prize competition and three papers that were finalists in the competition but did not win a cash award. The editor of this volume is grateful to those who served as judges for the 1979 Mitchell Prize competition: Robert Cahn, Environmental Writer; Murray Comarow, Distinguished Adjunct Professor in Residence, The American University; Robert W. Crosby, Department of Transportation; Victor C. Ferkiss, Professor of Government, Georgetown University; Peter Henriot, Director, Center of Concern: Michael Michaelis, Authur D. Little, Inc.; John M. Richardson, Jr., Center for Technology and Administration, The American University; Bruce Stokes, Worldwatch Institute; Albert H. Teich, Graduate Program in Science, Technology, and Public Policy, The George Washington University; Irene Tinker, Director, Equity Policy Center; and the Right Rev. John Thomas Walker, Diocese of Washington.*

It is not to be expected that a book authored by 13 strong-minded scholars from a variety of disciplines and from different parts of the world could, or would, present a monolithic view of what is wrong with the world's growth policies and what should be done about them. There is, however, a striking agreement on the propositions that sustainable growth is physically attainable and morally imperative.

The theme of these papers is diversity: diversity in approaches; diversity in priorities; the need for continued diversity in culture, values, and economic and political systems; and diversity on how to maintain diversity.

The hard part, all seem to agree, is managing ourselves. The quest for the sustainable society is finding ways to make complex decisions that do not require government to handle all aspects of governance for a necessarily pluralistic society in an increasingly interdependent world. Lao Tzu said it centuries ago: "Ruling a big country is like cooking a small fish," i.e., too much handling will spoil it.

James C. Coomer
Harlan Cleveland

NOTES

(1) Dennis L. Meadows, ed., Alternatives to Growth-I: A Search for Sustainable Futures (Cambridge, Mass.: Ballinger, 1977), p. xvii.

(2) In a companion volume edited by Harlan Cleveland, the key commissioned papers, together with two keynote statements, are published with a contextual introduction by the editor. That book is entitled The Management of Sustainable Growth, and is also published by Pergamon Press.

---

*Affiliation is for identification purposes only.

1 Introduction:
The Nature of the Quest
for a Sustainable Society
James C. Coomer

One of the unique qualities that separates man from the other animals on this planet is his capacity for self-transcendence: the ability to make himself his own object. Man can stand "outside himself" and evaluate where he has been and a direction in which he is moving. He can assess his impact upon those things which are around him and he can adapt to changes, either self-generated or externally imposed. Those changes in man's environment that are self-generated can be examined to determine if the changes are beneficial or detrimental to his existence. If beneficial, the change is held to be an advancement; if detrimental, a catastrophe. In his capacity to transcend himself, man has learned that some changes in his environment which were once embraced as beneficial have, over time, become catastrophic. Upon learning this, man has attempted to find an equitable relationship with the physical environment so that he will not generate changes that may seriously impair that which sustains him. Seeking that equitable relationship is the perpetual quest for a sustainable society. That sustainable society is one that lives within the self-perpetuating limits of its environment. That society, contrary to some popular opinion, is not a "no-growth" society. It is, rather, a society that recognizes the limits of growth. It is not a society that continues to seek alternatives to growth. It is, rather, a society that looks for alternative ways of growing.

The sustainable society recognizes that there is one primary environment - the physical environment - within which all other environments function. All other environments - political, social, economic, to name three major ones - exist within and act upon the primary environment.

The quest for the sustainable society entails a continual evaluation of a variety of social, economic, and political

1

events.   Many of these events, precipitated by or evolving
within the nation-states of the world, are viewed as "internal"
matters to be managed within some sovereign state.   The
peoples of the world are learning, however, some painfully,
that there are no longer discrete social, economic, or political
problems to be solved one at a time and at a leisurely pace.
The problems of the world's people are interrelated because all
draw sustenance from the same source, the Earth's physical
environment.   The seriousness of the interrelated problems are
compounded by two things: (1) the Earth is not conscious of
time and (2) nation-states are not designed to handle
horizontal problems.
     Within the life cycle allotted most of the Earth's in-
habitants, they must sustain and protect themselves using the
resources that are at hand.   As their numbers increase, the
use of resources increases and, although one resource may be
sufficient to sustain and protect the inhabitants through
several generations, the regenerative processes of the earth,
considerable though they may be, demand millions of years for
reproduction.   As a consequence, the history of mankind is a
history of consuming one resource after another to sustain,
protect, and perpetuate itself so that consequently, and within
a geological time frame a very short period of time, mankind
has threatened the very resource system it is dependent upon
for survival.
     The second thing that compounds the difficulty in the
quest for solving the world's problems is that societies of
individuals in various sections of the world have organized
themselves within homogeneous communities with designated
boundaries.   All of these societies have traditionally declared
that their primary responsibilities are to those within their
boundaries.   Those without must look out for their own needs.
     The various ways in which the communities of the world
have sustained and protected themselves with whatever resources were available and governed themselves with whatever
structure was maintained have, over generations, become a
part of that society's "way of life."   Any suggestion that what
has always been may not always be is perceived by many to be
a threat to a way of life that one has been taught and condi-
tioned to support all of one's life.   Social, economic, and
political infrastructures have developed over time to not only
support but to benefit from the way things have always been.
Change is usually believed to be negative and not positive.
But ready or not, the world must get ready for change.   One
way to do this is to know where to look for change.   Fore-
warned is forearmed as the old adage put it.
     One key aspect of growth change in the future will simply
be number of people.   The United States population growth has
slowed during the past two decades.   One might expect an
increase of about 15 percent over the next twenty years.

While the population growth is stabilizing, however, population character is changing; there is an increase in the number of people in the older age range. This is important because it offers a different connotation to growth policies in the United States than in the developing world where the population continues to increase with ever growing numbers of younger people.

What changes can the United States expect because of a stabilizing growth rate? Many of the physical structures and facilities to serve the United States population are already in place, which means, for example, there will be a shrinkage in the demands for educational facilities for the lower age ranges in the next two decades. Level and composition of the work force will change considerably with problems of unemployment and underemployment particularly. The major issues of the society will become those of retraining, retirement, pensions, social security, and all of the services that we require in our society for an aging population rather than a younger population - the opposite of the services needed in the developing nations.

What critical issues for American business underlie population decline or stabilization? All businesses that cater particularly to a younger population will experience change. A decline will come in the nursery industry, baby foods, toys, and all manner of infant services. In the United States, teenage and young adult markets will similarly shrink in the next two decades.

One interesting economic implication is that with less than 1 percent of population growth per year and a more stable and older population, lower economic growth rates may, indeed, be normal for the highly industrialized economies like the United States, with a resulting decelerating demand for energy and materials.

Apart from energy, the United States can sustain its population's needs for physical resources. Most of the metals and minerals required for the United States economy are price sensitive rather than reserve sensitive and the country is practically autonomous with regard to the kinds of metals and minerals needed. Nevertheless, most of the growth debate in the past decade has been preoccupied with the continuation, in industrialized countries like the United States, of high material demands and consumption approaching exponential levels and leading inevitably to resource scarcities and high environmental deterioration. These problems soon cease to be internal problems of nation-states and come to be the interrelated problems of the world community.

There are some signs that industrial countries are more aware of resource scarcity than most of the literature gives them credit for. The most critical literature on resource depletion has failed to take into account many technical and

resource changes. For example, the changing profile of resource needs becomes very marked as the technologies change;
the expandable nature of many reserves, increased recycling,
increased energy and materials intensity of use are particularly
apparent in the United States. There has been a growing
attempt to do much more for people with far less energy and
far fewer materials. One might hypothesize that, in the
United States, even with high living standards and a majority
of people at or above sufficiency levels, satiation or stabilization for many resource demands (with the possible exception of
energy), could be reached within two decades. To do this,
two key technological shifts are critical: one is the emergence
of information as the ultimate social resource, and the other is
the growing importance of the bioresources and biotechnologies
that are now emerging as the leading edge of innovation in
advanced industries.

Information as a resource has several surprise features
that are usually not associated with resource use. All other
resources are ultimately dependent upon information and communications for their recognition, evaluation, and use. In
addition, as a resource, information is not reduced or lessened
by wider use and sharing as are other resources. Its peculiar
quality is that it tends to gain in the process of being used.
Information/communication can also replace or reduce consumption of other resources either directly, by symbolic
substitutions, or by identifying other physical substitutions or
alternative resource uses. These three qualities are critical.
Where other resource bases, such as raw materials and energy, are by comparison potentially depleted, information and
knowledge, organized knowledge, are potentially inexhaustible.
The more you use it the bigger the supply becomes. The
properties of this new resource, or this new dimension of the
resource range, have profound implications for the structure
of our society and for the structure of our society's economy.
In advanced economies, such as the United States, the prime
innovation and growth sectors are already in what one would
call the electromagnetic spectrum industries: electronics,
telecommunications, computers, and automated equipment. As
these industries grow, they increase their energy efficiency.
Over a period of five to ten years, there is a tremendous
capacity in these industries to do much more with much less.
It has recently been calculated that information handling and
symbolic transfers in the United States now account for up to
30 percent of the GNP.

Information workers now overshadow most other kinds of
workers in the economy. Information use transfers and inter-
linkages have become a central nervous system which ties
together the whole economy. It ties together extraction,
production, commerce, banking investment, corporate organization, education, government, entertainment, and culture.

In many senses, the changed information environment itself has already had considerably unanticipated impact on both the United States policy and the economy. From the Pentagon Papers to ABSCAM there is an information debate that reverberates throughout the society: rights of consumers; questions on proprietary ownership of resource data, from military documents to personal financial disclosures. The structure of the business economy itself has been altered as new kinds of systems change the flow and immediacy of market data; industrial organization, productivity, and employment are only examples. One could hypothesize that the increased dependence on information and knowledge as central social resources will move U.S. society, particularly during the next few years, toward new kinds of institutions, new kinds of organizations, and other changes we can only speculate about at the moment. There has been and continues to be a curious lack of official policy in this regard, although the phrase, "the information society," has been floating about for the past ten years.

The second area which may have critical importance in the quest for sustainability is the emerging biotechnical revolution. Understanding this revolution and its potential consequences is compounded by the enormously wide spectrum of discoveries and processes. Ranging from greater uses of solar power for energy, through enhancement of photosynthesis to grow more food, to the use of microorganisms in increasingly diverse ways, the potential uses of biology in heretofore limited ways may be one of the keys to developing a sustainable society. Although it has been used for thousands of years in agriculture - food and drink fermentation and the use of bees and silkworms - the impetus toward becoming a new kind of industrial base has emerged particularly from the spectacular advances in biochemistry, microbiology, and genetics in the past few decades. One can now begin to see the outlines of a new, integrated biochemical, microbiological industry occurring at the world level. These outlines are represented by things like fuel production by plants providing alternative energy supply; the extraction of hydrocarbons from forestry products and agricultural wastes (an equivalent to the petrochemical industry); and hydrogeneration on large scale through photochemical means.

The impact of this biotechnological potential is less immediate than the information/communication developments. There is, however, a great deal of work underway: a sweetener made from field corn by enzymatic action; the oil and chemical industry spending approximately $500 million in single-cell protein development; farming of bacteria, yeast, and algae to produce feedstocks and human foods; a $3 billion investment by Brazil on alcohol plants to replace 20 percent of its gasoline consumption by 1985; Volkswagen investing heavily in research and development of an alcohol-powered car using biosources for that alcohol. These kinds of research investments, increasing as the quest expands for alternative ways of growing, are likely to impact significantly on the world's economies during the next decade.

If one limited one's prospects for change in the future to only these two areas, the information/communication area and the biotechnological developments, the growth questions for the highly industrialized countries might no longer be physical limits to growth in terms of sustainable future growth. Potentially, these countries may no longer be faced with a problem of a limited, fixed resource pie to be divided or a finite resource pool to be exhausted. There are now possibilities that, with the right kind of policies, a myriad of growth directions could be stimulated, based on an entirely new range of renewable and regenerative support systems. The question of sustainability is related to going about it in the right way. The central question is not so much technological, but how one may more directly relate physical, economic, and social growth to the actual needs of people. It is not a management of the environment; it is rather, a management of those myriad activities that impact on the environment. One could argue that this is a self-evident proposition. One often assumes that organizations are designed for the needs of people, that growth has to do primarily with the state of the nation, the health of the economy, or the production system; with business progress or the protection of the environment. One forgets that growth really has to do with human needs.

The range of human needs beyond affluence or sufficiency that one finds in the developed countries are much less materially defined than the sort of basic human needs one finds in underdeveloped countries. The needs in the industrial countries are much more qualitative needs: the need for meaningful work, for achievement, for affection, for security, respect, social justice and equity, and for those kinds of needs for self-realization and personal growth which determine the whole sum qualities of life's experiences. When one talks about sustainable growth for a society, one ultimately talks about how that growth is perceived and sensed, and how it may be realized in individual terms.

Individuals are now asking hard questions, not only about how society should grow but for what kind of purposes and for whom? This is evidenced by a series of trends which have now become apparent. One of these trends is the concerns that have been articulated over the past ten years regarding the quality of the physical and social environment; the quality of education, the quality of urban life, the quality of society. Material equity and justice are still pursued and still pursued vociferously, but the key debates which have traumatized the United States particularly for the past ten years have not been about material issues at all. They have been about the ethical uses of the power of the presidency; that traumatic division of the nation on the morality of a war; the right to live, work, and to be educated without discrimination; and the resistance to a growing invasion of personal privacy.

The significance of these debates and protests suggests that, philosophically, as people move toward a sustainable society at very high standards of living, large groups of society become preoccupied with issues that are nonmaterial. They begin to have the leisure and the security to focus on the philosophical issues, the ethical issues of how society is to be organized and administered. That, in my judgment, is one of the great hopes in questing for and moving toward a sustainable society. There is, in this movement, a shift from things to people. Once one has reached a certain adequacy in one's standard of living, once one moves above a sufficiency level, one is no longer worried so much about the things that sustain survival. As material goods become much more freely available, their value and importance to people decline. By way of illustration, let me suggest that previous generations prized things that were unique and enduring beyond a personal lifetime. These "heirlooms" were handed down from one generation to the next. So many of the things that the present generation has, uses, or wears are simply expendable. Little value is attached to them. In the past, people were expendable, things were unique. Today, particularly in the developed countries, the focus of concern has turned toward the human being rather than the things which subtend human survival. Goods, therefore, are expendable, people are unique.

In terms of work and the work ethic, whereas in the past material possessions were the goal for striving and the mark of life attainment, they are now much less important. Human development begins to be prized above material investment. This is expressed in a variety of ways although not every one agrees with all of them. These ways would include the human potential and awareness movement; the renewed concern for the family and child development; and a more sensitive awareness of the aging experience. There is also the declining role of racial stereotyping, which is another kind of facet of this value shift as people seek to be less limited by sex, minority, or occupational role and to seek more individualized and qualitative lifestyle commitments according to their personal predilections.

One other trend is the reevaluation of work toward intrinsic satisfactions and interests. Work is now seen by more people in the developed world as providing meaning and self-fulfillment as well as providing economic well-being. There is a demand for participation by those who work, not only in how work is organized but in what is actually being produced by their work.

Underlying these trends, particularly in the United States society, is a questioning of the traditional production and consumption patterns that have developed as an industrialized America developed. These patterns evolved and were developed to meet the demands of a much different era and considerably different socioeconomic conditions. There are indications that, almost immediately, there will be less need to expand consumer product ranges by businesses. People, on the whole, no longer seem to want or expect more of the same. Business has become accustomed to and extremely efficient in doing what the public seems to have wanted for a very long time. That will all change. People are beginning to reject the idea that more might be better. That is a little against the business traditions of most developed countries.

One should be neither surprised nor alarmed by these societal and value changes. The perpetual quest for the sustainable society continually generates change. The only thing different about the present transition is the time frame in which it is taking place. More change is happening in one lifetime than most people are prepared to accommodate, physically or emotionally. That does not impede the change, however, only our capacity to deal with it. The trends outlined above are only scattered evidence of a much more fundamental transition in our society, not only in the United States but in the whole of Western society. There is a basic change underway in the ways in which we organize our social, political, and economic life. The world is moving into a very strange and unprecedented transition. It obviously will not be an easy one. We are entering a period of extraordinary dissidence and uncertainty accompanied by an enormously enhanced capacity for self-destruction within society unless we are able to guide and control it with adequate policies. The implications of these trends for the sustainable society are:

1. The redirection and rediversification of growth itself has already become a major social, political, and economic issue. It is not merely a question of alternatives to growth but of alternative ways of growing.
2. The continued technological growth direction is sustainable with lower investments of energy and materials and lower environmental impacts. The new ranges of electronics and the biotechnologies afford new modes of wealth generation which are relatively parsimonious and much more in harmony with the kinds of preferred qualities of life that are now being articulated around the world. Society possesses the physical means and resource possibilities to provide qualitatively high standards and styles of life to meet an even wider range of human needs and preferences than we now have.

3.   The essential challenge, then, for the next decade is to
     create the requisite sets of purposes. This is particular-
     ly what is presently lacking; new kinds of sets of
     socioeconomic roles, new political and institutional ar-
     rangements through which we may use these means to
     pursue new growth directions. And, then, to turn that
     kind of pursuit into a major social purpose in itself.

     The quest for the sustainable society continues unabated
by protest, threats, or misunderstandings. This book is
simply a chronicling of thoughts and activities of some actively
engaged in the quest. The purpose is to emphasize that, no
matter the task, they are all interrelated; no matter the
problem, they are all interdependent; no matter the goals, the
ultimate objective is the same, survival with meaning. That is
what makes the quest for the sustainable society not only
exciting, but essential.

I

THE ENVIRONMENT OF THE SUSTAINABLE SOCIETY

0114
7220

2 Diversity and the Steady State
Paul R. Ehrlich

In the world of biology, as in the world of
finance, diversity is the only protection
against the unknown, against a future risk situation.

J. A. Browning, 1974

The diversity of nonhuman organisms and the genetic, cultural,
and technological diversity of our own species are crucial to
the future health, happiness, and perhaps even survival of
humanity. Therefore, those concerned with planning for a
transition from today's growth-oriented society to a society
that might persist over the long term must give careful consideration to the roles played by various kinds of diversity in
human affairs, how diversity can be maintained, and how
diversity can be regenerated once it has been lost. This
essay attempts to provide a starting point for such consideration.

DIVERSITY OF ANIMALS, PLANTS, AND MICROORGANISMS

Civilization is utterly dependent upon the ecological systems of
the earth for a wide range of essential "public services."
These include moderation of the weather, maintenance of the
quality of the atmosphere, operation of the hydrological cycle,
production and preservation of soils, recycling of nutrients
critical to both agricultural and natural ecosystems,(1) disposal
of wastes, provision of food from the sea, control of more than
95 percent of all potential pests of crops and vectors of human
disease, and the maintaining of a vast genetic library from

which may be drawn new domesticated animals and plants, antibiotics, medicines, spices, and organisms for biomedical research. In many cases, the way in which the systems work(2) is not precisely known, and the technical know-how to substitute for these services in the event of ecosystem break-down is unavailable. In virtually all cases, if the requisite knowledge were available, it would not be possible to replace the services on the vast scale required.

The living components of these essential ecological systems are the between 2 and 10 million species (kinds) of organisms estimated to inhabit our planet. Most of these organisms carry on their jobs day in and day out unknown to the vast majority of human beings - indeed, most are unknown even to science in the sense that they have not yet been named and described. They include such unsung organisms as the predaceous mites that eat the eggs of plant-eating insects which might otherwise have populations so large that they would be pests. They include myriads of tiny arthropods, bacteria, fungi, and other organisms that break down wastes, and recycle nutrients, and make the soil fertile. They include green plants that have evolved complex organic chemicals to poison herbivores, chemicals that Homo sapiens put to such diverse uses as anti-cancer drugs and pesticides.

Nonhuman organisms play important roles in the running of complex biogeochemical cycles such as the nitrogen cycle - cycles whose proper functioning is essential to virtually all forms of life on earth including human life. Careful studies have shown how living systems control these cycles, changing inputs and controlling outputs so that, in the absence of gross disturbance, the cycles run in a predictable manner year in and year out.(3) Studies have also shown the catastrophic consequences for these cycles (such as losses of nutrients from the system) that the disturbance of an ecosystem can entail.(4)

Species diversity - that is, the diversity of <u>kinds</u> of organisms - is essential to the provision of ecosystem services. There are many different roles that are performed in the functioning of complex ecosystems; ecologists generally refer to these roles as "niches." They may be thought of as the characteristic ways in which a component organism obtains the resources it requires. But a species that can occupy a given niche in a tropical rain forest may be totally unsuited to play an analogous role in a tropical seasonal forest, to say nothing of a temperate grassland or coral reef.

A great deal is known about the overall organization of ecological systems, the general kinds of niches present, broad energy pathways, gross nutrient inputs and outputs, and so forth. For example, major ecosystems can be divided into a series of trophic (feeding) levels. The first trophic level is that of producers - green plants that bind the energy of the sun into organic molecules that can fuel the life processes of plants, animals, and microorganisms. The binding process, photosynthesis, is reasonably well understood, but scientists have not yet reproduced it in the laboratory. Energy and nutrients flow from producers to the next trophic level, that of the herbivores; after that come one or more levels of carnivores.

A critically important trophic level with links to all the others (which may process as much as 90 percent of the productivity of the producers) is that of the decomposers - small plants, animals, and microorganisms that make their living by extracting energy from the chemical molecules of the remains and wastes of other organisms. In the process, decomposers free nutrients which can once again be taken up by plants and thus recycled in the economy of the ecosystem. Energy proceeds through ecosystems in a one-way flow in which the availability of the energy to run life processes is continually and rapidly reduced. Materials, on the other hand, tend to move in cyclical paths through ecosystems.

While this basic "black box" structure of many ecosystems is known, the details of how the component species interact with each other ecologically and how they evolve in response to each other are generally not well understood. Niches are not static; they are in constant flux as population sizes vary and populations are transformed genetically - and it is extremely difficult to predict the consequences of these changes for the functioning of the entire system. Indeed, trying fully to understand a natural ecosystem is like trying to unravel the complexities of a gigantic computer that someone else has built and that cannot be disassembled for study. The problem of understanding is especially difficult because an ecosystem computer is one in which the numbers of each kind of component are perpetually changing, and in which the characteristics of each kind of component are also continually evolving in response to changes in the other kinds of components. One important result of these problems is that the relationship of the diversity of organisms in an ecosystem to the stability of that ecosystem is one of the most widely discussed and debated topics in population biology.(5)

Lacking full understanding of the earth's ecosystem computers but knowing they are essential to human life, ecologists generally tend to take a conservative view of their disruption. While it is true that removing certain components and altering others may not lethally disrupt the functioning of the system, the state of knowledge at the moment does not, in most cases, allow prediction of what can be safely disturbed. Indeed the only general prediction that can be made is that, if enough components are deleted or altered, eventually the entire system will collapse.

Considerable attention has already been drawn to the potential economic value of many species that are being driven to extinction. Almost half of modern drugs have natural origins in plants, yet only a tiny minority of plants have been screened for possible medically-useful compounds. Conservationist Norman Myers, writing of the tropical forests alone, stated that it is "a statistical certainty that [they] contain source materials for many pesticides, medicines, contraceptives and abortifacient agents, potential foods, beverages and industrial products."(6) The potential of the largely unknown alkaloids of tropical plants for the treatment of diseases ranging from hypertension to cancer might, in themselves, more than economically justify the preservation of Amazonia, African forests, and the remnants of tropical forests elsewhere. Compelling (as well as compassionate and esthetic) as these reasons seem to be for preserving species diversity, they are secondary to the problem of maintaining other ecosystem functions. Society could persist without new pesticides and anti-cancer chemicals. It might not survive widespread breakdown of biogeochemical cycles, rapid climatic changes, collapse of oceanic fisheries, or other catastrophic loss of ecosystem services.

GENETIC DIVERSITY

It is not only important that species themselves be preserved, but it is also important that genetic variability within the species be preserved. Genetic variability is essential to the capacity of a species to evolve in response to environmental change. Since environments are always changing, this means that the preservation of genetic variability is esential to the preservation of species. The problem of the loss (or, as it is more technically described, the decay) of genetic variability has received most attention in connection with crops.(7)

In nature, plants and herbivores (and plant pathogens) are engaged in a continuous stepwise evolutionary battle.(8) The plants' enemies are perpetually evolving new methods of attack to counter the constantly evolving defenses of the plants. Crops, likewise, are involved in a "coevolutionary race" with the pests and diseases that attack them. A resistant strain of a crop will produce high yields only until an organism that attacks the crop evolves ways of overcoming the resistance.

With domesticated plants, it is up to plant geneticists to create new resistant strains when the defenses of an old strain are breached. The raw material with which the plant breeders must work is genetic variability - variability that once was available in abundance in the multitudinous strains of the major crops that were planted all over the world, and in the wild ancestors and relatives of those crops.(9) In recent decades, however, in part as a result of the Green Revolution, the diversity of crop strains has been greatly reduced. In some areas of Turkey, for example, where numerous varieties of wheat used to be planted, now only one "miracle" strain can be found.

The problem is worldwide. In 1972, a committee of the U.S. National Academy of Sciences announced that "most major crops are impressively uniform genetically and impressively vulnerable."(10)   Simultaneously, habitat destruction and chemical herbiciding are reducing the availability of the wild progenitors and relatives of crop plants. This decay of genetic variability of crops is one of the least recognized but most important factors in the deterioration of the human environment. If it goes too far, Homo sapiens will be permanently out of the business of high-yield agriculture - an unprecedented catastrophe unless the size of the human population has been reduced to around two billion or less before it occurs.

While the problem of the decay of genetic variability in crops and, to a lesser degree, in domestic animals is recognized by many, the parallel problem in wild species has received must less attention. In the minds of many, conservation means simply the preservation of species, which, in turn, means keeping a minimum population of a particular kind of organism extant. But, for sexually-reproducing organisms, every population potentially represents a unique gene pool, adapted to local environmental conditions and often having distinctive morphology, behavior, and ecological relationships.(11) Every time such a population is forced to extinction, the ability of the species to persist is jeopardized, both because the species population is reduced in numbers and geographic distribution and because the total genetic variability theoretically available to the species at that time is reduced.

Although in the short and medium term there is little danger that Homo sapiens will become extinct, there are reasons to believe that, over the long term, care should be taken to maintain the genetic variability of our own species. The ability of humanity to evolve genetically depends ultimately on its store of genetic variability, at least until scientific advance can provide the technology for direct intervention in the DNA to create the required variability on demand. (A situation that many thoughtful biologists think is unlikely ever to occur.) But, fortunately, there is no need for concern about Homo sapiens' store of genetic variability unless humanity suffers a catastrophic reduction in numbers.(12) As with most sexually-reproducing species with enormous population sizes, Homo sapiens are not at all short of the raw materials of evolution - nor are they likely to be in the fore-seeable future.

I say "fortunately" because, at the moment, not enough is known by population geneticists for them to make any sensible recommendations about manipulations of the human gene pool. There is controversy, however, over what proportion of the human genetic variability is variability between populations and what proportion is within populations.(13) It is also not clear how much genetic variability there is for many human characteristics, including such widely discussed traits as intelligence, creativity, various kinds of mental illness, and so on.(14) The present state of human genetics allows only the most limited kinds of recommendations - such as counselling parents about the probabilities of their children inheriting certain types of genetic diseases, or generally warning that increased exposure to radiation or mutagenic chemicals is likely to be harmful. One might also caution, for esthetic reasons if for no other, against accelerating worldwide trends toward the swamping out, through migration, of some of the physical diversity that makes our species such an interesting one. But as long as there are billions of people living in diverse situations, there is no reason whatever to be concerned about the richness or quality of the human gene pool. Should a thermonuclear war reduce Homo sapiens to a few scattered groups of survivors, that statement would no longer apply. It seems unlikely, however, that any population geneticists would survive to worry about the consequences of human genetic depauperization.

CULTURAL DIVERSITY

While there appears to be no reason for immediate concern over the genetic diversity of Homo sapiens, there clearly is a need for immediate attention to humanity's <u>cultural</u> diversity. Cultural diversity can be thought of as an analogue of genetic diversity. In the same way that differences among genes are the raw material upon which biological evolution works, so can differences in the body of nongenetic information (that is, culture) possessed by individuals and societies be thought of as the raw material of cultural evolution.

By some measures, the body of cultural information possessed by humanity is growing exponentially. Consider, for instance, the explosive growth of science and technology in the last few decades and the computer revolution that continues to enhance human ability to manipulate and store information. But in other ways, humanity's store of cultural variability is clearly decaying. What might be called a fundamentally Western, industrial-scientific culture seems to be

in the process of overwhelming and replacing the wide variety
of other human cultures that existed a mere 50 years or so
ago.

Increasingly, one world view and one family of languages
is becoming dominant, and the speed with which this dominance
is being attained seems to be accelerating. One of the last
major holdouts against Westernization, the People's Republic of
China, with nearly a quarter of the globe's population, shows
distressing signs of caving in. With Coca-Cola already in, and
a plea for Western technology out, can English as a second
language and other Western ways be far behind?

Unfortunately, while too little is known about the process
of genetic evolution, even less is known about the process of
cultural evolution. Almost 40 years after the death of
Benjamin Lee Whorf, for example, the Whorfian hypothesis that
language is a major factor in shaping the worldview of a
culture(15) is still a matter of dispute.(16) Recently, however, L. L. Cavalli-Sforza and M. W. Feldman have begun to
forge a mathematical theory of cultural evolution analogous to
that already developed in population genetics.(17) Some of
their results support the intuitive view that various factors in
the modern world, such as the development of systems for
mass education, standardization of curricula in professional
schools, and especially the growth of the mass media, would
tend to accelerate the decay of cultural variability.(18)

In the face of what little is known about cultural evolution, it would seem wise for humanity to take a conservative
position on the preservation of cultural resources for the same
sorts of reasons that commend a conservative approach to the
preservation of biological diversity. One cannot be sure, for
example, that an Eastern philosophy might not provide a better
basis for human beings to orient themselves to a highly technological environment than a Western philosophy; there is no
guarantee that the secret for human beings living in peace
with one another is not buried deep in the culture of, say,
the gentle Tassaday of the Philippines. Once everyone is
Westernized, we will never know.

TECHNOLOGICAL DIVERSITY

Finally, it can be argued that there is considerable merit in
maintaining a high level of what could be described as "technological diversity," i.e., diversity in the physical and
political technologies employed by human beings in general and
Western nations in particular.(19) If people can use many
different means to achieve the same ends, there are manifold
benefits. Decentralization of physical technologies becomes
feasible, reducing vulnerability to accidental or malign dis-

ruption.   Social systems become less susceptible to massive
subversion.   Individuals gain more control over their lives and
are more likely to reap the benefits (and pay the costs) of
their own acts.   Diversity and decentralization permit, in
essence, parallel experiments that can supply humanity as a
whole with critical information on the advantages and disadvantages of different systems.

To date, the most thoroughly worked-out arguments for
technological diversity and decentralization have been made in
the context of energy technologies by energy specialist Amory
Lovins in his classic works on "soft" energy paths(20) and by
plasma physicist John Holdren in his cogently reasoned
discussions of the need to design systems that localize both
the costs and benefits of power generation in the same
population.(21)

It would seem wise to encourage as many parallel and
semi-isolated experiments as possible.   This would not only
maximize the yield of information, but would limit the probabilities of breakdowns in one area propagating to others.
Consider how much better off the United States might be today
if, in the early part of this century, it had found a mechanism
for encouraging some cities to use mass transit for commuting,
others to design around bicycles, and still other cities to plan
so that people could walk to work and commuting would be
unnecessary.   If that had been possible, it seems likely that
both the urban and the energy problems in the United States
today would be much less serious and much closer to solution.

On a grander scale, suppose that there had been
stronger barriers to cultural diffusion in the past few centuries so that virtually all societies would not have been
engulfed by one or the other of two major political-economic
ideologies.   How much better off might humanity be today if
its future political-economic choices were among dozens of
distinct systems rather than being constrained, in the eyes of
most, to variants of those two?   This restriction in choices is
especially tragic since both capitalism and communism may be
incapable of solving the most important problems now faced by
our species.(22)

Of course, humanity is neither inclined nor organized to
carry out such experiments.   One might ask, are there
courses society can select that will lead to and permit maximum
diversity to be preserved during a transition to a sustainable
society?

PRESERVING SPECIES DIVERSITY

The key to the preservation of biological diversity is simply
for humanity to reduce its now escalating assaults on the

ecosystems of the planet to a level where the natural resilience of those systems can easily permit accommodation. As long as those systems are being paved over, plowed under, and subjected to chemical warfare with everything from acid rains to PCBs, rapid deterioration will continue. To a large degree, this problem boils down to converting much of the remaining relatively undisturbed habitat on earth into preserves in which human activities are minimized and carefully regulated to prevent the decay of variability.

Some progress has been made by population biologists in planning the sizes and arrangements of preserves so that the conservation of diversity is maximized within each unit area.(23) However, the state of the art is such that, at the moment, the best rule to follow in most cases would seem to be to maximize the preserve area.(24) This is particularly so since it is becoming clearer that judgments of minimum preserve size made on the basis of information gathered in the relatively short term may be utterly erroneous. For example, observations during the California drought of 1975-76 indicated that some preserves in that state were too small to prevent, even over the medium term, the extinction of insect populations they contained(25) - even though before the drought they seemed quite adequate.

There is a growing tendency for some to consider maintenance of animals in zoos as an appropriate method of preserving diversity.(26) One notion is that species thus protected from extinction could eventually be used to "restock" nature after a secure habitat has been reestablished. There are several serious defects in this notion. First of all, the resources of the world's zoos are completely inadequate to the task - and there are few signs that the additional resources will be forthcoming to maintain even a small fraction of the vertebrates soon to be endangered. More important, animals kept in zoos are selected for docility and other characteristics that make them easy to keep in captivity - characteristics that would tend to make them utterly unadapted to the wild.

Of course, the ultimate folly of the "preserve-them-in-zoos" school is in believing that, once endangered species are ensconced in zoos, the habitat they have vacated will be preserved (or eventually restored). In fact, the presence of prominent endangered species is often the sole factor retarding the forces of development in a given area. Could anyone seriously argue that if California condors were announced as having been successfully preserved in zoos, anything would stand between oil companies and other exploitative interests and the present condor preserves in Southern California? Prominent endangered species are very often the key to preserving habitat for myraids of less well known but potentially even more important organisms.

PRESERVING GENETIC DIVERSITY

The problem of conserving the genetic diversity of crops is much simpler in theory than that of conserving natural species diversity. Three things seem to be required: One, the protection of wild relatives and progenitors of crops, would be taken care of automatically if steps were instituted to set up proper biological preserves, as previously mentioned; the second would be to accelerate the development and deployment of genetically highly variable crop strains that would show high resistance to both pathogens and insect pests;(27) the third would be the establishment of a special series of agricultural research stations around the world devoted to the genetic work that is essential to the maintenance of crop diversity. Storage of seeds of diverse varieties is not enough in the long term. Storage eventually leads to a decay of variability since the storage process selects for seeds that store well and the storage process itself may produce genetic damage in the seeds.(28) But if the stations had funds for maintaining experimental fields and subsidizing local farmers to plant less productive varieties, the crucial problem of maintaining crop variability could be solved. The price would be miniscule compared to the arms budget of even a second-rate military power.
On the other hand, conserving the genetic diversity of species in nature is part and parcel of preserving the species themselves. The fact that there is geographical variation with a genetic basis in most species is well documented. In itself this is a strong argument for not lightly exterminating any natural population. Costs that are hidden are, nonetheless, costs.

PRESERVING CULTURAL DIVERSITY

It is much more difficult, even in theory, to see workable ways of attempting to preserve human cultural diversity. To a degree, a biological preserve system might help since indigenous peoples could be "preserved" along with their natural habitats. But virtually all societies are now more or less in full contact with Western society, and putting people off into cultural "zoos" would present great practical and moral problems.(29)
To give just a single example, suppose that a large section of Amazonian rain forest were permanently set aside along with the Indian peoples inhabiting it. Would the Brazilian government have the moral right to prevent missionaries from entering the area and bringing the benefits of

Western medicine to the Indians? Would it be physically possible to do so, even if they had the right? I am inclined to think that the answer to the first question is yes, and the second is no, but these are points on which humane people are bound to differ. If a decision were made to introduce Western medicine, then not only would the cultural distinctness of the Indians tend to fade, but unless contraception were introduced simultaneously, their population size would probably increase to the eventual detriment of the biological preserve. Sad as it may be, it seems certain that the few remaining "primitive" peoples will undergo substantial acculturation - or disappear.

The prospect for preserving some cultural diversity in Homo sapiens is not entirely bleak. Many people concerned with the future of humanity have been distressed in recent years to see the goal of "one world," that so many hoped was close to realization after World War II, seemingly moving further and further from humanity's grasp. Everywhere, ethnic and religious distinctions appear to be increasing rather than diminishing. Francophiles want to secede from Canada; Black Power radicals reject the goal of assimilation into a white society in North America; the Ibos, Hausas, Masai, Kikuyu, and other African tribes maintain strong senses of ethnic identity; many Iranians have violently rejected Westernization in favor of a Moslem theocratic state.

Troublesome as these barriers are to those who are concerned about humanity triggering a nuclear Armageddon, they do have a positive side. People clearly have difficulty relating to a vast, amorphous world culture. The desire to identify with a more restricted group creates countervailing centrifugal forces that help to keep everyone from being sucked into the same cultural vortex. One viable strategy for attempting to maintain cultural diversity, then, is to work with those forces that are already present.

The West, in particular, must overcome the idea that there is something wrong if an Iranian prefers to live under a repressive religious ruler rather than suffer forced Westerniza-tion under an even more repressive Shah. Americans should not be amazed that French-speaking Canadians might wish to retain their cultural traditions and their beautiful language even at the cost of some confusion in air traffic control and some economic disruption. A middle-aged corporate executive sequestered in a coronary intensive-care unit might grow to appreciate that there is something very positive about a relaxed Polynesian culture. He might even realize that the lives of Australian aborigines or Masai tribesmen would not necessarily be enhanced by dressing those proud people in Western clothes and putting them to work in office buildings. In short, the world as a whole could come to learn that a high price is paid for the "creature comforts" of industrial civiliza-tion; that their benefits are very unevenly distributed within

the West; and that the best plan for a global sustainable
society is not to model the whole world after a mix of the Los
Angeles basin, Tokyo, and the Ruhr.

Indeed, some who have thought extensively about sustainable political systems see the maintenance of cultural (and
technological) diversity as a key element. It is generally
agreed that some form of redistribution of wealth will be
necessary if a successful transition to a sustainable society is
to be made. Today, the rich minority is attempting to "buy
off" the poor majority by promising that future growth will
enrich even the poorest of the poor. There is no reason to
believe in that "trickle down" approach, even if the requisite
growth were possible or desirable.(30)   But, in the absence of
substantial continuing growth, that promise of more for everyone becomes transparently absurd, and faith that some type of
redistribution will be possible becomes essential to maintenance
of the social contract. Political scientist Davis Bobrow, looking
toward a "coordinated redistribution," makes explicit the value
of diversity:

> . . . the politics of noncoercive redistribution
> are more feasible when preferences for particular
> commodities differ widely as do the preferred times
> for their receipts. Diversity across commodities and
> delivery times increases the possibilities of adequate
> supply and of consensus that restraint and modera-
> tion are working out well. Uniform preferences make
> general satisfaction unlikely in the absence of high
> throughput. Diversity makes possible a number of
> nonidentical benefit packages.(31)

Bobrow goes on to argue cogently that, under a "sustainable
society" (low throughput) vision of the future, monolithic
central authority must be avoided primarily because society
cannot afford to divert physical or social resources into the
massive instruments of oppression required to keep people on
the road to the steady state by force. Another reason, of
course, is that monolithic central authority would inevitably be
a homogenizing force.

It is hard to avoid the conclusion that nothing less than a
restructuring of Western ideals and values will be required if
the peoples of the world are to be satisfied with Bobrow's
diversity of commodities and delivery times. A demand must
be created for the cultural and other resources that can be
supplied by nonindustrialized peoples. People must come to
accept that not all areas can be industrialized or even be
economically productive in conventional terms. Some areas
within Western countries today are maintained at economic
expense because they supply other values. Certain parts of
the United States, for example, are preserved as parks or

wilderness while others are heavily industrial. Similarly, some
areas and peoples of the globe should be maintained at
economic expense in the future because they supply other
values: cultural   diversity,   biological   diversity,   natural
beauty, survival and happiness for other human beings, and,
in the long run, survival for everyone.

The notion that substantial progress can be made in that
direction is, to a degree, utopian. But so is the general
notion of moving toward a sustainable society, and many of the
steps that might help slow down cultural homogenization are
the very ones that most thoughtful people recognize as necessary if a steady state is to be approached. An outstanding
example is the development of a "spaceship" economic system
so eloquently espoused by Kenneth Boulding and Herman
Daly.(32)

Western nations push their culture and technology in
other parts of the world for economic reasons, in a never-
ending search for larger markets. If the press for economic
growth were eased, the whole process of Westernization would
slow considerably. If soft-drink manufacturers were not under
continuous pressure to expand, then the dental and general
health of the Chinese would be enhanced.

The deleterious effects of the growth-oriented system
were recently highlighted by events in Iran. There was
widespread official and unofficial distress in the United States
at the news that the Iranians were going to cancel the enormous orders for military hardware that the Shah had placed
with American companies. In the immediate reaction there was
not one word of whether it was good for humanity if the
United States distributed sophisticated nuclear-age weapons to
one and all - the main response was to ask whether other
buyers could be found to absorb the economic impact of the
lost orders.

PRESERVING TECHNOLOGICAL DIVERSITY

Some preservation of technological diversity will obviously
result if successful steps are taken to preserve cultural
diversity. But the reverse is also true. For example,
population biologist Peter H. Raven has eloquently advocated a
commitment by the United States to assist poor nations to
develop solar energy as a major route toward economic stability
and prosperity.(33) There is a wide variety of solar technologies, and many of them are suited to construction with
local labor that can be adapted to local conditions and can be
designed to require (compared with other technologies) relatively small amounts of capital. They do not require the
installation of permanent conduits to technological centers of

the West, in stark contrast to "hard" energy systems such as nuclear.

A transition toward a diverse array of renewable (primarily solar) energy technologies would also make rich nations much less vulnerable to interruptions of supply due to accident, terrorism, or political manipulation. Since energy plays such a fundamental role in all technological ventures, diversification of energy systems should have top priority. Another obvious area where technological diversification is desirable is transportation. Dependence on petroleum-powered vehicles - both trucks and passenger cars - must be reduced.

THE REGENERATION OF DIVERSITY

With present (and foreseeable) technologies, species and populations can be reestablished in some areas where they have become extinct, thus species diversity in an area may be partially restored. For example, the large copper butterfly Lycaena dispar became extinct in England but was successfully reestablished in a small area using stock from Dutch populations.

In the majority of cases, however, extinction caused by Homo sapiens results from habitat destruction and, therefore, even such limited regeneration of diversity is often impossible. Of course, once all the populations of a species have been extirpated, the situation is utterly irreversible. Furthermore, many human activities tend to disrupt the speciation process,(34) i.e., the natural evolutionary mechanism that for billions of years has created new species and compensated for natural extinctions. This is an ominous development indeed since, at present, humanity appears to have increased extinction rates by an order of magnitude far above historic rates.(35) It is the failure to appreciate the divergence of speciation and extinction rates that permits many commentators to view the continued extirpation of species with equanimity.(36)

The picture is not quite so bleak with respect to genetic diversity, since appropriate breeding programs (assuming large populations can be maintained) can increase the frequency of rare genes and increase genetic diversity. When genes have been lost entirely, however, one is reduced to waiting for random mutation to recreate them. The wait may be very long indeed (even though in some cases mutation rates can be accelerated) because not only are mutations rare events but many, if not most, desirable traits appear to have a complex genetic basis involving many interacting genes. Usually the individual genes involved cannot be detected, so that in practical terms, once the trait is lost through the decay of genetic variability, it might only reappear if several beneficial mutations occur simultaneously - an extremely improbable event.(37)

Cultural diversity might be regenerated in various ways without resorting to deliberately cutting off all communication between human groups and waiting for the inevitable divergence. In nations such as the United States, it might mean a weakening of central government (and national media) and a fostering of regionalism by programs designed to encourage most people to live their entire lives in the place of their birth.

But, as with species and genetic diversity, cultural diversity is clearly much easier to preserve than to regenerate. Only with technological diversity is regeneration easy in principle, usually requiring only the political will and the capital. The United States, for example, could easily move to a transport mix in which trains, buses, bicycles, and feet were all more important than private automobiles. It would require only political courage and some temporary economic dislocation (but nowhere near as much as usually imagined).

OVERVIEW

It seems certain that working toward a steady-state economy would automatically be a major step toward the preservation of diversity. In itself, however, it is unlikely to be enough. For one thing, the transition to a steady-state economy worldwide will occur over a relatively long term, several decades. During that time, the decay of variability is certain to accelerate. It may reach levels that will eventually lower the carrying capacity of the earth for human beings and also reduce the cultural resources that Homo sapiens will have at their disposal to deal with that lowered capacity. Therefore, much more must be done immediately to impress upon people, and decision makers in particular, that the fate of Western civilization is likely to be influenced by the fates of small organisms such as the snail darter and obscure peoples such as the Tassaday. Much of the emphasis in public education should be shifted away from the preservation of wilderness areas for recreation and for esthetic reasons (though both reasons are perfectly valid) to their role in the life-support systems that make civilization possible. Equally, those who wish to see other cultures and peoples preserved on compassionate grounds should make the case that it is in everyone's self-interest to do so.(38)

When a sustainable society is achieved, it should be one in which nature's economy is monitored as closely as the conventional economy is monitored today. Considerable human effort may have to go into ecosystem preservation and restoration, and the diversity of cultures and technologies should also be nurtured with care. Fear of loss of human diversity must come to override xenophobia. Fear of putting too many eggs in one technological basket must come to override the economic and political forces of centralization.

These notions will seem utopian to most, but humanity now finds itself in an ironic situation. The only practical solutions to its major problems are ones unrecognized or shunned by most people who think of themselves as practical. Nothing could be more impractical than for society to continue on its present course.

NOTES

(1) An ecosystem is the complex of the organisms found in a given area, the physical environment of that area, and all of the interactions between them. It is neither possible nor wise to give a more precise definition, and it is perfectly appropriate to refer to the ecosystem of the entire planet or the ecosystem of a single aquarium.

(2) For a discussion of how one ecosystem supplies some of these services, see F. H. Bormann and G. E. Likens, Pattern and Process in a Forested Ecosystem (New York: Springer-Verlag, 1979).

(3) See, e.g., G. E. Likens, F. H. Bormann, R. S. Pierce, J. S. Eaton, and N. M. Johnson, Bio-geo-chemistry of a Forested Ecosystem (New York: Springer-Verlag, 1977); W. J. Mattson and N. D. Addy, "Phytophagous Insects as Regulators of Forest Primary Production," Science 190 (1975): 515-22: J. F. Kitchell, R. V. O'Neill, D. Webb, G. W. Gallepp, S. M. Bartell, J. F. Koonce, and B. S. Ausmus, "Consumer Regulation of Nutrient Cycling," Bio-Science 29 (1979):28-34.

(4) A classic demonstration has been provided by F. H. Bormann and his collaborators through the experimental manipulation of the Hubbard Brook Forest ecosystem (see Borman and Likens, Pattern and Process for a summary).

(5) See, e.g., D. Goodman, "Theory of Diversity-Stability Relationships in Ecology," Quarterly Review of Biology 50(1975):237-66; G. W. Harrison, "Stability Under Environmental Stress: Resistance, Resilience, Persistence, and Variability," American Naturalist 113:(1979):659-69.

(6) An expanded approach to the problem of disappearing species, Science 193 (1976):198-202.

(7) See, e.g., O. H. Frankel and J. G. Hawkes, eds., Crop Genetic Reserves for Today and Tomorrow. (London: Cambridge Univ., 1975); and Peter R. Day, ed., The

Genetic Basis of Epidemics in Agriculture   (New   York: New York Academy of Sciences, 1977).
(8) P. R. Ehrlich and P. H. Raven, "Butterflies and Plants: A Study in Coevolution," Evolution 18 (1965):586-608.
(9) J. A. Browning, "Relevance of Knowledge About Natural Ecosystems to Development of Pest Management Programs for Agro-ecosystem," Proc. Amer. Phytopathological Soc. 1 (1974):191-99.
(10) National Academy of Sciences, Genetic Vulnerability of Major Crops (Washington, D.C.: NAS, 1972).
(11) P. R. Ehrlich, R. R. White, M. C. Singer, S. W. McKechnie, and L. E. Gilbert, "Checkerspot Butterflies: A Historical Perspective," Science 188 (1975):221-28.
(12) For an overview see L. L. Cavalli-Sforza and W. F. Bodmer, The Genetics of Human Populations (San Francisco: Freeman, 1971).
(13) For one view, see R. C. Lewontin, "For Apportionment of Human Diversity," Evolutionary Biology 4 (1967): 381-98.
(14) P. R. Ehrlich and S. S. Feldman, The Race Bomb (New York: Quadrangle, 1977).
(15) John B. Carroll, ed., Language, Thought and Reality: Selected Writings of Benjamin Lee Whorf (N.Y.: M. I. T. Press and Wiley, 1956).
(16) For a review, see George A. Miller's "Reconsideration" on Whorf, Human Nature, 1 (6) (1979):92-96.
(17) An overview is found in Cavalli-Sforza and Feldman, "Toward a Theory of Cultural Evolution," Interdisciplinary Science Reviews 3 (1978):99-107. Examples of more technical publications by the same authors are: "Cultural Versus Biological Inheritance: Phenotypic Transmission from Parents to Children (A Theory of the Effect of Parental Phenotypes on Children's Phenotypes)," Am. J. Human Genetics 25 (1973):618-37; and "The Evolution of Continuous Variation. III, Joint Transmission of Genotype, Phenotype, and Environment," Genetics 90 (1978):391-425.
(18) M. W. Feldman and L. L. Cavalli-Sforza, "Random Sampling Drift Under Non-Mendelian Transmission," Proceedings 41st. Session International Statistics Institute, New Delhi, 1977, see p. 161.
(19) The dangers of centralization of interconnections between technologies have been described by Roberto Vacca in The Coming Dark Age (New York: Doubleday, 1974).
(20) For example, Soft Energy Paths: Toward a Durable Peace (Cambridge, Mass.: Friends of the Earth, 1977).
(21) Observations for the California Energy Future Conference, Sacramento (May 20, 1978).
(22) For example, R. L. Heilbroner, An Inquiry into the Human Prospect (New York: Norton, 1974).

(23) Examples are J. M. Diamond, "The Island Dilemma: Lessons of Modern Biographic Studies for the Design of Natural Reserves," Biological Conservation 7 (1975):129-46; and A. L. Sullivan and M. L. Shaffer, "Biogeography of the Megazoo," Science 189 (1975):13-17.

(24) J. Terborgh, "Preservation of Natural Diversity: the Problem of Extinction Prone Species," BioScience 24 (1974):715-22; M. E. Soule, B. A. Wilcos, and C. Holtby, "Benign Neglect: A Model of Faunal Collapse in the Game Reserves of East Africa" unpublished, Biological Conservation 15 (1979):259-72.

(25) P. R. Ehrlich, I. L. Brown, D. Murphy, C. Sherwood, M. C. Singer, and R. R. White, "Extinction, Reduction, Stability, Increase: The Responses of Checkerspot Butterfly (Eyphydryas) Population to the California Drought," Oecologia 46 (1980):101-5.

(26) C. Wemmer, "Can Wildlife Be Saved in Zoos? New Scientist 8 (September 1972).

(27) See Browning, "Relevance of Knowledge"; P.M. Dolinger, P. R. Ehrlich, W. Fitch, and D. Breedlove, "Alkaloid and Predation Patterns in Colorado Lupine Populations," Oecologia 13 (1973): 191-204.

(28) E. H. Roberts, "Problems of Long-Term Storage of Seed and Pollen for Genetic Resource Conservation, in Frankel and Hawkes, Crop Generation Reserves, pp. 269-95.

(29) For some insight into these issues see Sheldon H. Davis, Victims of the Miracle (New York: Cambridge University Press, 1977).

(30) The "trickle-down" theory of spreading wealth has been thoroughly discredited. See, e.g., J. P. Grant, Foreign Policy, no. 12 (Fall 1973).

(31) "The Politics of Coordinated Redistribution." In The Sustainable Society: Implication for Limited Growth, edited by D. C. Pirages (New York: Praeger, 1977), p. 316.

(32) Most recently in H. Daly, Steady State Economics (San Francisco: Freeman, 1977).

(33) "A National Commitment," St. Louis Post-Dispatch, Centennial Edition, 25 March 1979.

(34) M. E. Soule, "Thresholds for Survival: Maintaining Fitness and Evolutionary Potential." Chapter 9 in Conservation Genetics, edited by M. E. Soule and B. Wilcox (Sunderland, Mass.: Sinaver Assoc., 1980).

(35) P. R. Ehrlich, A. H. Ehrlich, and J. P. Holdren, Ecoscience: Population, Resources, Environment (San Francisco: W. H. Freeman, 1977).

(36) For example, S. Witchel, "Give Me That Old-time Darwin," New York Times, 3 May 1979.

(37) This is an oversimplified discussion. For a brief introduction to some of the complexities of genetic con-

servation in wild and domestic populations, see O. H. Frankel, "Genetic Conservation: Our Evolutionary Responsibility," Genetics 78 (1974):53-65.
(38) Ehrlich and Feldman, The Race Bomb.

3 Social, Environmental and Economic Implications of Widespread Conversion to Biomass-based Fuels
Arthur A. Few, Jr.

INTRODUCTION

Botanical systems have evolved in local environments so that they tend to maximize the conversion of available solar energy into stored chemical energy contingent upon the availability of sufficient resources and constrained by the climatology of the local environment. When the capability of man to perform the same process with man-made, high-technology systems is closely examined - produce stored chemical fuel from available sunlight constrained by climate and resources - it is found that man is unable to surpass the performance of the biological systems without resorting to systems that cost hundreds of times more than biological systems with comparable output.

The realization of this concept and the recognition of the environmental desirability of increasing the total global biomass leads one to consider a strategy of growing biomass for fuels in addition to its use for materials, fibers, chemical feedstocks, and foods in regions of the world with insufficient rainfall or irrigation capabilities. But, can the development of a market for biomass fuel lead to an increase in biomass, or will it, instead, cause exploitation and decline in total biomass? To answer this question one will need to consider the economic, social, and policy influences on developing biomass and energy markets. Here the answer is clear. In a proper economic environment, where energy costs reflect actual values in terms of sustained yields of renewable resources, the economic forces should encourage the maintenance of and reestablishment of lands committed to production of biomass. In many situations this will mean forestland.

The economic, social, and policy implications of this biomass energy strategy are significant and widespread; ultimately, it leads to a value system related directly to land area, soil characteristics, the product of insolation with rainfall (or irrigation capacity), and, most importantly, wise and informed management of land and resources. These factors work to produce a nondepletable resource system and a more stable economic structure that rewards wise stewardship of our land and water resources; this is in contrast to current energy markets with the greatest profits going to those who most rapidly exploit our nonrenewable resources.

A preliminary analysis indicates that the energy market is approaching the point at which biomass fuels are practical and competitive with fossil fuels. In many regional and special applications, biomass fuels are already in use. It is important to begin a careful and thoughtful analysis of the potentials and implications of this energy resource.

THE SCIENTIFIC BASIS FOR SUSTAINABLE PRODUCTION OF BIOMASS-BASED FUELS

Before plunging into the technical discussion of this section, it is necessary to define the terms to be used and delineate the scope of the topics to be considered. The term sustainable production is used precisely as implied by its definition - the periodic removal from a managed land area that fraction of the total biomass, which on the average is the net biomass produced during that period on the land area, and the returning to the land such nutrients as required so that future biomass productivity is not diminished. One must accept at the onset that this concept cannot be compromised.

The hyphenated "biomass-based" fuels used in this chapter carries with it a specific concept and meaning. (In a sense, all fossil fuels are biomass-based; however, in this chapter they will be excluded from consideration because they are not renewable fuels.) Considerations are not limited to specifically proposed "energy crops" such as sugar cane, cassava, pineapple, Hevea, Euphorbia, and guagule;(1) although these crops and other specialty crops will surely play an important role in the biomass-energy future. In addition to these specialty crops, biomass-based fuels include: (1) primary sources from energy-farm production such as tree, kelp, or duckweed farms;(2) (2) secondary sources such as land clearing and forest improvement activities, forest residues, mill residues, and agricultural residues; (3) and tertiary biomass sources obtained by recycling biomass wastes from industries and cities. The term biomass-based fuels is used to include all of these sources.

Some secondary and tertiary biomass sources mentioned above are readily available today and are being utilized in limited quantities. A key element in the development of biomass-based fuel usage is the wide-spread recognition of the availability of an extensive sustainable biomass source; one that the public can depend upon. From examination of the various sources, some of which are previously listed, I have concluded that silviculture or tree farming can best provide this foundation resource. Spurr and Vaux(3) find that forests account for 67 percent of all dry matter production on the earth. Because of the perceived importance of the silviculture fuels, the use of the other sources will follow.

Solar Energy Conversion: Biomass in Comparison With Technological Systems

In considering the setting aside of large areas of land to produce fuel from biomass, an examination must be made comparing the efficiencies of other systems that are equivalent. If, for example, one is able to produce a man-made fuel from sunlight by a technological process at a lower cost per unit of output energy, then it would be hard for the biomass fuels to compete in the fuel market. A preliminary analysis indicates that this is not the case; we find that the biomass fuels are probably the most economic to produce.

There have been a number of important papers recently that discuss energy production by plants from both the theoretical and empirical points of view. From an excellent theoretical paper by Bolton(4), one can obtain an estimate of the potential or upper limit on the efficiency of conversion of solar energy to stored fuel. Bolton's analysis estimates this efficiency at 12 percent, but when plant respiration is taken into account Bassham(5) has estimated the net efficiency drops to 6.6 percent. The encouraging result of the very general treatment given the subject by Bolton is that photosynthesis has optimized the process of conversion of sunlight to chemical energy.

Within the kinetic and thermodynamic limitations on the conversion of light energy to chemical energy, I have shown that a reasonable goal for solar energy storage efficiency in a fuel-generation reaction would be 10 to 13 percent but probably not much higher than 13 percent. A consideration of various possible fuel-generation reactions indicates that the most efficient energy storage process would be one in which two photosystems operate in series in one-electron oxidation-reduction reactions much as photosynthesis functions, . . .(6)

There is a gap between this efficiency estimate and most of the reports on measured energy efficiencies for a variety of photosynthetic systems; for example, Bassham reports efficiencies on a range of .7 to 3.2 percent for various crops (alfalfa to sudan grass and corn). Rather than being discouraged by the gap between photosynthetic potential and the empirical results, this present difference can be viewed as an area where productive research can improve energy accounting and ultimately the productivity of biomass. Bassham comments,

> These measurements were all made in the United States in the temperate zone, where winter temperatures severely restrict growth for even plants such as sugarcane that grow year-round. The maxima lend credibility to the proposition that under year-round optimal conditions of temperature and growth, yields corresponding to energy conversion efficiencies of 4 to 5 percent would be achievable.(7)

An analysis of silviculture finds similar data and less consensus. Hellmers(8) has reviewed several determinations of forest efficiencies and concludes: "Results from the different sources suggest that over a growing season a stand of trees has a relatively high photosynthetic efficiency in comparison to that of an agricultural crop."(9) Hellmers's values, 2.2 to 3.5 percent, however, are referenced to visible light (4000 to 7000A) and when corrected for actual sunlight are 1 to 1.5 percent.

Values in the 1 percent range are generally accepted (S. H. Spurr, personal communication) as typical forestland conversion efficiency; they should not, however, be accepted as limitations. Research by Spurr and by Spurr and Vaux(10) have demonstrated that forestland productivity can be doubled or tripled by better silvicultural practices. Again, a need for additional research is seen in the evaluation of forest efficiencies to refine the data and remove the present discrepancies in their interpretations.

For biomass, we are certain of a 1 percent conversion capability, confident that 3 percent can be obtained with good management,(11) and hopeful that future generations may have available plants that are 5-6 percent efficient in the conversion of sunlight to chemical energy. Figure 3.1 provides a tally of the losses and residuals in the biomass energy conversion chain based largely on the estimates of Bassham.

After developing a range of efficiencies for the biomass conversion, a comparison of these figures with man-made technological solar energy conversion systems can be made. The solar thermal systems are now in the prototype stage of

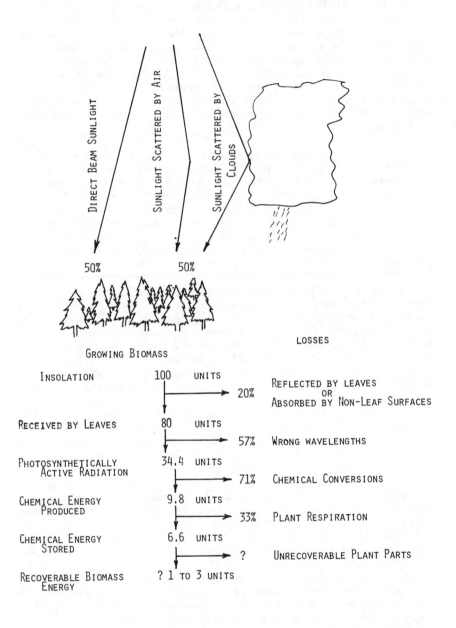

Figure 3.1.   Energy conversion process for biomass.   Percent
losses in right-hand column apply to the number
of energy units available at that particular stage.

development. These systems use large surface arrays of mirrors to focus sunlight onto boilers; the steam is then used to produce electricity. Europeans have had working versions of these systems for several years and Sandia Laboratory in New Mexico now has one under operational test for the U.S. Department of Energy. To obtain a chemical fuel for comparison with biomass processes, one must take the electrical energy provided by this solar thermal system and form hydrogen gas by electrolysis.

Hildebrandt et al.(12) performed an energy efficiency analysis of the Solar Power Tower Concept and found that electricity can be produced with approximately 30 percent efficiency from direct beam sunlight that falls on the surface of mirrors used to concentrate the sunlight. But this figure does not give us the true bottom-line efficiency for conversion to a stored fuel. Itemized below are other losses that must be added to their considerations in order to get a true comparison with the biomass systems:

1. In order to prevent shadows on the mirrors, they must be spaced apart; this results in 50 percent of the direct beam radiation during the course of a day falling between the mirrors.
2. Under average climatological conditions, only 50 percent of the insolation (total sunlight) is in the direct beam, which can be focused by the mirrors, with the balance being radiation scattered from clouds or the air itself. (This can be improved when operated at a desert-type site.)
3. Hydrogen gas is produced by electrolysis of water in a process that, under laboratory conditions, is 95 percent efficient at best.
4. The hydrogen gas must then be liquefied and stored in cryonic vessels in a process that is, at most, 70 percent efficient.

One can now see that the liquid hydrogen produced from sunlight in a typical U.S. site is accomplished with a process that is only 5 percent efficient. This efficiency should be compared with the 6 percent theoretical efficiency for photosynthesis. In an actual process, we know that there will be other losses so that our expectation for the technological production of fuel from sunlight by this method is realistically only about 3 percent, which is equivalent to the stored energy production of a field of irrigated, fertilized corn or a well-managed forest. Figure 3.2 exhibits the losses in the solar-thermal approach to solar fuels.

Similar efficiency estimates for two other solar energy conversion systems have been performed, each one representing the next step upward on the technological scale. The

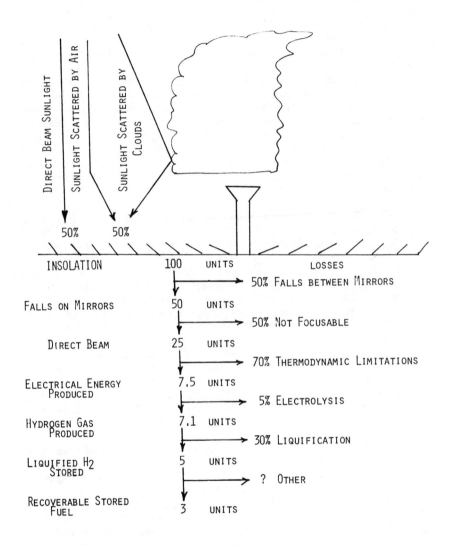

Figure 3.2.   Energy conversion process for the solar tower
power process.   Percent losses in right-hand
column apply to the number of energy units
available at that particular stage.

next step is to consider a conversion system utilizing large photoelectric arrays to produce electricity which is then converted to liquid hydrogen, which leads to the proposed solar power satellite that collects the full sunlight in space 24 hours a day and beams the energy to a large receiving antenna on the earth's surface using microwaves.

For the photoelectric system, the efficiency limitation is primarily a result of the choice of the solar cell that is used to produce the electricity. Johnston(13) has reviewed the wide range of materials that are available and concludes that the photovoltaic devices with efficiencies greater than 10 percent are all of very pure materials with the most efficient being made of single crystalline substances. These materials are not suitable for energy production because the energy required for their manufacture exceeds their expected lifetime output of energy. The photovoltaic cells that are inexpensive to produce with respect to both energy and cost are all in the 5 to 8 percent range of efficiencies. (Proponents of the photovoltaic approach are hopeful that there will be eventual breakthroughs in the production of low-cost, high-efficiency photo cells.) Using a solar cell in the 5 to 8 percent conversion range and then following that with the chemical storage part of the system brings the bottom-line efficiency into the 3 to 5 percent range. Again, the same value is obtained for our realistic expectation of solar-fuel conversion efficiency.

The final system that needs to be examined for comparison is the space solar power concept. An assumption is that the more expensive solar cells can be justified for space operations; thus, one starts with an 18 percent efficient solar cell array in geosynchronous orbit. The microwave power transmission is hoped to be 85 percent efficient.(14) On the ground, the very large receiving antenna (30,000 acres) receives sunshine in equal amounts to the microwave power; since this solar energy is unutilized, one must discount the efficiency of the total system by another 50 percent. The system is now seen to produce electricity at an efficiency of 7.6 percent. To obtain the efficiency for fuel production by this path, it is necessary to once again go through the process of hydrogen production and storage. The bottom-line efficiency then comes to 5 percent. Again, an answer essentially equal to our other results.

To paraphrase Bolton's conclusions: The conversion of sunlight to fuel is a process that is fundamentally limited by the laws of physics and chemistry and that 13 percent is an absolute upper limit; furthermore, realistic expectations should be in the 6 percent range where the photosynthetic process seems to have already maximized the process.

Before leaving this subject, it is important to state there is no wish to downplay the importance of the technological systems for the utilization of solar energy because each of the systems has its best use: the space solar power for the production of electricity, photoelectric for local on-site use of low voltage DC electricity; and the solar tower power for high temperature applications and electrical power in dry climates. These estimates and comparisons clearly demonstrate that for the production of chemical energy, attention and effort should be turned to biomass production.

Estimates of United States Silvicultural Productions

An essential element in the development of biomass usage is the recognition and appreciation of the magnitude of the biomass resource. In the preceding subsection it was suggested that a 1 percent conversion efficiency for forests was a conservative estimate. Noting that one-third of the land-area of the United States (754 million acres) is forested,(15) it is a simple, straightforward matter to use these two figures plus the observation that the average insolation for the forested areas of the United States is 400 ly/day(16) (ly=cal/cm) to compute the annual energy production by U.S. forests. This computation yields 178 Quads (1 Quad = 10^{15} BTU); for comparison, the total gross energy consumed in the United States during 1970 was 67 Quads. Had the more optimistic 3 percent conversion figure been used in this computation, the result would have exceeded the U.S. energy consumption by 8 times.

This example is given to draw attention to the fact that biomass energy has a great, unused potential for serving man, not to advocate turning over our forestland to supply the insatiable energy demand in the United States. The intent is not only to demonstrate the potential of biomass but to also encourage thought and research into the impacts that this resource will have on the economic, social, and policymaking elements in our civilization. One must also remember that, although we are working with energy units to measure the biomass production, the output has many uses and its use as energy is probably the lowest value that it has compared with food, building materials, fiber, pulp, and chemical feedstocks.

One final example will be given to complete the discussion of this subsection. In 1974, the United States consumed 75 million cords of pulpwood for the production of paper products. If all of this energy were recovered by recycling the used paper products, nearly 3 Quads of energy could be recovered. For comparison, in that same year the United States imported approximately 7.4 Quads of energy in the form of crude oil.

Environmental Impacts of Biomass-Based Fuels

Upon initial examination, one would conclude that extensive use of biomass-based fuels should have no impact on the global environment. The basis for this is that worldwide photosynthetic activity continues at an almost constant pace with the energy content of the biomass being recycled at an equal rate, mostly by decay of biomass materials. From this simplified point of view, the use of biomass-based fuels only perturbs this system by concentrating part of the decaying matter so that the energy may be put to some useful purpose.

Upon closer examination, it can be seen that the problem is more complicated and the chief problem of concern is a consequence of deforestation. Even though a field of soybeans may be as photosynthetically active as a forest of equal area, the forest builds a reservoir of standing semi-permanent biomass year-after-year in the large stems and trunks of the trees; whereas, the soybean crop produces very little biomass that is carried beyond its annual cycle. Since all of the carbon in the biomass reservoir comes from the CO_2 in the atmosphere, and since the other carbon reservoirs interact with the atmosphere with very long time constants, the biomass reservoirs are the primary modulators of CO_2 in the earth's atmosphere. Figure 3.3 illustrates not only the increasing trend in the global CO_2 concentration but also the annual cyclic variation in concentration due to the seasonal changes in photosynthetic activity in the hemisphere where these measurements were made. The upward trend is attributed to two sources: (1) the burning of fossil fuels, and (2) the deforestation process.(17)

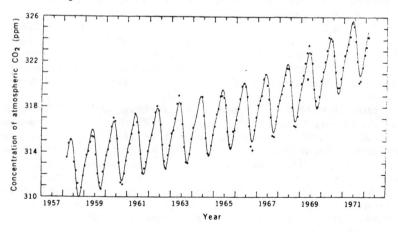

Figure 3.3.   Long term variation in the CO content of air measured by Eckdahl and Keeling at Mauna Loa Observatory in Hawaii. Figure is from note 17.

The carbon dioxide problem is the one that comes immediately to mind when considering biomass fuels. It is a problem of great concern to scientists because atmospheric CO_2 is a major regulator of the earth's climate. And, indeed, there have been a number of scientific papers that ascribe a large fraction of the increase in atmospheric CO_2 to deforestation; these scientists[18] would urge us not to use biomass for fuel. I am in complete agreement with them regarding deforestation and the concern for the CO_2 increase in the atmosphere, but I do not agree with their recommendation regarding biomass fuels. First, the industrialized world is not using biomass fuels now and yet deforestation is progressing rapidly. The fossil fuels are being rapidly depleted and the atmospheric CO_2 is increasing. So, not using biomass fuels is not providing the desirable solution. Second, economic instincts tell us that there is no way to stop the depletion of biomass until it becomes profitable to produce biomass. As mentioned previously, by linking the costfloor or base of biomass to the rising energy market, a climate for profits in biomass production can be created. By this process the nations of the world may be able to reverse the downtrend in biomass.

When biomass-based energy is compared with some of the other energy sources on the point of heat rejection into the atmosphere, it is found that biomass-based energy is the most environmentally compatible of all systems. All forms of fossil fuel usage, nuclear energy, and the proposed space solar power system introduce into the atmosphere heat energy that otherwise would not be present; whereas, most solar energy conversion systems are making use of energy that would have been absorbed anyway. This does not have a large effect globally, but might produce some local or regional effects.

The atmospheric emissions from the controlled burning of biomass are innocuous when compared to burning coal or high-sulphur fuel oil. Most of the expensive emission control devices are not needed, and the fly-ash content is below that of coal.

Fuel storage and transportation of biomass-based fuels are simple and environmentally desirable. First of all, the source is widely distributed and should not require long-haul transportation. Secondly, the fuel is self-storing almost indefinitely. Thirdly, with the exception of the possible hazard of forest fires, the fuel is completely safe and provides recreational benefits in its primary form. Contrast these environmental aspects to very large arrays of antennas, or mirrors, or photocells, and the problems of storing and transporting liquid hydrogen.

Another environmental consideration that is affected by the biomass fuel concept is the utilization of refuse. If a market is created for biomass fuel, the biomass processing facilities can be utilized for processing refuse with slight modification or preprocessing. The balance of the refuse, sewage sludge, and feedlot by-products provide another problem in current use patterns that can become an important resource in a biomass energy strategy. These by-products are usually not allowed to be used as fertilizers for food crops, but are acceptable for use in crops producing fiber, building materials, or energy. Rather that being a refuse problem, these items can become a resource if biomass energy is developed.

Concluding this subsection on environmental issues, I view the development of biomass-based fuel as being environmentally positive provided the prevailing economic environment encourages the production of biomass for its lowest value-energy. After all, in such an economic environment, the result might be a slow restoration of the world's biomass reservoir.

Some Comparitive Costs of Solar Produced Fuels

In my research on the comparative assessment of biomass-based fuels with higher technology systems, I have also looked closely at some of the cost factors associated with fuel production from these systems. It is an easy task to show the economic advantages of fuels from biomass in comparison to the high-technology solar fuel systems. One has only to imagine the differences in production costs of a large tree farm compared to an equally large array of solar tracking mirrors with all of the associated towers, generators, electrolizers, hydrogen liquefiers, and cryogenic storage and transportation facilities.

Rather than discussing these estimates in detail, which is akin to "beating a dead horse," the results of this exercise are presented in Table 3.1.

POTENTIAL ECONOMIC RAMIFICATIONS RESULTING FROM WIDESPREAD USE OF BIOMASS-BASED FUELS

At several points in the development of this chapter, it has been stated that the success of biomass-based fuels as a sustainable resource depends critically upon the economic environment. We now need to look closely at these economic requirements and any evidence that is available to guide us in discerning the best economic environment for the development of biomass-based fuels.

At the very least, biomass-based fuels must be profitable for the producer and competitive with other fuels. To be more

Table 3.1.   Comparisons Sunlight to Fuel, 1 GW Capacity

	Biomass	Solar Thermal	Photo-electric	Space Solar Power
Efficiency	3%	5%	5%	5%
Land required in acres	41,500	24,900	24,900	5000 (+2700 in space)
Characteristics	Forest	5 million mirrors 50 towers (450 M high)	100 billion solar cells	Extensive space operations
Estimated Construction Cost in Billions	.11	3.5	13	17.4

specific, it should be possible for an investor to (1) purchase or lease land; (2) prepare, plant, and maintain the land, using appropriate silvicultural or agricultural practices; (3) periodically sell a portion of the biomass to a fuel buyer; (4) receive from the transactions sufficient income to amortize indebtedness for the land and equipment, pay interest on indebtedness, pay all salaries and expenses, pay income taxes, and retain a respectable balance as a profit on his investment. The fuel sold to the buyer in step (3) above must be harvested, processed, transported, and sold to an end user at a price significantly below that of natural gas, which is unquestionably the superior fuel, and at a price approximately equal to coal, but perhaps higher, since coal is environmentally less desirable for most applications. The fuel buyer-processor must also receive a net profit sufficient to encourage future investments in this phase of the activity. These specific requirements will be examined in a later subsection.

Assuming, for the moment, that the above-stated conditions are met and the timing is correct (this will also be discussed later), one is faced with what appears to be a Catch 22. If profitably produced, biomass can be sold for fuel, which is its lowest value; why not produce, instead, pulpwood or, better yet, timber, and realize even greater profits from the same lands? People who have faced this proposition in the past have tended to fall into three groups; two are wrong and one is correct.

The Fuels for Biomass Program at the Department of Energy for years stoically maintained one of the wrong positions. (There has recently been a turnover in the administration of this branch and a 90° change in the point of view on this matter.) The position was that, if a biomass farm was to produce biomass fuel, it should be operated solely for that purpose and no other. Their studies(19) had convinced them (one assumes) that biomass for fuel could be produced in sufficient quantities that the profits would match or exceed those from a timber operation with a correspondingly lower yield.

The traditional foresters and wood products industries tended to take the opposite (also wrong) point of view. They had studied their accounting sheets and knew the source of their profits; anyway, as a group, they are the largest users of biomass fuels in their own plants. Why should they be interested in any activity that might ultimately compete against them for the biomass resource providing them with their profits?

In the third group (the correct one) we find (1) the informed, progressive foresters who view biomass fuels as the opportunity to finally practice silviculture at its best;(20) (2) the small forestland owners who see the chance to obtain income from the forest without completely destroying its character; and (3) the entrepreneurs who recognize the possibilities of this large, underutilized resource, and see an opportunity to get involved in a growing industry before the "Corporate Energy Giants" move in and take over. The view taken by this group is that a healthy forest can provide any and all of these products, and good silvicultural management can produce the maximum income from the land by selective and timely harvesting of specific components.

In addition to the requirements of profitability and competitiveness, the timing of emergence of biomass fuel into the market is extremely important. If the move is made too soon, heavy financial losses will occur and only the wealthy corporate participants will survive the competition. If the move is made too late and the demand is high, then the probability of exploitation by the get-rich-quick crowd increases and the concept of sustained production will suffer a major setback.

The Biomass-Based Fuel Infrastructure - Developing A Supply Line

Natural gas is clean but, most importantly, it comes out of the end of a pipe on demand. There are literally millions of miles of pipelines of all sizes crisscrossing the land areas of this world, with their many compressor stations that transport natural gas from the producer to the user. There is no corresponding infrastructure for biomass-based fuels; not yet.

Crude oil is trucked, railed, and piped from producer to refinery, where it is made into a thousand different materials; then trucked, railed, and piped to a nationwide network of retail and industrial users. There is no corresponding infrastructure for biomass fuels; not yet.

These complicated infrastructures for the oil and gas industries did not develop overnight; the process was slow and required large quantities of investment capital. The same process must occur for biomass-based fuels. Biomass is a more versatile resource than oil or gas, and we will ultimately find many more uses for biomass than are presently envisioned, but the initial uses must be very simple and require a minimum of processing. The necessary infrastructure will be built by a long series of individually successful (i.e., profitable) enterprises that utilize the biomass resource.

The starting point is the use of densified biomass by medium-size facilities as a source of process heat or electrical generation with the cogeneration of process heat. Steps beyond that are synthetic natural gas, methanol, and ammonia. Beyond this step, the opportunities mushroom as biomass essentially replaces oil as a chemical feedstock.

The Present Economic Environment – How Does It Look Now?

The present environment for biomass production is, in a word, marginal. There are several special situations where biomass-based fuel is being used today. A look at these situations provides information on the present environments where biomass is profitable.

The wood products industries are the largest users of biomass energy in the United States today (other than, perhaps, the general public's use in the home fireplace). I have interviewed several managers of these facilities and find that they are extremely pleased with their successful trials using biomass fuel and are planning to expand their use as rapidly as is practical. One user interviewed used all of the waste wood from their facility plus waste wood purchased from most of the nearby (50 miles) smaller operators, and occasionally took a large chipping machine into the woods to recover timber residues for additional supplies in order to provide the required fuel for their operations. Another user was utilizing all of their waste wood for process heat and was still using natural gas for other operations; they were planning to convert totally to biomass fuels in the future.

These cases are not good test cases for exposing economic parameters because the biomass fuel is available to these users at extremely low costs. However, these efforts are important steps in building the necessary infrastructures; in this case, it is the experience with burners that use unprocessed waste wood. These industries have invested in special burners; they have turned off the natural gas; and they are pleased with the results. If the other levels of infrastructure existed at this time to provide these industries with densified biomass at prices below natural gas, for example, they would probably buy the biomass fuel to supplement their own supplies.

There are small electrical generating plants in New England that are successfully operating on biomass fuel. In this situation, there are local sources of biomass fuel (principally waste wood from wood products operations), and the cost of imported oil or gas is very high. This provides a somewhat better test because economic pressures provided the motivation for the switch to biomass fuel. Because of the local nature of the operation, very little infrastructure is required to support it.

There is an effort underway in the United States to develop an infrastructure on the theory that, if it were there, then a lot of potential users would convert to biomass fuel. The leader in this effort is the Bio-Solar Research and Development Corporation; this firm is constructing biomass pelletizing plants in various regions of the United States to provide a source of densified biomass in a convenient form. These efforts will provide several good tests of the economic climate for biomass fuels on regional bases.

Across the southeastern part of the United States, the major wood source of the U.S., both natural gas and coal are plentiful. If biomass energy can acquire a permanent part of the non-special energy market, then indications are positive that it will be ultimately successful.

The Department of Energy has completed a rather large study of the economics of fuel farm operation which provides us with additional valuable data.(21) One output from this study is that a biomass fuel farm (totally dedicated to fuel production) could be profitable (9.7 percent return on investment) in Louisiana on land purchased for $300/acre if the unprocessed fuel was sold for $1.21/MMBTU - a typical natural gas cost in this area, for comparison, is $2.80/MMBTU. This study contains lots of assumptions and does not include some of the infrastructure costs, but it is, nonetheless, encouraging.

The Ownership of the Land and Clouds on
the Horizon

Assume that a small landowner has a biomass farm that converts sunlight to fuel with 1 percent efficiency. The annual average insolation is 400 ly/day which translates into an exposure of 24,000 MMBTU/ac yr. At 1 percent efficiency, the biomass should be produced at 240 MMBTU/ac yr. If the biomass is sold to the fuel-processor-distributor for $1.00/MMBTU, the landowner should receive $240.00/ac yr. income. This should be sufficient income on land purchased at $1,000.00/acre to encourage investment in biomass production. (These are approximate calculations used to illustrate that at some point biomass becomes profitable.)

When the condition of profitability to the small landowner occurs, we have the essential ingredient that is needed to motivate a reversal in the steady decline of forestland that has been occurring during the last several decades. It becomes possible to support a family on several hundred acres of land if the land is properly managed. The conditions are then suitable also for a reversal in the shift of the population to the cities and suburbs. A larger segment of the population can live outside major cities, and more people will be employed in occupations directly related to the production of a basic commodity. These demographic shifts will assist in stabilizing the economy and cooling inflation.

There is a cloud on the horizon. Some regions of the United States have seen a substantial shift in the land ownership patterns. For example, in east Texas, a few large wood products industries now own most of the land (approximately 70 percent). If the managers of these large corporations perceive and appreciate the opportunities that lie ahead for biomass fuels, the land ownership pattern may continue to shift to the large corporate investors. An even darker cloud, possibly, is that the energy corporations will see these possibilities and swallow up the small landowner and the wood products industries. There is evidence in the financial sections of the newspapers that this process may already have begun. It would, indeed, be ironical if the profits from the exploitation of our fossil fuels were used to purchase control of our future biomass fuels. It could be happening.

From one standpoint, such a process might not be all bad. Historically, the wood products industries have been good managers of the land that they own. Because their future supply of biomass depends to a large extent on their silvicultural practices, they have been much more diligent than the private landowner. I suspect that the energy corporations would have a similar motivation for land management.

The Inflation Impact on Wood Products, Fibers, and Foods

If the landowner receives $1.00/MMBTU for biomass, this corresponds to $20.00/cord for pulpwood (1 cord = 1.25 tons at 16MMBTU/ton). In 1976, $10.00/cord was an average price paid for pulpwood in the southern United States. It is easily seen that wood prices are generally depressed relative to energy costs, and that an adjustment will occur in the future. In fact, from this example one would predict that a market for biomass fuel will immediately cause a doubling of the cost of all wood related products. Although this inflation will affect all, it will have a good effect in the long run because the price of both fuel and wood products will eventually be governed by a renewable resource – biomass.

The impact of this jump in wood products prices will eventually reach all forms of biomass production (foods and fibers) as land use adjustments occur in response to the new values of biomass-based products.

SOCIETAL IMPACTS AND RELEVANCE TO GROWTH POLICY RESEARCH

In the current economic situation, it is difficult to purchase land to be held indefinitely for biomass production and expect to make a reasonable profit on the investment. Profits in land are made chiefly by buying and selling, not in holding. There are a few exceptions where land can be purchased and farmed intensely with profits earned by the farmer. But the clamor produced by the American farmers recently indicates that the profitability of the smaller, unincorporated farms is disappearing.

The situation is similar in forestland. Only the large timber and pulp companies who purchased large land areas several decades ago and who operate vertically integrated industries are able to hold land for its production capabilities and make a profit. The smaller timber operators must constantly buy and sell the land and, in some cases, exploit the biomass in order to survive. One result of the current economic situation is that nearly half a million acres of forestland are lost each year in the United States to other uses.

Developing a biomass energy market in an economic situation when energy costs reflect the true replacement cost of the energy will actually reverse the current trends in silviculture and agriculture. Land could be purchased and held indefinitely for the production of some form of biomass with the energy value of the biomass providing a cost base underriding all other forms of biomass. The profit production capability of the land would then be tied to the cost of energy.

To a very large extent, the growth history of the industrialized world is rooted in progressive exploitaiton of one natural resource after another: labor, land, wood, coal, minerals, oil, gas, and water, for example. Until this century, it was possible to move on to new lands when the earth's resources were depleted; in this century, the appetite for the earth's resources has grown exponentially and expand into the national and international political areas. Daily, one can witness a fragmentation of this system; a cure for the obese growth-based energy economy must be found. Diet is part of the answer and it is surely on the horizon, but the long-term answer lies in the utilization of fuels that are renewable at a fixed sustained rate.

It is the biomass fuels that have all of the proper attributes of the ideal fuel for the future.

1. Biomass fuels have a global distribution that reflects the population distribution; it is an extensive as opposed to intensive energy source.
2. Biomass fuels are renewable; under careful and informed management practices, the earth can produce a constant, sustained yield.
3. Biomass fuels utilize lower technology and require a dispersed labor force.
4. Biomass fuels are nonpolluting; in all known aspects, they are preferable to all other energy systems.
5. Biomass fuel economics can promote an increase in the global biomass reserve and ameliorate the atmospheric CO_2 trends.
6. Increased biomass production causes shifts in local climatology toward more humid conditions; reclamation of lands lost to deserts may be possible.
7. Biomass fuel economics can allow the smaller landowners to hold onto and return to the land.
8. Biomass fuel economics can lead to a stable, noninflationary, world economy.

Most importantly, the widespread use of biomass-based energy can lead to a value system that is related directly to land use, soil characteristics, water resources, and informed management; the rewards of this value system would go to those practicing wise stewardship of these resources.

NOTES

(1) W.G. Pollard, "The Long-Range Prospects for Solar-Derived Fuels," American Scientist 74 (1976): 509-13; Melvin Calvin, "Photosynthesis as a Resource for Energy and Materials," American Scientist 64 (1976): 270-78; D.L. Marzola and D.P. Bartholomew, "Photosynthetic Pathway and Biomass Energy Production," Science 205 (1979): 555-59; A.L. Hammond, "Alcohol: A Brazilian Answer to the Energy Crisis," Science 195 (1977): 564-66; T.H. Maugh, "The Petroleum Plant: Perhaps We Can Grow Gasoline," Science 194 (1976): 46; and W.J. Broad, "Boon or Boondoggle: By-gone U.S. Rubber Shrub is Bouncing Back," Science 202 (1978): 410-11.

(2) R.E. Inman, Silviculture Biomass Farms (Contract EX-76-C-01-2801, report to the Energy Research and Development Administration, Washington, D.C., 1977), Vols. 1-6, available NTIS, Springfield, Virginia; Calvin, "Photosynthesis as a Resource"; and W.S. Hillman and D.D. Culley, Jr., "The Uses of Duckweed," American Scientist 66 (1978): 442-51.

(3) S.H. Spurr and H.J. Vaux, "Timber: Biological and Economic Potential," Science 191 (1976):752-56.

(4) J.R. Bolton, "Solar Fuels," Science 202 (1978):705-11.

(5) J.A. Bassham, "Increasing Crop Production Through More Controlled Photosynthesis," Science 197 (1977): 630-38.

(6) Bolton, "Solar Fuels," p. 710.

(7) Bassham, "Increasing Crop Production," p. 633.

(8) Henry Hellmers, "An Evaluation of the Photosynthetic Efficiency of Forests," Quarterly Review of Biology 39 (1964): 249-57.

(9) Ibid., p. 256.

(10) S.H. Spurr, "Silviculture," Scientific American 240 (2) (February 1979): 76-90; and Spurr and Vaux, "Timber."

(11) P.H. Abelson, "Energy from Biomass" (Editorial), Science 191 (1976).

(12) A.F. Hildebrandt, G.M. Hass, W.R. Jenkins, and J.P. Colaco, "Large-scale Concentration and Conversion of Solar Energy," EOS Transaction, American Geophysical Union 53 (1972): 684-92.

(13) W.D. Johnston, Jr., "The Prospects for Photovoltaic Conversion," American Scientist 65 (1977): 729-36.

(14) Solar Power Satellite Concept Evaluation, Vol. II. Lyndon B. Johnson Space Center, Houston, 1977.

(15) Spurr and Vaux, "Timber."

(16) Climatic Atlas of the United States, U.S. Department of Commerce (Washington, D.C.: U.S. Govt. Printing Office, 1968).

(17) Bert Bolin, "Changes of Land Biota and Their Importance for the Carbon Cycle," Science 196 (1977): 613-15.

(18) Ibid.; and J.A.S. Adams, L.L. Lundell, M.S.M. Matovani, "Wood Versus Fossil Fuel for Excess Carbon Dioxide," Science 190 (December 19, 1975), letters section.

(19) Inman, Silviculture Biomass Farms.

(20) W.E. Towell, "Energy From the Forest" (Editorial), American Forest 84 (October 1978): 14.

(21) Inman, Silviculture Biomass Farms.

6212
UK

4 Some Implications of Low Economic Growth Rates for the Development of Science and Technology in the United Kingdom

Michael Gibbons

INTRODUCTION

To examine the history of the United Kingdom during the last fifty years is to discover a nation in the throes of deep-seated social, economic, and political changes.(1)   To understand the meaning and implications of these changes has occupied the minds of two generations of scholars whose reports, diagnoses, and remedies would by now fill a good-sized library.   One family of diagnoses which is gaining some currency, possibly because of its implication of moral superiority, suggests that the United Kingdom is in transition from an industrialized to a postindustrial society.   What precisely this means is far from clear but, in general terms, it describes a change from the growth goals of industrial society to the improvement goals of postindustrial society; from concern with production, quantity, monetary values, work, discipline, and competition to concern with distribution, quality, human values, self-realization, and cooperation.(2)   An impressive array of evidence could be brought forward to show that Britain has, by comparison with her European partners, achieved lower values of productivity growth, experienced chronic failure in international trade, and undergone a progressive deterioration in industrial relations. On the positive side, however, greater energy than previously has been directed toward redistribution of incomes and the provision of medical, educational, and welfare services to all who desire them.   The Welfare State is a contemporary British achievement and is regarded by many as signaling the beginning of the end of an industrial society.

There is, as yet, no consensus as to whether the failure of British industry to achieve comparative growth in productivity or to maintain her position in international trade is due to widespread disillusion with the goals of industrialized society, as some have supposed, or to the inability of management to come to terms with the realities of international competition in technology which have dominated world trade since 1950. Whatever the full explanation, the outcome - persistently sluggish economic performance - is undisputed.(3) It is also clear that, whatever changes in attitude toward the growth values of industrial society may have taken place during the last 25 years, successive governments have never wavered in their commitment to high economic growth rates through the application of the latest advances in science and technology. Indeed, with regard to the latter, one student of British technology policy has concluded that politicians, civil servants, and industrialists alike appear to be in the grip of a "technology opportunity syndrome" as a result of which decisions concerning future directions of technological development were taken without due attention to basic commercial considerations.(4) For example, between 1945 and 1974, Britain invested 1,505.4 million in civil aircraft and engines and received only 141.9 million in receipts. This is perhaps sufficient to indicate the reality of this syndrome.

Although the recent "affair" with high technology for its own sake may now be over, it provides a leitmotif against which subsequent changes in policy toward research and development generally may be comprehended. Our concern in this chapter is with a general problem which will confront any nation which seeks to create an alternative society based on a low growth scenario: the mobilization of research and development behind new types of industrial products and processes. The contemporary British experience of trying to control the direction of government research and to orientate it in the direction of social and industrial needs provides an important historical exemplar of some of the difficulties involved.(5) The fact that Britain is attempting to do this in the context of low economic growth rates provides additional interest because low growth rates mean that existing resources will have to be reallocated. In the voluntary transition to low growth scenarios, few countries will be able to build up their research capability ab initio. The consequences for research policy of greater concern with energy and resource conservation, with environmental purity and "quality of life" factors generally will mean the channeling of existing resources into new areas. Perhaps, then, this brief description of events in Britain will be of some benefit to those who have, so far, not attempted such changes.

THE END OF A GLAMOROUS ADVENTURE

In order to better appreciate the problem that faced Britain with regard to research and development expenditures, it will be helpful to present some of the general features of this investment as it evolved from the end of World War II. Although, in terms of expenditure on industrial research and development, Britain is now relatively far down the international league table and is surpassed in absolute terms by the United States, Germany, and Japan, this was not always the case; in the immediate postwar period and later during the 1950s and 1960s, Britain spent considerably more both absolutely and as a percentage of gross national product. If a suitable time lag, say five to ten years, is allowed, then it would not be unreasonable to expect this investment to be reflected in trade and general economic performance during the middle and late 1960s.(6)   Instead, there was the "British paradox." For the first time publically, the possibility was raised that Britain might be overcommitted to research and development; that technological innovation might be as dependent on good industrial housekeeping as on research and development; and that, in any event, research and development might have been directed to areas which had little or no relevance to the improvement of economic performance.(7) Although the political push given by the Labour Party to the technological transformation of British industry from 1964 onwards did much to obscure the situation, both the absolute magnitude and the distribution of research and development were out of line with respect to her principal European competitors as well as Japan. The principal dimensions of this misalignment may be summarized thus:

1. by comparison with Germany and Japan, Britain's R & D effort was highly concentrated in aircraft;
2. a very high proportion of government supported R & D was directed at a few areas of high technology - nuclear, aerospace, and computers;
3. R & D in mechanical engineering was low and after 1966 continued to decline in real terms for another decade;
4. the problem of R & D expenditure did closely resemble that of the United States with whom, for a variety of reasons, Britain was unable to compete;
5. the absorption of scarce scientific and engineering manpower into government laboratories and industries related to government high technology had the effect of starving private industry of the benefits of this resource;
6. subsequently, Britain was unable to derive commercial successes from her high technology investments.(8)

During the first ten years after World War II, Britain had developed a set of research priorities which reflected her intention to compete in the first league of advanced industrial nations. Alas, it was not be be. Reluctantly, it came to be recognized that the expansion of the economy was likely to be far more responsive to technological innovation in mechanical engineering, motor vehicles, textiles, chemicals, and other traditional industrial sectors. Yet, in these very sectors, R & D expenditure continued to decline in real terms from 1966 onwards.(9)

The basic problem of overcommitment to high technology was traced to, among other things, a series of inept public decisions; and it was this situation, perhaps more than any other, which provoked the debate over accountability in British government which led, in 1971, to proposals for a complete reorganization of the mode of allocating resources to government-funded scientific and technological activities.(10) Through this reorganization, it was hoped to provide an administrative framework within which priorities for research and development could be changed to bring them more into line with the nation's industrial capabilities and needs.

The Rothschild Reforms

During the early 1970s, the movement was in full spate to bring all government-funded research and development under the "customer-contractor" principle as formulated by Lord Rothschild, the head of the Central Policy Review Staff, the government's "think-tank." In attempting to enhance public accountability, Lord Rothschild argued that all government research should be related to and justified in terms of departmental objectives. In principle, this had always been the case. The novelty lay in bringing additional visibility to research and development, an activity which heretofore had been identified with the creativity and insight characteristic of science. Consequently, government laboratories had enjoyed a large measure of independence over the direction of their research program.(11)

Lord Rothschild, in introducing the customer-contractor principle, sought to constrain this independence and to give the departments a greater say in the direction of research. The idea was a simple one; the departments as customers would identify research problems and put out contracts to the scientific establishments for the execution of programs aimed at solving these problems. This amounted to applying to research and development the well-tried commercial principle that the customer knows best what he wants and is prepared to pay (for research in this case) in proportion to his need for it. Conversely, if a scientific team wished to pursue a given problem, it would be incumbent on it to demonstrate that the program was relevant to some departmental objective. So it was that scientists and administrators were to be drawn into close and continuous dialogue in the articulation of research programs and accountability attained.

The most important aspect of the new arrangements, for our present concern, is that the customer - i.e., the department - was now in a position, through the Office of the Chief Scientist, to formulate long-term research goals and to require its own laboratories to adjust its research activities accordingly. The new scheme would replace, in large part, the system of committees which had grown up to <u>advise</u> the government about the programs of its establishments but which, nevertheless, had no executive authority over how resources would be spent.

This, at least, was the intention. In the next part of this chapter, the impact of the customer-contractor principle to two areas of particular relevance to the changing research priorities will be discussed; industrial research and development, and basic research of the type usually associated with universities. In the former, we will be concerned with the Department of Industry, in the latter with the Science Research Council, the nearest equivalent in Britain to the National Science Foundation in the United States.

Industrial Research and Development

It was T. S. Eliot who wrote, ". . . between the idea and the reality falls the shadow." The idea behind the customer-contractor principle was to ensure the orientation of research and development to national needs. The shadow of reality intruded itself almost immediately in the case of industrial research and development. In Britain, something in excess of 50 percent of all industrial R & D is funded by the government and is carried out in the Department of Industry's own research establishments, such as the National Physical Laboratory and the National Engineering Laboratory. The implication of the Rothschild reforms was that, under the current system of controls, these laboratories were not as efficient in allocating resources to industrially-relevant projects as they might have been. Indeed, there had been a tendency for them to evolve in directions determined more or less by the intrinsic interests of the problem itself; that is, they tended to become centers of curiosity-oriented rather than mission-oriented research.

The customer-contractor principle was supposed to remedy this "drift" in the industrial research establishments - i.e., the contractors - toward pure science. But, who, in this case, was the customer? In other government departments,

such as those concerned with health or the environment or
defense, the department itself has a specific need for research. The Department of Industry, by contrast, has itself
no need of research; rather, its function is to promote research of interest to industry. Clearly, the Department
cannot function directly as a customer in the sense intended
by Rothschild. This problem was resolved, administratively at
least, by the establishment of Research Requirements Boards
to serve as proxy customers for seven designated sectors of
industry.(12). The boards would be composed of scientists,
industrialists, and civil servants and would have executive
authority to allocate resources. In particular, the laboratories
of the Department of Industry would have to develop their
research programs along lines established by the boards if
they expected to maintain their operating budgets. The
boards themselves set about developing research strategies.
Thus, the dialogue between customer and contractor as originally envisaged by Rothschild was restored.

The Strategies of the Boards

The boards became responsible for a set of research programs
which were already underway and, apart from any new money
which they might receive, they were confronted with the
problem of redeploying resources to new programs of greater
value to industry. They spent the first 12 to 18 months
familiarizing themselves with their areas of responsibility, but
were not allowed the luxury of doing this before assuming
executive responsibilities for those areas. This meant that
they had, from the outset, to respond to requests from
research establishments for continuing support for existing
programs. In view of the volume of submissions and the need
to maintain continuous use of staff at the establishments, it
was inevitable from the point of view of the boards that most
of what was initially submitted to them was accepted.
    This is not to say, however, that in their haste to
implement the new arrangements, the boards were uncritical of
existing programs. As one official put it, many submissions
had a "very, very rough ride," largely because the establishments (and, one suspects, the boards themselves) were not
entirely clear about what information was wanted. Thus, one
board observed that it was "not fully satisfied with the form in
which proposals were first submitted and asked that the jus-
tification for the work and the case for Government funding
should be brought out more clearly."(13)
    Presentation apart, the boards were clearly determined to
make their mark as early as possible, and their first annual
reports contained numerous statements of dissatisfaction with
parts of existing programs. One board observed that, even
though it had only processed programs to the tune of some 77

percent of its £5.5 million budget, it had already made modifications values at 800,000 million.(14) By the end of 1973, most of the boards were well-advanced in their reviews of their areas, and all were beginning to pay serious attention to their future strategies.

In 1974, after about 18 months of activity, the boards began to make serious efforts in special meetings to clarify their criteria for choice. This proved to be more difficult than had been expected, but they were able, in 1975, to publish a document outlining their interim strategies. In the foreword to this document, it was pointed out that the boards were beginning to develop criteria for the deployment of funds "which need not necessarily imply an extrapolation into the future [of] the needs of the past." These strategies should, however, be regarded as tentative, and the purpose of publishing them was to "initiate an expanding dialogue" between the boards and industry so that policy would be broadly based and well-informed.(15)

The centralized control of research should not, however, be exaggerated. While the research establishments are not nearly as autonomous as, say, before 1965, nevertheless, the initiative over research programs remains largely with them. It was considered inappropriate for the boards to concern themselves in too much detail with the programs of the establishment. Though, as we shall see later, there are some ways in which greater involvement is necessary, the boards, in general, aim at identifying areas of work that are important enough to support, leaving the detailed research proposals to the establishments and other contractors. This, indeed, is the basic understanding of the intention behind the strategies exercise, and it is reasonable to expect that, in this way, the balance of influence over the overall shape of the Department's research programs will, over the next few years, continue to tip toward the boards.

Will the overall shape be arrived at sensibly? The problem of criteria for choice, or of strategy, as it is termed here, is of comparable difficulty in this field to its counterpart in the field of basic research. One reason for this is our lack of understanding of the factors which affect industrial performance, and of the role of science and technology therein. Another is the lack of a clear industrial policy to which the boards might try to respond. The current attempt to develop an industrial strategy offers some hope of guidance for the boards. Progress to date has not been striking, but the industrial strategies exercise is still very young. One ground for curbing undue optimism, however, is the lukewarm enthusiasm which British industry has traditionally expressed for government research establishments and their work.

In order to fill out the picture presented here, it will be important to keep in mind, the overall pattern of government

research support for civilian industry. A breakdown of
expenditures on R & D by sector in the early 1970s would
reveal that about 86 percent of the Department's research and
development effort is concentrated in three sectors: nuclear,
aerospace, and computers. The remainder, classified as "other
industry," represents the budget of the Research Requirements Boards which we have been discussing so far. Although
all of the Department's research and development spending is
supposed to be allocated using the customer-contractor principle, it is difficult to discern what mechanisms have been
introduced to coordinate the budget so that, overall, the
expenditure is matched to the propensity of the economy to
grow. As far as one can see, no strategy exists in the case
of nuclear, aerospace, and computer technology comparable to
that which has emerged in the Research Requirement Boards
for "other industry." These investments represent an enormous fixed cost and any administrative mechanism would be
hard pressed to dismantle or redistribute it.

Basic Research

The bulk of Britain's basic and long-term applied research is
administered by the research councils and carried out in
council-operated laboratories, universities, or institutes associated with universities. The customer-contractor principle
which was intended to be implemented across the whole range
of government R & D caused a tremendous furor within the
scientific community when Lord Rothschild recommended that a
fraction of each council's budget be transferred to the appropriate departments. Whether it was due to the intensity of
the furor or not, the budget of the Science Research Council
(SRC) - a council concerned predominantly with basic research - was left intact. Nevertheless, the SRC presents some
very interesting phenomena to those who would contemplate
changing the rate and direction of basic research activities.
     Although formally exempt from the Rothschild reforms,
the SRC was, in the early 1970s, an organization under
pressure due to a declining growth rate in its budget coupled
with pockets of strong criticism from within the scientific
community itself over the distribution of resources among the
various disciplines. At that time, about 40 percent of the
Council's budget was devoted to nuclear physics, and many
scientists publicly expressed their doubts about benefits to the
country at large of so lop-sided a pattern of distribution.(16)
     The main instrument devised to handle the problem of
declining growth rate in the budget was the policy of selectivity and concentration. The guiding idea was that certain
areas of science and engineering should be selected for priority funding and resources concentrated in a few centers of

excellence - university departments - where research of the highest quality would be carried out. Although the criteria for priority selection were never made explicit, it is clear that the intention was to increase support for engineering research and certain areas of "small science" such as polymer chemistry which were seen to have industrial relevance. Resources for this increased funding were to be transferred from the budget of the Nuclear Physics Board.

The effect of this policy on the national nuclear physics capability was devastating. Since 1971, nearly all of Britain's domestic nuclear physics program has been stopped and laboratories closed. Soon, all that will remain will be a base level of support to enable British scientists to take part in CERN, the European nuclear facility in Geneva. There can be no doubt that, in terms of facilities, machines, equipment, and laboratories, domestic nuclear physics is coming to an end.

But when one looks at the evolution of the pattern of research grant funding for nuclear physics, the picture is somewhat less clear. Currently, I am involved in an examination of all the peer-adjudicated research grants awarded by the SRC over the decade 1964-1974; a period in which 12,000 grants involving an expenditure of £120 million were allocated. In terms of priorities, three things stand out. The Engineering Board failed to maintain its early growth (in terms of percentage of total SRC commitments) and support has now slumped to pre-1970 levels. Further, the grants awarded by the Nuclear Physics Board, despite drastic cuts in expenditures on facilities, managed to hold their own or even increase slightly. The Science Board, on the other hand, which may be said to support "small science" generally, has remained constant in terms of its percentage of total SRC commitments. In particular, the Chemistry Board - which would have an important stake in funding of polymer chemistry - actually decreased as a percentage over the decade. Overall, little change has occurred in the pattern of allocation during the post-Rothschild period as far as peer-adjudicated grants are concerned. In terms of selectivity, it seems reasonable to conclude that, if priorities have changed, they have somehow been completely masked in the grant allocation patterns as they have evolved over the last decade.

Concentration - the percentage of grants given to a percentage of the funded community of scientists or university departments - also presents some interesting features. An analysis of the changes over time in the distribution of grants among scientists, university departments, and universities shows that concentration has remained virtually constant at all levels of aggregation over the past decade.(17) What this means is that the same proportion of scientists, university departments, or universities have been in receipt of the same proportions of SRC funds for the past ten years. In view of

declining growth rates in budgets, one might have expected,
for example, that scarce resources would have become concentrated in the elite institutions and that the "second-best"
would have gradually been starved of this sort of support.
This appears not to have happened.

On the basis of this empirical work, one is forced to
conclude that, in terms of the intentions of the policy of
selectivity and concentration, resource distributions have been
stubbornly resistant to change, despite a considerable effort
by the SRC. It is possible to believe that the policy was mere
rhetoric, designed to show that the Council was trying to
accommodate the spirit of the Rothschild reforms or, alternatively, that the Council was unable to direct its funds
according to policy, but neither conclusion is really tenable.
The answer lies in the structure of the SRC and its relationship to the scientific community. On the one hand, the
SRC makes almost exclusive use of the peer-review system for
identifying projects of scientific merit, and it is clear that this
system is more competent at identifying scientific merit than it
is at balancing it with commercial or industrial merit. On the
other hand, the SRC is a responsive system and, as such,
must wait upon the scientific community to produce proposals
for research. The scientists, in their turn, are fully con-
versant with the operation of the peer-review system, and
know that their success in getting a grant as well as their
professional advancement depend on the judgments of their
colleagues as to the scientific excellence of their proposals.
The consequence is that, as long as the SRC relies on the
peer-review system, it will, de facto, be supporting projects
which arise within the various scientific specialisms. It is,
perhaps, not too big a step to say that, once the pattern of
support among the specialisms has been established, it will
change according to its own rules and time scale. What we are
faced with here is not resistance to change but the social
dynamics of the scientific community for whom significant
changes in cognitive interest involves a more complex process
than is allowed for in the policy of selectivity and concentration.

DECISION MAKING IN KNOWLEDGE COMMUNITIES

In making the transition from the case studies to the implications for policy, it will be helpful to summarize the main
developments to date concerning the implementation of the
customer-contractor principle. First, we have observed a
thoroughgoing attempt to establish a need-oriented framework
for the guidance of research. Secondly, the criteria for
choice within this framework are not yet fully worked out.

Thirdly, in both the cases considered, it has been left to the scientific and technological communities to interpret general objectives and to respond to them with proposals for research. Fourthly, the principal incentive used to induce changes in research priorities has been to increase or decrease the funds available for certain areas of research. In the Department of Industry, research directors are still required to bid for resources, albeit now with some knowledge of the general interests of the requirement boards, while the SRC has limited itself primarily to announcing its <u>intention</u> to support certain areas of research. In the end, however, both must wait on the decisions of the scientific and technological communities for proposals to indicate whether and how the shift to newly defined areas will be accomplished.

If one accepts that, because of the uncertainty of research activity itself, the coupling between needs and research programs must remain somewhat loose, then the problem of changing priorities in research and development can be seen to hinge on the ability to influence the behavior of scientists and engineers. This behavior has two dimensions: motivation and cognitive expectations. With regard to motivation, the traditional ethos has it that scientists are seekers after knowledge of the natural world for its own sake, while engineers pursue technical efficiency. The oversight, which is currently being clarified by the sociology of science, has been that, in the twentieth century, both science and technology are fully professionalized activities and that this brings a distinct social dimension to the motivation of scientists and engineers. No longer is the pursuit of scientific knowledge or technical efficiency the domain of the disinterested amateur or the "inspired tinkerer" which characterized science and technology throughout most of the nineteenth century. Scientists and engineers now work in teams, usually in large institutions, and seek, among other things, identification with and recognition from their peer group. The point to be made is that, in the professional community which characterizes scientific and technological activities today, knowledge and social organization have become mutually self-defining: what constitutes an interesting intellectual problem area needs the assent of a community of inquirers without whom the problem would remain a fringe activity. Conversely, those communities which have established themselves have an important influence not only over what the interesting areas are but what methods will be considered appropriate as well as who shall be admitted to the specialty and according to what criteria. It follows from this that purely monetary incentives of the sort we have observed in the two case studies can be expected to have only a marginal effect on the motivations of scientists and engineers. One consequence of this which has been observed many times is that the scientific or technological community comes into conflict with institutional goals established at an earlier time; de facto, the institution has undergone a goal displacement – though annual reports couched in the language of the original mission of the laboratory continue to be written.

Turning now from the motivational to the expectational aspects of behavior, economists and policymakers have long been aware that motivational patterns are strongly affected by the expectations of the business community toward likely future changes. For example, decisions about buying and selling are critically dependent not only on prevailing prices but also on expectations about changes in these prices. In an analogous way, scientists and engineers have cognitive expectations; expectations about the pattern of scientific or technological developments which are likely to occupy their profession in the future. As in the case of a businessman, a scientist will embark on a problem area with as clear an idea as possible of costs and benefits involved. After all, he knows well enough that he will obtain little in the way of professional rewards for tackling problems which are judged to be passé or routine by his peers; neither will he receive much encouragement if he embarks on too radical a departure from existing judgments about what is worthwhile. Although these patterns of cognitive expectations (for there are many of them) may not be explicit, they, nonetheless, define a crucial input into policies aimed at changing research priorities.

SOME SUGGESTIONS FOR POLICY

There is clearly a close connection between motivation and cognitive expectations. One hypothesis is that the motivation for change is critically dependent on cognitive expectations. Let me illustrate this in a general way by reference to two examples of change: one scientific, the other technological.

Scientific Change

It is to Thomas Kuhn that we owe the idea that scientific development might be discontinuous; an activity that is rooted cognitively in a paradigm - a kind of open-ended puzzle - and socially, in the adherence of groups to a paradigm.(18) What Kuhn postulates is that, most of the time, scientists are busy in a puzzle-solving manner working out the implications of some more general framework which he refers to as a paradigm. From the point of view of policy, this is a valuable insight because it suggests a correlation between the cognitive and social dimensions of science. Indeed, it suggests an alternative way of classifying the activities of the scientific community. Rather than relying solely on the traditional method of classification by discipline which is static, an alternative would be to identify "active research groups": individuals who are in close contact intellectually with one another. Such individuals may not belong to the same discipline, nor need they all be members of a university, but they would define a problem area. There is already a considerable literature about how such groups are formed, how long they endure, and how they come to be regrouped in new combinations.(19) Although there is much more to be learned about the dynamics of these groups, it is clear that problem areas identified in this way tend to be fluid and to change more rapidly than either disciplinary labels or committee names.

Such a procedure could be used as a basis for planning. If the scientific community were encouraged to classify itself in this way, policymakers would have a much better grasp of where, at any time, the efforts of the scientific community are concentrated. This could be important for two reasons. First, it is possible to show that the advance of science depends critically on the adherence of a group to a set of problems, methods, or techniques; unless scientists are motivated to make this commitment, the set of ideas involved will not be tested thoroughly enough to discover how good they really are - hence, no development of the problem area will occur. Conversely, once the groups are formed, it may be very difficult to shift them to something else. Nevertheless, it is possible to hypothesize that, when the details of a problem area are becoming exhausted, the specialist group may be particularly prone to look for (i.e., it is motivated to seek) a new direction. Indeed, it may be possible to identify this empirically by observing changes in the pattern of intellectual contact between members of different groups; perhaps the interaction between groups is greatest during a time of intellectual transition from one problem area to another.

These changes in intellectual association are the direct expression of changing cognitive expectations: judgments by the members of a group that a particular line of inquiry is coming to an end. There is a growing literature which suggests that the propensity of a specialism to respond to socioeconomic goals is strongest during these times. For example, a recent study of the origins in Germany of the discipline of chemical engineering as a professional subgroup from its parent (chemistry) shows in detail how theoretical developments in chemistry were related to the emergence of the economically important, industry-oriented science of chemical engineering.(20) Similar data would be of immense help in informing policymakers of the propensity of scientific disciplines or subdisciplines to respond to social goals. In terms of resources, it would cost very little and, perhaps most important of all, it would not impair the normal operation of the peer-review system.

Technological Change

In the theory of technological innovation, the notion of discontinuous development extends back to Schumpeter in the 1920s.(21) Whereas, for scientific development, the key distinction is between "normal" and "revolutionary science," in the study of technological innovation, the key distinction is between incremental and radical innovation. The analogue in technology to the paradigm in science is the dominant design. Engineers, like scientists, appear to spend a good deal of their time elaborating either a single or a family of related designs which engages their attention for a considerable period of time and provides a natural trajectory for a whole range of innovations.

The Model T Ford provides an excellent exemplar of the existence of a dominant design and of the effects of its presence on the motivations of a whole range of Ford Motor Company employees. The Model T, viewed as a dominant design, also illustrates the importance of the cognitive expectations of engineers to which we referred earlier. The perceived potential of this design resulted in a continuing and heavy investment of resources in the Model T for a period of nearly twenty years. The benefits of elaborating this design were continually falling prices despite overall increase in both the weight of the motor car and the horsepower of the engine. On the other hand, it should be noted that these technological expectations eventually became so fixed in the fabric of the organization that, in the end, they became a major stumbling block to further innovation.(22)

From the point of view of the firm, the acceptance of a dominant design tends to establish a pattern of incremental innovation, while its absence provokes the search for radical innovations. In the context of industrial research strategy, it makes a considerable difference whether an industry is in a predominantly incremental or a predominantly radical mode of innovation. Stated briefly, a different pattern of government support would be required to help an industry solve a major problem associated with a dominant design from that required to identify a dominant design. This is precisely the sort of industrial information which is not available to the Research Requirement Boards at the moment, and it is difficult to understand how their strategies can fully influence the direction of research in their laboratories when they possess no coherent data on the technological expectations operative in the relevant industries. The precondition of a successful industrial research strategy is a group of current dominant designs and the patterns of natural trajectories of technical development that derive therefrom.

CONCLUSIONS

Whether our current economic malaise is due to the problems of the "fifth Kondriatieff upswing" as Rostow has suggested,(23) or to the abandonment of the industrial ethos as Dahrendorf has indicated,(24) or whether low economic growth rates are forced on the major economies of the world by resource limitations of various kinds, the conclusion remains that, in the next 25 years, a "different composition of output" will be required. The first consequence for research and development strategy will be a need to change priorities. But, the general conclusion to be drawn from the cases presented in this paper is that, in two crucial areas - industrial research and development, and basic research in science - changes have been slow in coming. We have suggested that the reason for this lies not in the natural resistance of organizations to change but in the dynamics of the scientific and technological communities. The cognitive orientation of these communities at any time, we observed, was embedded in the long process of socialization which transforms high school students into members of professional elites. One implication of this is that the natural rhythm of change takes place over generations rather than decades. A major problem arises here because it is widely believed that the pressure on world resources is such that changes on the time scale of decades rather than generations is imperative.

A second consequence is that governments will have to become more deeply involved in the planning of research and development. The ability of governments to do this successfully will depend in large part on the theoretical tools which are available to them. Unfortunately, the tools that have been developed so far tend to deal with the problems of the level of output; changes in composition of output which are likely to accompany low resource growth rates will require a deeper understanding of the nature of scientific and technological activities.

In focusing as we have on the dynamics of scientific and technological change, there is no intention of revising the spirit of technological determinism. The substance of science and technology - theories, instruments, methods, and machinery - cannot by themselves provide an easy transition - a technological fix - to a low growth economy. What we have been trying to indicate is that, in the contemporary context, science and technology are thoroughly institutionalized and professionalized and that this, in turn, implies that there is an intrinsic social process at work which conditions behavior and constrains the rate and direction of innovative activity, whether scientific or technological. Policy for science and technology, we have said, has been based on an analogy with economic exchange mechanisms. But, if the clarification of the motivations and expectations of businessmen and consumers as economic actors is considered central to economic policy, does it not follow that similar clarification with respect to scientists and engineers would enhance the prospect of reallocating scientific and technological resources?

Yet, here we must face a paradox. The developed countries of the world describe themselves as technological societies, thereby giving expression to perhaps their essential dynamic. But if that is the case, it is hard to understand why so little attention is devoted to understanding the nature of those scientific and technological processes on which they are so clearly dependent. It would be ironic indeed if our prodigious technological civilization were to falter because it failed to accept the seriousness of this challenge.

NOTES

(1) A. Marwick, The Deluge (London: The Bodley Head, 1976).

(2) R. Dahrendorf, The New Liberty (London: Routledge and Kegan Paul, 1975) passim., but especially p. 41.

(3) A. Singh, "U.K. Industry and the World Economy: A Case of De-industrialization," Cambridge Journal of Economics (June 1977): 113-35.

(4) A. Mencher, "Lessons for American Policy Making from the British Labor Government's 1964-70 Experience in Applying Technology to Economic Objectives," London Graduate School of Business Studies, London, 1975.

(5) N. K. Gardner, "The Economics of Launching Aid," in The Economics of Industrial Subsidies, edited by A. Whiting (Dept. of Industry, H.M.S.O., 1975).

(6) C. Freeman, "Technical Innovation and British Trade Performance," in De-Industrialization, edited by F. Blackaby (National Institute of Economic and Social Research, Heinemann, 1979), pp. 56-73.

(7) B. R. Williams, Technology, Investment and Growth (London: Chapman Hall, 1967).

(8) Freeman, "Technical Innovation," p. 66.

(9) D. L. Bosworth, "Recent Trends in Research and Development in the United Kingdom," Research Policy 8 (1979): 164-85.

(10) A Framework for Government Research and Development, Cmnd. 4814 H.M.S.O. 1971.

(11) R. Williams, "Some Political Aspects of the Rothschild Affair," Science Studies 3 (1) (January 1973): 31-46.
(12) The seven Research Requirements Boards represent Ship and Marine Technology; Chemical and Mineral Processes; Engineering Materials; Mechanical Engineers and Machine Tools; Computer Systems and Electronics, Metrology, and Standards. The Chief Scientist's Requirement Boards handle a range of topics including those which fall between the existing boards.
(13) Department of Industry, Reports of the Research Requirement Boards, 1973 (London: Department of Industry, 1974), p. 5.
(14) Ibid., p. 41.
(15) Department of Industry, Interim Strategies of the Research and Development Requirements Boards (London: Department of Industry, 1975), p. 5.
(16) E. Jones and R. Nyholm, "Minority Report" in The Proposed 300 G & V Accelerator (Department of Education and Science, Cmnd. 3503, H.M.S.O., 1968).
(17) C. Farina, "Selectivity and Concentration: Patterns in the Science Research Council's Allocation of Resources" (Ph.D. diss., University of Manchester, 1978), pp. 212-72.
(18) T.S. Kuhn, The Structure of Scientific Revolutions (Chicago: University of Chicago Press, 1962).
(19) B.C. Griffith et al, "The Structure of Scientific Literatures II: Toward a Macro and Microstructure for Science," Science Studies 4 (1974): 339-65.
(20) K. Buchholz, " Vehrfahrenstechnik (Chemical Engineering): Its Development, Present State and Structure," Social Studies of Science 9 (1) (1979): 33-62.
(21) J. Schumpeter, The Theory of Economic Development (Oxford University Reprints, 1974), pp. 57-94.
(22) W. Abernathy and Kenneth Wayne, "The Limits of the Learning Curve," Harvard Business Review (September-October 1974): 111-20.
(23) W. W. Rostow, Getting From Here to There: A Policy for the Keynsian Age (London: Macmillan, 1977), pp. 20-37.
(24) Dahrendorf, The New Liberty.

6210

5 Science, Technology, and the Emerging Postindustrial Society
Tom Stonier

THE TECHNOLOGICAL HERITAGE

The relationship between society and its environment is primal. However, this relationship is altered by the introduction of technology. As far as humanity is concerned, that process is ancient. The reduced canines of the early hominids imply that they used weapons. Three million years ago, there emerged a creature able to walk upright as we do. Undoubtedly, the selective pressure for this development stemmed from the parallel evolution of the musculature of the arm, wrist, hand, and fingers. These developments allowed our proto-human ancestors both to throw things accurately and to manipulate and shape objects. Throwing objects and manipulating arti- facts represent the beginnings of human technology. Using technology for making our environment more suitable and productive has become a major feature of the human heritage.

It can be argued that the use of technology is the major feature of our human heritage. For example, it took the development of two major technologies – fire and language – to provide the foundation for human culture. Of the two, fire was perhaps the most important, although current opinion favors the latter. In fact, it is often claimed that language is unique to humans. This is in contradiction to the evidence obtained over the past two to three decades on members of the dolphin family, creatures whose brain to spinal chord ratio is comparable to ours. The fact that the ability to communicate a wide range of information by abstract auditory symbols is not unique to the human species should, in no way, detract from its significance from one generation to the next in parallel to, but outside of, the genetic system. It represents a form of paragenetics which begins to alter the mechanics of evolution.

For one thing, it permits the Lamarckian heresy to operate -
acquired characters <u>are</u> inherited.

Dolphins may have the brains and language with which to
analyze their environment, but they lack the hands with which
to shape it. Of all the miracles fashioned by human hands,
the greatest must have been the controlling of fire. Not only
are all other higher animals afraid of fire, no other creature
has harnessed a nonmetabolic energy source which is not a
regular feature of its environment (e.g., sun, wind, currents,
gravity). No wonder the gods were angry with Prometheus.

With the exception of those animals at the top of the food
chain, all animals face two major problems: getting enough to
eat, and not being eaten. The use of fire solved the second
problem for our prehistoric ancestors, and helped enormously
with the first. Fire not only frightened away predators, it
would stampede game over cliffs or into swamps or traps. Fire
made food more digestible (e.g., meat), palatable (potatoes),
even converted the poisonous into something nutritious (cassava). It could also help preserve food by drying it. Fire
provided the warmth necessary for expanding the geographic
range, and it could make smooth and hard the points and
edges of weapons and tools. Last, but not least, our ancestors no longer were forced to sleep at nightfall. By the
light of the fire, what was probably the first human language,
mime, developed, perhaps re-enacting the day's hunt for the
wide-eyed young. Also, by the flickering flames, the moving
shadows of the human psyche, by now comprehending fully its
own mortality, must have developed religion, engaged in feasts
of food and sex, devised group vocalization, developed laugh-
ter and language, and become human.

Other advanced primate societies continued to adapt
themselves to their environment. Human societies, in contrast,
began to adapt the environment to themselves.

In due course, our human ancestors solved the basic
biological problem of getting enough to eat. The domestication
of plants and animals provided a stable, year-round food
supply. Following the completion of the Neolithic Revolution
and settlement life, further increases in levels of production
began to produce surpluses. The establishment of trade was
facilitated by technological improvements, not only in food and
materials production, but also in transportation. Thus arose
the foundations of economic interactions.

THE DYNAMICS OF CULTURAL EVOLUTION

Ecological, technological, and economic interactions provide the
basic determinants from which all further sociocultural patterns derive. These include customs, belief systems, be-

havior patterns and, in particular, the cultural institutions of society. There are feedback loops; for example, changes in technology may themselves be caused or influenced by a variety of economic, social, and political factors. New technological advances may reflect the commercial exploitation of economic opportunities, political decisions to develop a new military technology, or they may reflect the accidental spin-offs of scientists who, for reasons of professional advancement or just plain intellectual curiosity, have uncovered new information. But irrespective of the reason for technological advances, such advances always precede major changes in lifestyle. Changes in technology provide the major driving force for cultural development.

The rise of the major civilizations has been characterized not only by the invention of physical technologies such as mining, metallurgy, irrigation, road building, and shipping, but, perhaps even more important, the invention of social technologies generating three new major institutions - war, slavery, and the state.

War as an institution arose in late Neolithic times. Prior to that, intergroup conflict had involved merely territorial skirmishes, not much different in principle from that observed among other primates engaged in group territorial behavior. By the late Neolithic times, the very success of having solved the two basic biological problems of getting enough to eat and not being eaten led to a systematic overcrowding. As the anthropologist Robert Carneiro has pointed out, from this point, the principal new environmental determinant for societal success or failure became a society's enemies. Those who could organize themselves most successfully could put the maximum number of warriors in the field. Survival no longer depended on physical technologies alone but on social, political, and military ones as well.

These developments occurred in "circumscribed" geographical areas where it was not possible for subgroups to move out without considerable hardship. Smaller social units were subdued or assimilated by larger ones, who, in turn, might be forced to submit to still more powerful neighbors. Thus, the formation of tightly hierarchical, centralized states, the emergence of a warrior class and standing army, and the requirement for coerced labor (usually in the form of serfs and slaves) combined to produce the "great" ancient civilizations.

The eight millenia, or so, comprising this Agrarian Era were filled with military violence in which competing groups fought interminably over limited resources. Nowhere was this more true than in Northern Europe. A thousand years ago, however, a fortunate series of technological developments produced the Agricultural Revolution of the ninth and tenth centuries. Europe emerged from the "Dark Ages." Centered on the deep plow and ancillary technology, the fertile plains of

Northern Europe became available for excess food production. Prior to that technological breakthrough, Europe was condemned to be a poor and backward area. After, it began to grow prosperous.

THE RISE OF THE MECHANICAL ERA

It was in the middle of this millenium, following the remarkable technological progress of the Middle Ages and the Renaissance, that Europe began to move into the "Mechanical Era," characterized by the development of mechanical devices and the institutionalization of science. The epitome of the Mechanical Era occurred in the eighteenth century with the invention of the steam engine.

The steam engine represents a paradigm for the concept of a "metatechnology," a concept useful in understanding what is happening to contemporary society. Initially, the steam engine was merely another clever device for pumping water out of mines; for about half a century, that is all it was used for. Then it became a metatechnology: it was applied to a large number of existing mechanical devices. Coupling a steam engine to a wagon created a locomotive; coupling a steam engine to a loom created a power loom. Over the next century, or so, most major mechanical devices became power-driven devices. This is what we call the Industrial Revolution.

A parallel today is the emergence of the computer as a metatechnology. Initially, the computer was merely utilized to do some sophisticated and rapid computations. Gradually, however, its true significance as an information machine has been realized. What society is now seeing is the coupling of information machines to power machines, displacing the human operators who used to guide the machines.

Actually, the "Information Revolution," generating the information society, represents the second of two major technological breakthroughs. The first was the "Electronic Revolution" which, although it can be traced back into the nineteenth century, gained momentum in the twentieth. The Electronic Revolution differs from the Industrial Revolution in that the latter involved the invention of devices which extended the human musculature - devices which related to physical manipulation. In contrast, the Electronic Revolution involved an extension of the human nervous system - radio and telephone as an extension of the ear; film, an extension of the eye and the ear; and, of course, the computer, an extension of the brain. This analogy is not superficial; to be able to extend neurological capabilities is qualitatively different from extending physical capabilities.

THE RISE OF THE COMMUNICATIVE ERA

The major impact of extending neurological capabilities is in the organizational capacity of human social groups. In a sense, a caricature could be made of the late Mechanical Era: a Frankenstein monster heedlessly devouring our planet, characterized by an emerging nuclear missile technology which could destroy civilization without having developed the social technology to make sure that this would not happen. However, the emerging "Communicative Era," which began around the middle of the twentieth century, has reversed this imbalance at an amazingly rapid rate. Areas of traditional bloodshed and conflict, such as Western Europe, have emerged as an island of peace in a world still racked by strife. The reasons for this are self-evident if one recognizes that one of the consequences of the improved communication, transportation, and advanced production technologies has been the creation of an economically interdependent Europe, a Europe in which the traditional nation-state has become as irrelevent today as the feudal state became economically irrelevant following the rise of mercantilism. In addition, there is also the military reality. The feudal state became militarily nonviable after the advent of modern military technology (including the use of gunpowder). Similarly, the modern nation-state has become increasingly military nonviable with the spread of more sophisticated nuclear weapons powered by cheaper delivery systems.

The negative pressure of the military technology, however, is not as important as the positive cooperative interactions elicited by modern productive systems which draw components and raw materials from many other countries, generating a new form of interdependence. Traditional enemies, such as France and Germany, whose hatred reached peaks of virulence in the past, have not only become each other's largest trading partners, but in the process, developed harmonious relationships. People who cooperate to solve mutual problems tend to become friendly; people who compete for limited resources tend to become hostile. The greater the stakes, the greater the hostility, so that if the stakes begin to verge on matters of life and death, then killing becomes easy. In that statement is the greatest hope for the disappearance of war as an institution, at least in those parts of the world sufficiently technologically advanced to create affluence. One American farmer, for example, now feeds 59 people.

It is for this reason, the profound increase in materials productivity, that one sees the disappearance of war as a social institution during the Communicative Era. Earlier, during the Mechanical Era, that other ancient social institution, slavery, disappeared. Slavery was a social necessity because the ancient civilizations, at the beginning of the "Agrarian Era," needed a large pool of coerced labor to provide the extra food and other economic necessities for sustaining their military establishments, governing bureaucracies, and other concomitant activities. With the advent of the Industrial Revolution, the increasing productivity of wage labor coupled to machines obviated the need for slavery.

An increase in productivity is not enough if there is also an increase in population. It was only with the advent of still more efficient production systems that the Malthusian nightmare has been reversed; in technologically advanced societies, resources are, in fact, outstripping population. Therefore, the primary social motivation for war, the extension of resources demanded by expanding populations (secondary causes involving defense, revenge, struggle for status, etc.) has now been obviated by technological ingenuity. This explains why the technologically advanced sector of the world is now unlikely to become involved in military confrontations.

There is yet another aspect of the Communicative society which is attractive: an increasing tendency to diffuse power throughout society, that is, an increasing democratization. The most recent countries to begin entering Communicative society are the Southern tier European states: Greece, Spain, and Portugal. As the new communications/information technology overtakes the Soviet Union, we may expect profound political changes before the end of the 1980s, which will very quickly bring alterations in other Soviet bloc countries as well. That is not to imply that these countries will give up planned economies, or even sweep away all vestiges of authoritarianism. Nevertheless, the new technocratic rulers of Soviet society, which will replace the present gerontocracy, will bring about a profound liberalization of the political structure.

The reasons behind the pressure for democratization of the political structures of Communicative societies are not entirely clear. First, there has emerged an enormously efficient, complex, and leaky information network. Characteristic of Communicative society is the fact that the majority of households have telephones, the vast majority have television, and everybody has radios. These electronic systems are augmented by a flood of printed media and, more significantly, an advanced transnational transportation network with a steady stream of visitors moving around and in and out of the country.

Information is the new coin of power, just as money or ownership of land used to be in earlier eras. Widespread and advanced public education, plus massive communication networks (particularly TV), which will shortly be coupled to new home-based electronic data systems, assure a further diffusion of information over the entire society. As more and more people partake of higher education, as the communication/

information networks expand (including electronic polling techniques), as an increasingly complex economy requires more and more significant specialists' inputs, the society will continue to move toward consensus democracy. Orwell's 1984 paradigm is an extension of late Mechanical society; it does not portray what is actually happening.

This optimistic picture is, of course, in great contrast to what is happening in the Third World which is presently leaving the Agrarian period and moving into the Mechanical/Industrial phase of human society. In the process, Third World societies exhibit an increase in authoritarianism, nationalism, militarism, internal strife, and international war. To compound the problem, the introduction of modern medicine has depressed death rates sufficiently to cause a population "explosion." It is a moral obligation, as well as a matter of self-interest, that technologically advanced countries help Third World countries move as rapidly as possible through the Industrial phase into the Communicative Era. This involves not only a transfer of capital but also a transfer of technical information.

THE ROBOTS ARE COMING

For the technologically advanced sector of the world there are also pressing economic problems. Chief among these is the displacement of labor by the accelerating development of the microelectronics-based information technology.

Predictions that automation would create serious unemployment have abounded for decades. They were premature, however. Computers were too expensive. The microprocessors have changed all this. Compared to ENIAC, the world's first electronic computer, the price has dropped by a factor exceeding 10,000. The microprocessor is 20 times faster, has a larger memory, is 1,000 times more reliable, occupies a thirty-thousandth of the space, and consumes the power of a small lightbulb rather than that of a locomotive.

The rate at which a new technology displaces an older technology is a function of how much better it is. Better may mean cheaper, faster, more accurate, more reliable, or longer-lasting. Coupling the new information devices to machines has become all of these: coupling microprocessors to either a drill press or a typewriter makes it cheaper to operate than when it is coupled only to a human operator. Furthermore, machines can work 24 hours a day, 365 days a year, never go on strike, never report in sick (unless they are badly designed), and do not complain if they are shut off for six months because of altered production schedules. Nor does one robot displace one worker. That is not the way the field is developing. For example, a company making a complex facing for a piece of automated mining equipment used to employ six men to make that facing - four skilled and two unskilled workers. The entire team was displaced by a single robot requiring only one semi-skilled worker. In spite of the relatively high initial cost, the company manager felt that the machine paid for itself in about 18 months. This reflected, for the most part, savings in labor costs. There was also, however, a saving in materials and reduced rejects because the robot was more accurate.

The automotive industry is one of the major industries affected: Fiat, Volvo, Saab, VW, Nissan, Mitsubishi, Daimler-Benz, Renault, and others are installing automated equipment. In the case of Fiat, the "Robegate" concept takes advantage of the programmable feature of the microprocessor and does all the welding during framing so that 25 men, including maintenance personnel, replace 125 men. The Robogate system also reduces the cost of changing the body design. Robotized systems are emerging in many parts of the world. In television manufacture, one finds that automatic sequences, automatic insertion of components in printed circuit boards, wave soldering equipment, and computer-controlled automatic test equipment have eliminated most of the manual labor. A single machine can insert components into a printed circuit board at a rate of 72,000 pieces an hour. It would require 240 workers to achieve that rate, yet the automatic insertion machines can be operated by as few as 11. Not only does an automated process of this sort save labor, it also reduces the number of rejects, upgrades quality, and reduces maintenance cost.

It is not only in manufacturing, but also in services and offices that the microelectronic revolution will have an impact. For example, the British Post Office will introduce in the 1980s its systems X telephone equipment. Not only will it require only 4 percent of the work force needed to build the current electromechanical Strowgear, but once it is installed, the new equipment will require hardly any maintenance. The U.K. Post Office has also begun to install its computer-based PRESTEL information-communications system. Such a system will obviate the need for many middle-men. In the long-run, one would expect the vast bulk of the real estate, travel agents, and other similar services to become obsolete. The use of computerized cash checkouts in supermarkets, stockroom controls, etc. will greatly reduce the number of unskilled and semi-skilled service jobs available. The traditional office jobs are also rapidly shrinking. Not only have computers replaced hordes of payroll clerks, Xerox machines, and rooms full of copy typists, but now the word processors are beginning to enter the market. One department in the local city government of Bradford, England, introduced a word processor system into its typing pool. As a result, the work force of 44 girls was reduced to 22. This was accomplished with an overall productivity increase claimed to be 30 percent and an annual saving to the city of almost £ 60,000. Not to be over-looked is the fact that whereas personnel turnover rate amounted to 30 percent the previous year, it dropped to zero once the system was installed. The women enjoy working with the new equipment. What will happen when the vococoders allow a direct voice-to-type system?

The outstanding problem confronting Western societies in the 1980s will be the unemployment resulting from the rapid displacement of machine and low-grade information operatives by the new information technology. This process is not too different from the displacement of labor over the last few centuries by improved machinery and productive methods; first from farms, more recently from factories. What gives the matter greater urgency is the shrinking timespan. Whereas it took over 60 years in the United States for farm labor to decline from its peak in absolute numbers around World War I to its present level, it is likely that the corresponding decline in manufacturing and office labor will take place in a 15-30 year period.

At the beginning of the eighteenth century, it took 80 to 90 percent of the work force to feed a country. Today, in the United States, it takes less than 3 percent. What this will mean is that electronic systems will replace people carrying out routine jobs in offices, factories, mining, and transportation. The spread of the new metatechnology will mean that, by early in the next century, it will require no more than 10 percent of the labor force to provide society with all its material needs; that is, all the food we eat, all the clothing we wear, all the textiles, housing, furniture, appliances, automobiles, etc.

THE POSTINDUSTRIAL ECONOMY

The technologically-advanced sector of global society has moved into a postindustrial economy with the following fea-tures:

1. It is primarily a service economy rather than a manu-facturing one, with the knowledge industry predomin-ating.
2. As reflection of (1), the labor force is no longer dom-inated by machine operatives who work with machines but by information operatives.
3. It is a credit-based economy characterized by a flow of credit information rather than by large cash transactions.
4. It is primarily transnational rather than national.

5. It is characterized by unprecedented affluence both at the private individual level and in the public sector.
6. Changes are taking place at an exponential rate rather than linearly.

It is not the function of this chapter to describe these features in detail. It is, however, important to consider further several points in the above list. Knowledge, for example, has become the most important single input into modern productive systems, increasingly displacing the traditional inputs of land, labor, capital, materials, and energy. The displacement of land by knowledge is exemplified by skyscrapers. Automation will continue to displace labor, as mechanization did before. The reduction in capital, materials, and energy production is best exemplified by advances in the computer industry itself. Increasingly, information will be used to substitute for expensive materials or brute energy.

There is another highly significant feature of the information economy: When one consumes food or manufactured products, the monetary value of the item decreases as a result of being consumed, and the act of consumption increases entropy in the universe. The reverse is true when one consumes information and integrates it into the existing store of knowledge. This is true at the individual as well as at the societal level. The new information economy requires new paradigms and new concepts.

Over the last two centuries, there has been a shift from farm workers to factory workers to people who work in offices, classrooms, laboratories, etc. This shift reflects the emergence of information and knowledge as the most important asset of modern society. Even on farms, the American farmer has become the most productive worker in the world, not because he works longer and harder than his forefathers or his Third World contemporaries, but because of his knowledge base. At harvest time you might well find him driving an air-conditioned tractor and listening to his transistor radio. But he has an enormous information backup system including, not least of all, his own education. He knows how to drive a tractor and maintain a combine harvester which does the work of fifty men breaking their backs with a sickle. He knows about fertilizers, hybrid seeds, pesticides, and world market conditions. He knows how to run cooperatives to obtain cheaper supplies and store his crops for the right world prices. He may use a computer to optimize feed patterns and, in general, has the accumulated knowledge and information of many scientists and technicians behind him. He is himself the product of an advanced educational system.

Similarly, highly productive enterprises (such as pharmaceuticals, electronics, petrochemicals, and computers) represent an enormous investment in knowledge which has

accumulated over generations, including the knowledge inside
the heads of the Ph.D. engineers, and other technical workers
who invent, design, and operate the system. It becomes
apparent why the service sector which generates this knowledge is so important to the economy. Knowledge represents
an investment item, and government is the institution for
organizing that sector. People can readily understand that,
when the government builds roads, airports, and harbors, it
is contributing to the strength of the economy and constitutes
an investment. What is not yet understood is that an even
more vital investment is made when the government organizes
education to improve the skills of its people. These skills are
a nation's most important resource in a postindustrial society.
They are what makes the American farmer and the Japanese
shipbuilder the most efficient in the world.

Once this is understood, it becomes apparent what the
bulk of the work force will be doing in the next century.
Most people will be engaged in the knowledge industries,
specifically in education, research and development, and the
health services.

THE EXPANSION OF EDUCATION

Society is now subjected to an increasingly steep rate of
change. This reflects the fact that the accumulation of knowledge and the rate of invention is a function of how much
knowledge already exists and how many devices have already
been invented. The more that is known, the easier it is to
know still more; the more that has been invented, the easier it
is to invent still more. One of the inevitable consequences of
this exponential change is "cultural lag," clinging to cultural
patterns and belief systems which are no longer relevant. The
disparity between the new reality and the belief systems
results in what Alvin Toffler has called "future shock."

Toffler himself has suggested the answer to future shock.
It is to educate for the future; specifically, to educate for
the changing future. This must be one of the major new
functions of education. There must be other changes as well.
Education must become a cradle-to-grave proposition which
begins in the home under the supervision of paid professional
"grandmothers" coupled to home-based computers linked, via
television and telephone, to local, national, and global information resources. The traditional skills of reading, writing,
and arithmetic, as well as introduction to science, history,
geography, etc. can all be done singly or in small groups at
home. Children will go to school primarily to play with other
children, to engage in sports, dramatics, public speaking, and
to learn skills which cannot be learned as well at home. Edu-

cation must not be viewed merely as a front-end exercise at the beginning of life. The need for retraining will be paramount in a society where technology is continually closing off some areas of employment while opening up new opportunities elsewhere. Human beings should never stop growing. An attractive education system favors recycling in and out of learning experiences to meet the varying needs at different stages of life.

It is beyond the scope of this chapter to discuss in further detail the new educational structures which are likely to emerge over the next two or three decades.(1) What is important at this point is to describe the advantages of a massive expansion of education:

1. Education can provide millions of jobs in an area where it makes sense to be labor intensive, ranging from canteen personnel to computer professors.
2. A system of education which is sufficiently attractive to encourage young people to stay in and to encourage older people to return to full-time education will reduce the size of the labor pool. If one assumes a working life of 50 years, then every year added to full-time education represents 2 percent of the labor force.
3. An expanded education system creates a versatile labor force able to exploit rather than suffer from changing technological forces.
4. We need to educate for a much more sophisticated citizenry; one which understands the political processes, how the media work, and one which recognizes that we are members of a global society and must solve problems on a global basis.
5. We need to educate for leisure and for pleasure. As the formal work time decreases and as the standard of affluence increases, we need to train people how to enjoy themselves and how to develop their own talents and possibilities to maximum advantage.
6. We need to educate for survival, both at an individual level, to face a highly complex and psychologically taxing society, and as a global society living on a fragile planet floating in a hostile black space.
7. It takes education to increase a society's total data base. This improvement in mass data store, once coupled to research and development, will begin to solve a wide range of problems - physical, biological, social, economic, political, personal, and psychological. Expanded education coupled to R & D also becomes the basis for generating the wealth necessary to pay for the massive expansion of public service sector spending.

TECHNOLOGY AND GLOBAL RESOURCES

In a world now relying on nonrenewable resources, such as oil and gas, it becomes imperative to develop new sources of energy and stablize consumption while these new sources are being developed. High among these new sources is cheap oil from coal. Although coal, too, is a limited resource, there exist huge reserves throughout the world which would enable us to buy time. Of the renewable resources, wind energy and utilizing agricultural or other wastes (e.g., for producing methane or alcohol) hold promise. The most important form of renewable energy, however, is probably the sun. It is only since the Arab-induced oil crisis of 1973 that solar power has begun to be taken seriously in the United States. Extracting energy from ocean waves is another major source of renewable energy, as is extracting energy from the temperature differentials between the warmer upper layers of tropical oceans and the cooler deeper layers. Both forms of oceanic energy represent a way of utilizing energy trapped by the planet itself.

We live, in fact, on a highly energetic planet. Potential terrestrial energy sources include tidal and geothermal energy, particularly if techniques could be developed to exploit the heat of the deeper layers of the earth. Similarly, in nearby space both collecting direct solar radiation (which is then transmitted to earth as a microwave beam) and harnessing the solar winds could provide for a great expansion of the world's energy base. Nuclear energy seems undesirable for a number of reasons, but it illustrates the principle that new forms of energy may develop rapidly once they have been conceived and there is sufficient motivation to develop them.(2) Fusion energy is appearing on the technological horizon. What other forms of energy are available but not yet conceived of?

Other potential resource shortages must be viewed against a background of rising prices and developing technology. Just as drilling for oil under the North Sea became viable as the price of oil rose and the technology advanced, so have some companies begun to mine for manganese nodules in the deep, north equatorial Pacific. Other companies are contemplating extracting the brine pools of the Red Sea. A second approach to materials shortages involves substitution; the use of optical fibers to replace copper cables in telecommunications systems is a prime example. The other major human requirement, food, should involve a massive expansion of coastal and other forms of fish farming, and the expansion of the effort to develop safe and economically-viable single-cell protein techniques to permit the release of a vast acreage currently devoted to growing cattle fodder. Added to these two categories of technology is the development of new techniques to make deserts productive.

One hundred and fifty years ago, the idea of actually drilling for oil was of no value. Oil had not yet become a valuable resource. Fifty years ago, the idea of drilling for oil underneath the stormy North Sea seemed lunacy. Ten years ago, the idea that we should shortly begin mining for manganese in the depths of the oceans seemed highly unlikely. Yet, advancing understanding and techniques changed our perceptions. We should now, therefore, think of what mineral wealth lies underneath the ice sheets of Antarctica, the deep layers of the earth's crust, or on the moon. Why should resources always remain inaccessible?

We are developing highly sophisticated "coupled systems." Whole industrial complexes are being automated. Decentralized control, distributed data acquisition, and distributed information processing allow an entire plant, such as the Kimitsu works of the Nippon Steel Company, to be run automatically. Thousands of microprocessors carry out individual control, monitoring, and operational functions, sending information through a network of control computers. These, in turn, are linked via another network to master computers, completing a highly advanced coupled system. Similar systems are being worked on to create totally automated coal mines with no workers underground.

Similar principles could be applied to coupling wave power to coastal fish farming. The wave power devices extract enough energy off-shore to calm the coastal waters to facilitate fish farming, while the automated coal mines provide the basic raw materials from which to synthesize organic compounds which, when added to the coastal waters, favor the growth of certain plankton, thereby providing food for the fish (fin or shell).

A more extensive system could make the most barren part of the globe into one of the most productive. The deserts could be made to furnish humanity with much of its needs by coupled systems: Solar furnaces melt sand into glass; the glass is used for glass houses designed to act as solar stills; solar-powered pumps bring seawater into the glass houses where it is distilled to fresh water to be used in growing crops using thin film irrigation. The concentrated brine, developing as a by-product of this process, represents a valuable source of minerals which include potash and a variety of metallic and nonmetallic chemicals. The only reason the ocean waters are not mined now is because it takes too much energy to concentrate them. In the coupled desert system they would be a by-product. Solar energy can also be used for converting atmospheric nitrogen into ammonia. There is often a fair amount of phosphate available in desert regions. Such phosphate combined with the seawater-derived potash plus the air-derived ammonia provides fertilizer. The world's deserts would thus become major exporters of food, energy, and inorganic chemicals.

The problems of the Third World will not be solved by going backward. Once the West introduced medical technology, a population explosion was inevitable. The answer is not to stop vaccinations, nor is it just to ask parents to restrict themselves to only two children when there are no provisions for pensions or other forms of old age security. Furthermore, traditional farming needs the labor supplied by a large number of children and young adults. The developed nations have no right to deprive families of that resource. The only moral and sensible answer is a marked expansion of regional productivity. Societies in late industrial and post-industrial phases exhibit a demographic shift which is characterized by a leveling off (and sometimes even a decline) of the population.

To increase productivity in the Third World, we sometimes will need to introduce high technology such as the coupled systems previously discussed. In other cases, it may involve simpler technology, such as the use of solar-powered pumps for irrigation.

SUMMARY AND CONCLUSION

The emerging information society will usher in an era of peace and prosperity unprecedented in previous human history. Economic growth will be sustained, not in terms of an infinitely increasing materials production (and consumption), but by an expansion of services in general, and the knowledge industry in particular.

As a consequence of the expansion of the knowledge industry, we will find new methods for conserving existing resources and, more importantly, discover or create new ones. It also becomes increasingly possible to create a global community which is both truly global and provides a real sense of community. Traditional economic, social, and political ills also become soluble as a host of new intellectual, problem-solving technologies appear. The technology of the Communicative Era has already made remarkable strides: Around 1950, as the Mechanical Era was drawing to a close in Western society, the idea of putting men on the moon or of creating a United States of Europe seemed impossible - or at least a century away. Both happened within a generation.

There are immediate problems of some urgency. It must become the major task of Western societies in the 1980s to effect the orderly transfer of labor from the manufacturing to the knowledge industries. The most efficient way to accomplish this is by means of a major expansion of the education system which is coupled to an expanded R & D effort. The education system itself must be drastically overhauled to meet the requirement of the twenty-first century. Finally, the number one problem confronting global society is to close the gap between the rich and the poor of the world. Third World countries will require a massive infusion of information as well as some material aid to help them industrialize, then move on to Communicative society.

This chapter began with the theme that to be human means to be technological. The nightmare of St. John's Revelation envisioned the four horsemen of the Apocalypse: Famine, Pestilence, War, and Strife. We tend to interpret the Apocalypse as an event of the future. In fact, humanity has been living through it since the rise of the great ancient civilizations. During the Mechanical Era, science and technology slew Famine and Pestilence. Although the Industrial Revolution created much misery, it also abolished slavery. Now, the rise of the Communicative Era will see Isaiah's vision "they shall beat their swords into plowshares . . . " come to pass: War and Strife shall also disappear. Technological ingenuity will reverse the Malthusian nightmare stalking the Third World. Communicative societies already have demonstrated that they are able to find alternative resources, attain zero population growth, form stable, democratic governments, and develop complex transnational economic networks favoring cooperative and harmonious interactions.

The question remains: Can we educate ourselves and our political leaders to understand these new concepts?

NOTES

(1)   See T. Stonier, "Changes in Western Society: Educational Implications," in World Yearbook of Education 1979, edited by T. Schuller, and J. Megarry, and Kogan Page (London: Evans Brothers, Ltd., 1979), pp. 31-44.
(2)   In 1933, Lord Rutherford, the dean of nuclear physics, when asked how soon the atom might be harnessed, replied "Never." Nine years later, the first thermonuclear pile was operating in Chicago.

II
QUALITATIVE COMPONENTS OF SUSTAINABLE SOCIETIES

6 New Metaphors, Myths, and Values for a Steady-State Future

Robert L. Chianese

Values lag behind the genius of technology.

--A. Resnais, Hiroshima Mon Amour

MYTHS OF THE FUTURE

Our visions of the future reveal our dreams, fears, and realistic expectations about the place and time in which we hope to live out our destinies. The longing for a better future, usually with vast material and social improvements, informs the heart of Western thinking from Plato and Thomas More to B. F. Skinner and Buckminster Fuller. The history of Western thought looks backwards in time and deep into human nature to discover essential contours of our being that could enable us to design a future compatible with our best and most characteristic qualities. This quest is utopian, scientific, and religious, and it marks a long commitment to material and spiritual values which shape and color our images of the future.

Signs of the powerful influence of these values on our notions of the future, though often hidden, can be found everywhere, for values pervade language, thought, and action. Visions of the future in popular films, for example, reveal familiar assumptions. Luke fights Darth Vader in Star Wars, and Apollo fights the Cylons in Battlestar Galactica, where human intuition and individual bravery combat villainous arch-antagonists who are soulless machines programmed to destroy. This apocalyptic battle pits the artful intelligence of freedom-loving human beings against the limited responses of beasts and automatons, and reaches back into prehistory to reveal Ulysses, Beowulf, and King Arthur as the ancient forebears of Luke, Apollo, Flash, Buck, and their kin. The depiction of the future itself in these films, however, is more revealing than the dialogue or action, for it looks incredibly man-made. Space operas feature totally fabricated worlds and giant vessels, where computers, power sources, battlements, and other technical hardware constitute the living environment. Indeed, human beings in the future live by means of machine microcosms even as they do battle with mechanical demons.

Perhaps such a vision points to current ambivalence about technology, and anxiety over our loss of freedom in depending on it. Kubrick's 2001 makes this theme its subject, and, like the other films, defines the future in a by-now familiar way: first, that the future unfolds up and out among the planets and stars through technological advances; second, that the unspoiled Earth is either a distant memory or a future dream; and third, that our old, deep-rooted problems will continue to haunt us like unremitting ghosts, though we will become wizards of applied science. This view of the future epitomizes the principal and often unacknowledged assumptions of many scholars, writers, technicians, scientists, professional futurists, and ordinary citizens: technical progress will proceed apace, the Earth will recede in importance as a theater for the drama of humankind, and people will remain much the same – particularly in maintaining current racial, sexual, economic, and class power structures as they continue to search for freedom and peace out in the stars.

These ideas about the future, which together form the outline of a pervasive myth, capable of many plots and stories, may be so popular because it seems such an inevitable step from our previous history, embodies so many of our values, and posits continuity in the face of tremendous change. Presumably, it is comforting to imagine the wielder of a photon weapon having trouble getting a date, and it is reassuring to see women and blacks in less than command positions, still supporting white, male leaders. Nevertheless, this vision of the future derives its appeal from an even more widespread assumption most people make about the future itself – namely, that it represents a "natural" growth and expansion of the present. This concept reveals the linear and materialistic bias of Western thought, even as we attempt to define metaphysical abstractions such as space and time. In sum, we define the future as more, later! Almost every chart and graph in the West moves from left to right, from less to more, from the past or present to the future. Time moves away and out for us, like a seed growing in the ground, ramifying into a splendid tree. Time bears fruit and is pregnant with importance. These ideas coalesce into a nexus of assumptions that forms a mythology of growth. This mythology, which permeates modern culture and often serves as its official and acknowledged creed, gives growth, expansion, and progress the status of world metaphors for success in life.

It is no great leap from this idea to believing that growth occurs best without restraints, and that life itself is a struggle for unlimited expansion through individual competitions over

territory and resources. In the West, Nature herself is
believed to operate by the presumed law of exploitive self-
preservation, and we hold that human life should be modeled
on evidence we find in nature for an opportunistic and ex-
pansionist life-process. It is no wonder that screen battles in
the future, where resources and space would presumably be
inexhaustible, still take the form of imperial struggles for
territory, material wealth, and a way of life. Space, itself a
metaphor for infinitude, becomes the ultimate booty for victors
whose motives are clearly colonial.

Evenmore sober accounts of our "conquest" of space
highlight the increased energy, mineral, and food supplies that
space factories could provide us in much the same language of
the corporate executive projecting future business growth.
Indeed, space in America has become a commercial enterprise,
with scientists, astronauts, and lecturers on the futurist
circuit extolling the investment benefits and social virtues of
the exploration and exploitation of space. J. Peter Vajk, in
Doomsday Has Been Cancelled, presents an elaborate defense
of space colonization as the natural continuation of our quest
for unlimited material prosperity, which he sees as the means
to our growth as a species, including the development of a
higher consciousness. In a chapter significantly entitled "The
Endless Horizon," Vajk draws this portrait:

> As the human population of the solar system
> grows, and as the total economy of the space com-
> munities expands and becomes more intricate and
> complex, small groups of people will have the op-
> portunity to set out on their own, homesteading the
> asteroid belt or various orbits around other planets,
> to pursue whatever visions or lifestyles they may
> choose. In less than a hundred years human set-
> tlements will be found in most parts of the solar
> system, with no possibility of crowding - after all,
> more than just a little bit of space is available out
> there.(1)

This scenario projects the myth of the frontier into the extra-
terrestrial dimension, where Vajk's homesteaders brook no
restrictions on their freedom of choice. All limits or value
conflicts are avoided through continued growth and expansion,
and all hope for the future depends on having "more": "If we
are to have a humane and positive future, the production of
food for human consumption must expand as the population
increases."(2) These good intentions Vajk wants to achieve
through "social reforms," which do away with mismanagement
and "inequities" in food distribution in backward nations. But
to solve other problems, Vajk's space explorers will have to
turn a profit and, with exclusive access to the bounty they

discover there, they will be able to use their privileged van-
tage point in space to exact a high price. Would they, once
at home in their self-contained and efficiently designed col-
onies, want to rescue the messy and problematic Earth? The
personality of the space-merchant - the competitive, materialistic, progress-oriented, business-adventurer - puts grave
qualifications on the conquest of space as a final solution to
the energy, environmental, and social problems that beset us.
Finally, Vajk provides surprisingly few examples of how the
space program will actually solve present problems, for his
real mission is offering positive countervisions to the dooms-
days he finds in other writers on the future, particularly
those advocating limitations to growth.

STEADY-STATE CULTURAL CENTERS

This sketch of the origins and pervasiveness of the mythology
of growth is meant to suggest the extent of the difficulty
confronting world leaders who are preparing the way now for
viable steady-state societies in the future. People will resist
"no growth" and "steady-state" as philosophies fit for a de-
feated race if the metaphoric equations between the future and
natural expansion, between growth and unlimited competition
are allowed to stand. In such a context, steady-state is seen
as a stalemate against the human spirit.
    This is more than an image problem for steady-state,
though the term, with its unfortunate suggestions of an
austere and colorless standstill, needs to be replaced. If, for
instance, we substitute the term "dynamic equilibrium" for
"steady-state," we clarify and add attractiveness to the idea of
limits. A dynamic equilibrium describes a condition of balanced change along defined limits; it adds action and motion to
the concept of "steadiness" and characterizes the manner by
which change proceeds as a harmonious balance of all moving
parts within a self-contained system. (Calder's mobiles are
sculpturally dynamic equilibriums, whereas "steady-state"
seems sculpturally analagous to a static monolith.) The new
term more accurately conveys the nature of a "no growth"
society, which will change and continue to present risky
challenges to the imagination and stamina of its inhabitants as
they strive to maintain a balance.
    Growth has other forms besides unlimited material ex-
pansion, and freedom can be defined as the opportunity to
cooperate and not compete. Natural growth can be shown to
be dependent on strict laws that regulate recycling ecosystems
within the balance of the Earth. Unlimited expansion of a
single part at the expense of the whole is one way of describing cancer. Inner growth, the expansion of mutual

interdependencies, and the development of the human character free of material definition are versions of growth that involve the quality and depth of our lives and not quantities and products. Such modified myths of growth are compatible with a steady-state future and need to be shown as attractive alternatives to the destructive ones that dominate us now.

The contest between these two views of growth pits expansion, territoriality, competition, and exploitation on one side against steady-state, shared resources, cooperation, and interdependence on the other. The conflict points to a much larger issue than the solution of environmental problems, or population pressures, or unequal distribution of goods. It reveals our current dilemma to be a crisis of our basically dual nature - selfish and altruistic, acquisitive and generous, hostile and gregarious, repressive and ecstatic, impulsive and thoughtful. It is as if, after 8 million years of evolutionary and cultural history, we must, in the next 50 or 100 years, face the ultimate issue: ourselves. The choice will be whether our capacity for rational cooperation in the art of living on Earth, or even in space, can win over our proclivity for competitive self-interest which will destroy us. The problem is power, not energy, greed, not resources; and solutions must fit the political and cultural nature of the problem at the persuasive level of values and fundamental assumptions.

The project envisioned here addresses this need directly by founding steady-state cultural centers throughout the world to foster new habits and attitudes about cooperative coexistence in a world of limits. The centers would attempt to become a source of cultural transformation through the critique of destructive myths and the promotion of alternative ones. In revising the "mythology" of modern society, the centers would provide models for change that reach society's very core - its shared inner life. On one level, this mythology consists of actual legends and stories which entertain people and instruct them in their collective origin and history. (For example, the myth of the virgin land and the story of Paul Bunyan.) This kind of myth is often seen merely as a fanciful diversion from reality or an imaginative remolding of it. Others view such myths as products of "primitive" minds, using magical tales to quell the gods or expiate natural forces. Freud saw myths as public dreams, signaling pathological disorder in the body politic. Still others grant myths the status of careful descriptions of reality or prescientific explanations of empirical phenomena. The centers would be guided by the notion that mythical stories and legends continue to exert strong influence on people because their imagery and plots reveal the life-fulfilling needs and healthy longings of the human psyche. Such a view holds that the essential purpose of myths is to improve the dialogue between the holistic and integrative unconscious and the analytic and linear conscious and that myths guide us in forming a cosmos, or a unified world view, out of the disorganized flow of experience.

On another level, the mythology of modern society comprises its characteristic "fictions" and its accepted and inherited fixations, which may or may not surface as manifest tales. These "ideas" constitute the fundamental assumptions that people think with rather than think about. They may be said to structure consciousness itself and thereby organize the human environment in pervasive ways. (For example, "good is straight and true and right.") They at once fuel a society, channel its driving energies, and mark its ingrained prejudices. The basic values of a society find expression in these assumptions. Both a society's "ideas" and its legends represent adaptive forces of stability and act to resist change. The centers will, therefore, attempt to modify them and graft new varieties to existing stock, in the belief that the appropriateness of this revised mythology will enable it to serve as a catalyst for the change of values and habits of thought required for the creation and maintenance of a steady-state society.

The centers would be dedicated to the following set of principles and ideals:

- life is an infinite mystery, full of paradox, which art, science, and human understanding only partly comprehend; respect for and love of that mystery must be a central human concern;
- human potential is unlimited and is developed by challenging the unknown;
- the goal of human life is full exploration and uninhibited satisfaction of one's capacities, talents, and desires through enduring relationships with others;
- material acquisitiveness is the greatest deflection from such a goal and the transformation of people into dull, anxiety-ridden consumers its sorriest consequence;
- one of the most complex things in the universe is human, pluralistic community, which presents the ultimate challenge for thinking, moral creatures today;
- no individual human being can be whole or complete until all are so, for humanity is a single creature;
- human survival is at stake because of greed.

This collection of statements would serve to guide the centers in their operations, informing them with a general outlook rather than defining a specific creed.

These centers would serve society somewhat in the way organizations for institutional development serve a business, a region, a profession, or a university. Led by a director or coordinating team, they would offer selected people the opportunity and resources to launch planned social change. In their commitment to a particular set of values, the centers differ from the typical "think tank," since the task forces developed through them would be the actual source of change. To be effective, they would address a wide audience through the mass media, the arts, drama, films, books, lectures, and exhibitions, where myths and values are most powerfully communicated. They would try to revolutionize culture not through force, but through the persuasiveness, quality, and ethical soundness of an art, mythology, and new order of ideas that celebrate the values of cooperative restraints in a sustainable society.

The pool of people to direct or work at the centers is large: it includes everyone with a basic commitment to co-operative coexistence. Since this principle is not overly restrictive, the various projects the centers would sponsor would be extremely diverse and treat a wide range of issues from different approaches, thus allowing numerous people with heterogeneous backgrounds, personalities, and talents to participate. This would include a large segment of women, who might find the centers a unifying vehicle for their own liberation activities, one that many men would support just as enthusiastically. It would also include retired people and those who have left lucrative careers, dissatisfied with "the system," and those who have as yet been unable to find one. Artists, intellectuals, and academics, as well as people in professions, government, and business, who are critical of a wasteful and debilitating society, would find a creative outlet for their ideas and talents. Many people already working in areas such as consumer advocacy, alternative energy technologies, and environmental and health movements would discover strong affinities between their goals and the goals of the "steady-state" centers. In essence, many people in our society who at this point have rejected the reckless consumption and self-serving profiteering of the establishment, in spirit if not in fact, and who now seem diffused and isolated in single-issue politics or narrow social experiments, would discover a focus and a constructive form for their energies. Indeed, the founding of this loosely organized counterestablishment would galvanize a large segment of people in search of new ideals and could alter significantly the collective psyche of society by bringing a critical and creative mentality to the forefront of social consciousness.

Once chartered by a regional or national coordinating committee to undertake specified tasks, a center could start work with a handful of personnel. People would apply to join work groups by explaining their ideas about announced projects to the center's local coordinating team, which would make the selection. Depending on the nature of the project, people would work at the center, at home, or elsewhere. Since much

of the effort would result in public entertainments and educational materials and programs, the center could preview its
productions with the help of an advisory board. This board,
made up of people dedicated to the center but with limited
time, would offer suggestions for improvement but would not
have veto authority. The coordinating team, working with the
participants themselves, would be responsible for quality
control. Conflicts over content would seek resolution through
the regional committee, which would be charged with applying
the widest interpretation possible to what constitutes effective
"steady-state" material.
        In an example of the kind of work these steady-state
cultural centers could produce, a task force or a whole center
might undertake to revise the traditional concept of the hero.
Hero-myths usually involve a male quester searching for
himself. The archetypal pattern of this myth sets tests of
strength and prowess as impediments in the hero's way to
self-discovery. He must realize and accept hidden aspects of
his own nature before he wins the sacred treasure of freedom
and understanding. The story often becomes a paradigm of
individual (male) acsendancy and a symbol of psychological
growth - from dependence to independence, from youth to
maturity. It is enacted by heroes from many cultures and
eras: from Gilgamesh, Prometheus, Buddha, and Christ to
Huck Finn and Superman. The embellished biographies of
historical figures such as Lincoln and Mao, Rembrandt and
Beethoven, and Darwin and Einstein erroneously stress their
self-made character; and types such as the knight, the
samurai, and the cowboy glamorize self-sufficiency. This
nearly universal myth, which is essentially an initiation rite
into experience itself, stars, as Joseph Campbell has said, a
hero with a thousand faces.(3)
        To make this myth more compatible with a steady-state
society requires an important shift in emphasis. (Replacing
the male hero with an androgynous quester improves it but
does not change the basic pattern and point of the story.)
The self-reliant figure often discovers that the crucial parts of
himself with which he must come to terms are embodied in
others, and that his growth depends upon the integration of
them into his own personality, usually through love. This key
aspect of the myth must be stressed - that personal freedom
and the fulfillment of one's inner desires require other people.
The myth's paradoxical conclusion defines growth and personal
freedom as the extension of one's responsibilities to others.
Thus, in a revision, the collective aspect of the self (psyche)
needs emphasis, as well as the collaborative nature of the
quest. The "hero" cannot be allowed to forget his dependence
on others, whether it be in the form of servants, sages,
companions, combatants, or society and tradition themselves.
A refocused initiation myth must place emphasis on the con-

clusion of the quest and reveal the sacred treasure as interdependence. A team of male and female characters as the
protagonist could itself make this point, especially in a story
of collective self-discovery and an assault on group fear and
ignorance. The challenges could involve the solution of technological, environmental, or social problems rather than the
destruction of some villainous scapegoat. The crisis would test
the bond of cooperation and synergy between them rather than
individual might. None of the vigor and danger of the old
stories needs be sacrificed, especially their mystery, frivolity,
sensuousness, and their joy in eccentric personality. "Re-
visions" must avoid the clinical purity, the jargon, and the
dogmatism of the zealous ideologue.

In this example, the centers would then seek ways to
promote the new myth, mainly through commercial ventures.
The range of possibilities is enormous: exposure in popular
entertainment, the creation of schools of art, the development
of toys and games, and the production of educational materials. Revised versions of familiar tales, stories, and legends
that employ the hero myth could be used, or altogether new
stories could be written and illustrated for young audiences in
book or comic book form, along with action-figures and games
that feature the protagonists. New scripts for those current
television series that are most adaptable to the redesigned
content of the myth can be written and completely new series
can be introduced. Even quiz and game shows that involve
tests of collective knowledge and ability could be devised.
Stock situation comedies, soap operas, and talk shows are
prime sources of popular attitudes about cultural values. No
serious attempt at cultural transformation can ignore them; and
the centers could introduce their own or promote the introduction of new material in these and other popular art forms.

Other notions that reinforce exploitive growth need to be
analyzed and countered: for example, the one that defines
early middle age as full maturity and sees youth and old age
as less than ideal states; the one that sees change as only for
better or worse; the one that worships quantity over quality.
These ideas not only shape the theme of stories, but give
form to institutions, policies, and laws, as well as provide
structures for our very feeling, thinking, and seeing. Films,
plays, street theatricals, pageants, and radio dramas could be
sponsored that challenge the myths directly by emphasizing
other values related to the success of a sustainable society:

- complexity as a value, as opposed to simplicity
- life as a process of deepening significance and con-
  nections, as opposed to accumulation of products and
  experiences
- the excitement of long-term ventures
- the dependence of creative imagination on discipline and
  detailed work

- life as continual goal-setting rather than reaching a single goal
- acceptance of contradiction as fundamental to life
- the wholesomeness of instinctual gratification when free of repressive domination
- reflection on goals, choices, and consequences of actions.

These suggestions for the new content of art, mythology, and values for the future are not limited to verbal forms. Dance, sculpture, photography, music, architecture, and interior design can be made to reflect these concepts. They are general enough to find expression in all art, since they do not posit specific "programs" for reform or force the artist to create in the service of a narrow doctrine. (Indeed, the reinterpretation of much great art would find evidence for them.) Art by its nature is fundamentally noncompetitive and nonprogressive - Picasso is not an "improvement" over Turner; art changes without getting "better" or "worse." Art is an instrument of change essentially compatible with steady-state values.

Other means of reaching popular audiences need to be explored. The centers could publish national magazines that feature human interest photostories like Life, People, and Us, but which do indeed focus on the material suggested by the titles of these magazines and not on the loves, tastes, and narcissistic aspirations of "stars." The centers could also promote singing groups and other musical talent to vie with the current trend of flagrantly commercial performers. Textbooks and anthologies that present historical and political events from a less ethnocentric outlook are needed, as well as collections of literature that enable one to compare the new mythologies with past examples. Exhibitions of art, particularly Third World and non-Western, with detailed explanations of the background and values of the artists and cultures could provide needed education about the variety and homogeniety of people. Exhibits of rarely treated subjects such as community or collective heroism could be assembled, featuring works like Rodin's Burghers of Calais and paintings by Breughel and Chagall. Soviet and Chinese Communist art need to be displayed if the West is to find ways to understand and coexist with our supposedly most dangerous competitors.

A NEW ORDER OF IDEAS

The centers would augment this effort to transform society through the creation of a new mythology with an equally ambitious and complementary effort at forming a new order of ideas. New intellectual syntheses are the vanguards of major

social changes and the world views that emerge from them.
On the horizon are unified field theories in the biosciences and
physics that promise new definitions of human life. The
centers can become the coordinating impetus behind this search
for coherence, uniting the sciences, arts, and the study of
values into a modern and radical humanism - one that is
understood by and responsive to a wide and popular audience.
     This role of catalyst in intellectual discovery needs to be
taken on by an organization like the centers, since the university and the scientific communities have nearly abandoned
it. These two institutions have a strong investment in the
present order of ideas, which features narrow specialization
and compartmentalization of knowledge, territorial divisions
between areas of inquiry like the humanities and sciences,
standards of proof requiring quantification, and evaluation of
ideas based on utility. This intellectual schema is a major
factor in the vocationalization of the university and the
commercialization of knowledge, scientific and otherwise. As
long as society requires that education serve the job market
and science serve industry, knowledge, at least official knowledge, will remain circumscribed by the laws of supply and
demand.
     The nature of the intellectual discoveries now being made
requires not only new approaches suited to a less mechanis-
tically-determined and materially-constituted universe, but the
inclusion of previously excluded areas of human understanding
such as metaphysics and ethics, which are already entering
scientific thought. (The humanities will have as much catching
up to do as the sciences will have reviewing traditional
wisdom.) Subatomic particle physics borrows poetic metaphors
and mystical insights to describe for itself the paradoxes of
the electron and the quark. Behaviorism and sociobiology
treat "facts" of human behavior and social interaction that
inherently involve "value" considerations. Theories of per-
ception and learning in psychology make assumptions about
human seeing and knowing that the artist and the philosopher
could help to clarify. Objectivity (an impossibility) may itself
give place to another mode of vision, deliberately interacting
with the subject under scrutiny and capable of perceiving a
wider spectrum of phenomena than science chooses to examine.
     As medicine shifts from cures to preventive treatments
and includes the whole of the human organism in its view, the
definition of health itself will change and may involve factors
that only shamans or savants have seemed to understand.
Deeper understanding of the human cell may bring genetic
engineering and - along with the synthesis of information from
the fields of nutrition, stress management, brain research,
physiology, and psychology - it may lead to prolonged life
span and a redefinition of life, aging, disease, and death.
These theoretical breakthroughs involve a number of social,

political, and ethical concerns that necessarily intrude upon
the "value-free objectivity" still claimed essential by much of
contemporary science.

To explore the implications of these new ideas and
theories requires interdisciplinary efforts among many currently isolated fields, and the adoption of a more unified view
of existence. The traditional dualisms of mind and body,
living and nonliving, metaphysical and physical, value and
fact, and subjective and objective are breaking down, and the
content, mode of inquiry, and form of the new knowledge
depend upon synthesis. In helping to foster this intellectual
activity, the centers would work to remove knowledge from the
control and interpretative framework of the scientific, business, and academic establishment, which is committed to the
economic utilization of ideas and the maintenance of the existing intellectual power structure. The centers could finance
reports, debates, and conferences; and sponsor greatly needed
books and educational materials that explain current theories
and ideas to the general public; and place them, where possible, in a coherent system of thought. Fellowships could be
offered to promote the collaboration and cross-fertilization
necessary to accomplish this. The effort to lessen the influence of the materialistic and rationalistic values of our modern
technocracy upon what we know and how we know it is an
inevitable extension of the contest of values the centers will
wage through the creation of new mythologies for the future;
the new knowledge will inevitably be formed by and influence
that mythology.

SUMMARY

If the centers are to bring about significant social change,
they will need funds, and, as in any venture, generating
resources will represent a major challenge. The centers can
begin with volunteers and benefactors and with contributions
of talent and work by artists, musicians, writers, and intellectuals who are dedicated to steady-state reforms. Once
launched, the network of centers could model itself after a
nonprofit foundation, relying on volunteers, and fund drives,
grants, and bequests for revenue. But such a status could
result in limited activity and the imposition of restraints on the
centers' radical purpose. Moreover, the change in attitudes
the centers wish to foster must take place at the leading edge
of a completely commercial society. Nonprofit status would
confirm the suspicion of many that steady-state alternatives
are unworkable in the "real" world. The centers, therefore,
need to turn a profit, however modest. As they support and
expand programs largely on their own, the centers will provide

a model of a nonexploitive, cooperative enterprise that can sustain itself and thereby pave the way for others to launch more centers with very limited resources.

The sale of the art, entertainment, books, and educational materials produced by the centers would be a major source of revenue. The centers would also sponsor events ranging from exhibits, concerts, and lecture series to noncompetitive sports shows, festivals, and fairs. Once underway, the centers would offer stipends or royalties to people for their work, with staff members receiving salaries commensurate with financial need and the desirability of the tasks they perform, rather than according to rank or status. As the centers grow through the investment of profits in new programs, they would make flexible financial arrangements to accommodate various kinds of working relationships, often on a contractual basis. To sponsor and produce major ventures in television, publishing, entertainment, sports, and the arts will require the centers to form companies, with the difficult challenge of adapting the economics of what is essentially a network of community cooperatives to a large-scale operation.

This assortment of artistic, educational, and cultural activities constitutes an area where the main resources are, at least ideally, human talent and imagination. While growth in this area can be conventionally defined as capturing a larger share of a market, competitive expansion here does not necessarily lead to monopolistic control. The opportunity for wide participation in the art, education, and entertainment business is implicit, though present practice often reveals the most ruthless competition. There is room for as many good artists, stars, heroes, sitcoms, singers, films, and books as appear on the scene. The growth of the centers' efforts in these areas would be a model of the kind of growth needed in a sustainable state: shared, nonpolluting growth of human resources, which promotes greater insight, pleasure, knowledge, and connectedness between people. Eventual alliances with other industries, such as those involved with pollution control and alternative energy sources, could give the centers a strong economic base.

Activity on all these levels could be the catalyst for major social changes. Schools of art, psychology, philosophy, and economics could evolve out of the programs sponsored by the centers, and the separate forces of cooperative coexistence that already exist could find a means of organization. An intellectual, cultural, and political movement of the sort that accompanied and propelled the Renaissance could emerge. The movement envisioned here, with its commitment to change that gradually transforms society through new ideas and attitudes, stresses constructive alternatives and options and the formation of a highly visible counterculture within the existing order. It places its faith in the aesthetic, moral, and intellectual education of humankind, rather than in revolution or coercion. It presents a working model of social cooperation for the established culture to emulate and join and looks forward to joining and being joined by the main stream. But, the first stage of that eventual and productive confluence requires the organization of the talent and techniques of the modern world against its most self-destructive actions. The centers attempt to do this by providing a means of transition to a sustainable social order. The represent more than the limited hope of human survival; they offer a version of growth and change that will enable the human spirit to thrive.

NOTES

(1)   J. Peter Vajk, Doomsday Has Been Cancelled (Culver City, California: Peace Press, 1978), p. 166.
(2)   Ibid., p. 67.
(3)   Joseph Campbell, The Hero With a Thousand Faces (New York: Pantheon Books, 1949).

7 The Issue Is Human Quality: In Praise of Children

James Garbarino

INTRODUCTION: WHO CARES?

In their manifesto for the future, Human Growth: An Essay on Growth, Values and the Quality of Life,(1) Cleveland and Wilson argue that the "Good Society" is visible on the horizon. They argue that: "Such a society is bound to move away from 'growth' defined as quantitative product irrespective of what and whom it is for. Such a society is bound to consider basic human needs a first charge on available recources. Such a society is bound to bestow its highest priority upon the development of human resources - on enhancement of the human environment."(2) When it comes to human resources, the bottom line is the welfare of children. A society that does not do well by its children forsakes the quality of its future.

In sharp contrast to the optimistic and glowing vision of Cleveland and Wilson stands a rather more pessimistic observation offered at a recent marketing institute by Mary Ellen Burris, and based on public opinion surveys.

> A happy marriage, an interesting job, and a job that contributes to the welfare of society - each of these factors decreased in the percentage of people naming them as ingredients of the good life. In contrast, these things increased in importance; a color T.V., a lot of money, really nice clothes, a second color T.V. and consider this: in late 1975, more people named children as an ingredient in the good life than a car; now it's just the reverse.(3)

Is this the beginning of an ugly future in which we turn our backs on children in favor of material aggrandizement? Or,

103

is this simply a transitory, darkest hour before a new dawn? In this, the International Year of the Child, it is only fitting that our efforts to design a sustainable society focus on the role that children will play in that world to come, knowing as we do that in the long run, color T.V.'s, cars, and nice clothes are a losing proposition when contrasted with children on both practical and moral grounds.

Why care for children in the first place? Why indeed. At the heart of any discussion of a "sustainable society" lies the development of human resources and the issue of where children fit into a modern, social, and technological environment. The issue of human quality is inseparable from the well-being of children: Children are the future. The well-being of children is both the principal challenge faced by a modern society and the principal focal point for a society that can fulfill Cleveland and Wilson's mandate to "move away from growth defined as quantitative product irrespective of what and whom it is for."(4) Children must have first claim on such a society if it is to be both physically and socially sustainable. Children are the issue on both moral and practical grounds. And if children are to have first claim, then parents and the conditions of parenthood must be in the forefront of our consciousness. The topic is families.

I write in praise of children, yet I begin with families because neither has meaning without the other. Although 1979 has been proclaimed the International Year of the Child, it is foolhardy to think of children apart from the conditions of life for their parents. This theme emerged clearly when a panel of child development experts was interviewed on their views concerning the status of children in this International Year.(5) Although they all began from different theoretical perspectives and research interests, all returned inexorably to families when asked about the status of children. These experts recognized, as must any serious student of the topic, that for this or any other year to be devoted to our children, it must also be devoted to the people who care for those children. As Arthur Emlen, one of our children's best friends, puts it: "If you care for children, then care for parents."(6)

Children provide the focal point for assessing the quality of life for adults. By looking at children - and the people who care for them - we gain a finer appreciation of what matters and what doesn't; what is genuine and what is ephemeral; what is qualitative and what is simply quantitative. Children tell the story, for better or for worse. Child abuse is the worse.

Commenting on domestic violence in the animal world, Desmond Morris makes the following observation: "The viciousness with which children . . . are subjected to persecution is a measure of the weight of dominant pressures imposed on their persecutor."(7) Complementing this observation is Rock's report(8) that, when gorilla mothers are socially impoverished by being isolated from their peers, they have a striking propensity to mistreat their infants. However, when restored to the simian community, these mothers perform adequately. Social impoverishment is equally detrimental to human child rearing. Domestic violence among humans is also an indication of oppressive stresses and strains.(9)   Both abuse and neglect are associated with isolation of the parent-child relationship from the nurturance and feedback provided by "potent pro-social support system."(10)   On the negative side, the evidence is clear that when the quality of life for adults suffers, children suffer.   In the lives of children we see mirrored the lives of those adults whose job it is to care for them.

Any discussion of children, parents, and families is, of necessity, dialectical.   For the thesis presented by Burris that valuing things is taking the place of valuing children, there is the antithesis presented by public opinion polls that continue to show family life at the top of people's lists of what is important.   Based on a recent nationwide survey, Harris(11) concludes that, "Clearly, the most satisfying part of life to many Americans today is family life.   A substantial 92% of the public say this is very important to them.   And 67% say they are very satisfied with the way their family life is going." Despite flirtations with materialism, most of us recognize that color T.V.'s and the like are simply, as one Eastern philosopher puts it, "the unreal objects of this world."   The challenge in designing a sustainable society is to bolster and clarify that recognition, not obscure it by exploiting and falsifying people's basic material needs.

There is a real cultural struggle here.   The things of real value we have, and thus can offer to our children, are our time, our interest, and our attention.   The conditions of life - the very structure of the society - determine how psychically rewarding it will be to invest ourselves in social rather than material projects, in children and community life as opposed to cars and televisions.   To understand the dynamics of this process of investment we must understand the sources of meaning in adult life.

WHAT IS THE GOOD LIFE?

Searching for the meaning of the "Good Life" has been the traditional philosophical issue.   The search for the Good Life, while largely abandoned by contemporary philosophy, has been taken up by psychology.   In its "soft" side under the guidance of the gentle theorists, Abe Maslow and Carl Rogers, modern psychology has sought to provide psychological an-

swers to the eternal question, what is the good life? The
psychology of self-actualization is an ethic of existential
meaningfulness. There is, however, even within the "hard"
side of psychology, a growing appreciation for the centrality
of this most qualitative of issues. "Quality of life" is an
important and growing research issue in its own right. To
ask "what is the good life?" is to pose the fundamental issue
of psychological quality. It is to ask what brings meaning to
human experience. It is to ask what makes reality a positive
experience. Once this question is posed it opens a whole new
vista, or rather reopens it.

The issue of quality in a psychological context has new
implications in the modern era. however. In the past, considerations of quality were intrinsically elitist. The material
conditions of life did not permit a widespread dispersion of
qualitative concerns. The promise (and premise) of the
modern era was its tantalizing prospect of making available
adequate material conditions to permit quality of life to become
a concern for the masses. Indeed, the whole corpus of
utopian writing dating from the eighteenth century is built on
the premise that technological improvements permit the dispersion of human quality.(12)

It is ironic that the same technology that offered the
promise of the good life for all is now seen as the principal
threat to that life in the future by making us hostages to an
energy-intensive, unsustainable economy. Universal dispersion
of the benefits of technology was (and still is) presumed to be
the shortest route to widespread qualitative improvement in the
human condition. It is precisely this qualitative improvement
that is the rationale for the modern social engine. This
ideology permeated even to the creation of statistical indicators
for measuring the day-to-day life and future of societies. As
Campbell(13) has noted, as early as 1798, Sir John Sinclair
described statistics in the following language when he introduced them in his Statistical Account of Scotland: "The idea I
annex to the term (statistics) is an inquiry into the state of
the country, for the purpose of ascertaining the quantum of
happiness enjoyed by its inhabitants, and the means of its
future improvement." This is important because it establishes
measurement of a "quantum of happiness" as the target for
social indicators.

As is often the case, the fullest picture of reality comes
not from social science, but from fiction, where the rough
edges of incomplete factual information can be smoothed by the
visionary imagination. Some of the best thoughts on the
sustainable society in which quality predominates over quantitative concerns come from the utopian novelists. Austin
Tappan Wright's Islandia(14) presents such a totally sustainable society, one in which the pursuit of human quality is
totally preeminent over concerns with quantity. Islandia

presents an alternative to all the superficial trappings of what we consider the modern society. On the other hand, it incorporates the fundamental thesis of the modern society, namely, universal dispersion of quality through a social organization and material technology that permits the dignity of economic adequacy to all. The two characters are discussing how Islandia would change were it to become "modern" in the sense of the term understood by John, the contemporary American.

Dorn: "Why should I change?"

John: "Progress!" I said.

Dorn: "Speed, is that progress? Anyhow, why progress? Why not enjoy what one has? Men have never exhausted present pleasures."

John: With us, progress means giving pleasures to those who haven't got them."

Dorn: "But doesn't progress create the very situation it seeks to cure - always changing the social adjustment so that someone is squeezed out? Decide on an indispensable minimum. See that everyone gets that, and until everyone has it, don't let anyone have any more. Don't let anyone ever have any more until they have cultivated fully what they have."

John: "To be unhappy is a sign we aren't stagnating."

Dorn: "Nor are we. 'Happy' wasn't the right word. We are quite as unhappy as you are. Things are too beautiful; those we love die; it hurts to grow old or be sick. Progress won't change any of these things, except that medicine will mitigate the last. We cultivate medicine, and we are quite as far along as you are there. Railroads and all that merely stir up a puddle, putting nothing new in and taking nothing out."(15)

The essential issues of human experience are direct, simple, universal, and unchanging: mating, child bearing, child rearing, puberty, adulthood, and, once again, mating. Wright's

Islandia envisions a society in which technology is selected to
permit a style of life in which those fundamental human concerns are the principal agenda for the human community,
unencumbered by false issues of social change and social
development. Wright's vision of "what matters" for quality in
human life is paralleled in the "scientific study of human
experience." Psychology merges with ethics.
     In a paper entitled "Subjective Measures of Well-
being"(16), Angus Campbell reviewed the limitations of modern
objective measures of human society. He noted their fundamental falseness because they cannot attend to the subjective
experience of reality, the ultimate criterion of judging meaning. Campbell builds on the findings from national surveys
showing that, during the period between 1957 and 1972 when
most of the economic and social indicators were moving rapidly
upward, the proportion of the American population who described themselves as "very happy" declined steadily, and this
decline was most apparent among the part of the population
that was most affluent. Moreover, when people living in those
states (primarily in the Southeast) that have the lowest "objective quality of life" were asked about the subjective quality
of their life, they reported more positive experiences than did
their counterparts in the more affluent "developed" states.
Campbell concludes that we need indicators of personal well-
being to complement conventional social indicators.
     The "subjective measures" will, in large part, tell us how
things stand between children and their parents. Rather than
being the simple collecting of characteristics, human development is the process by which an individual constructs a
picture of the world and acquires the tools to live in and with
that picture. Child psychologist Urie Bronfenbrenner defines
development as: ". . . the person's evolving conception of
the ecological environment, and his relation to it, as well as
the person's growing capacity to discover, sustain, or alter its
properties."(17) This concept of development will figure
prominently in efforts to understand how the future of a
sustainable society depends upon the quality of life it offers to
children. Although children develop abstractions, they do not
develop in response to abstractions. They are a genuine
reflection of the actual quality of life as it is directly experienced. The "problem" of adults is that they are much
more liable to delusion, to being drawn away from "the
basics." But just what are "the basics" that bring about the
experience of quality for the subjective human organism?
Campbell concludes that they are "the presence or absence of
those various forms of interpersonal exchange that provides
psychological support to people."(18)
     Those interpersonal supports are just the things that
provide a positive influence on human development, as Bronfenbrenner defines the term. They both enlarge the capacity

of the developing human to utilize the environment, and provide the raw material that humans need to fashion a satisfying existence. The need for interpersonal support is the fundamental human need, satisfaction of that need is the foundation of social quality. Campbell was concerned with this fundamental need in adults. When we transpose his findings to the world of children, we find that the same kinds of interpersonal factors dominate the scene.

For adults to serve the basic needs of children (to play and develop competence) in a way that does not rob them of their own satisfaction requires a supportive community. The other interpersonal features of life must complement rather than compete with child rearing. For the child to flourish, the parent must have access to the social riches of family or family surrogates, kin and kith. Just as child and family are inseparable, both in interests and in functions, so family and community are wedded together by a functional connection. Unless a society provides parents with the means to rear children, it will be faced with an unfortunate mixture of unhappy parents and inadequately prepared children. Both are a direct threat to the goal of quality in the human experience.

It is reassuring to know that the fundamental needs of children and adults are relatively simple and basically unchanging. It is a challenge to simultaneously meet both those needs. To meet those needs for the mass of the population - a quantum leap in happiness - is a still further challenge to the skill of society's social engineers, managers, politicians, and individual citizens. The task is not an easy one and it demands a more precise examination of the conditions favoring an intensive social investment by parents in children without psychological bankruptcy to those adults. To that task our attention next turns.

MAKING THE NECESSARY INVESTMENT IN CHILDREN

We know that poverty is bad for people; children, and adults alike. And, we suspect that being rich has its own liabilities.(19) We know poverty is bad for children because it undermines their health and well-being.(20) It subjects them to damaging stresses, both directly by placing them in threatening situations and indirectly by undermining the ability of their parents to give what children rightfully deserve - a finely attuned and affectionate responsiveness. Severe economic deprivation robs families of the social necessities of life; it leads to social impoverishment. Social impoverishment is the principal direct threat to human development. The economic needs of children are actually quite limited: a socially rich child is better off developmentally than a socially impoverished one, even if the latter is materially wealthy. Of course, we can justifiably agree with Sophie Tucker when she said, "I've been rich and I've been poor, and rich is better." Nonetheless, child rearing is fundamentally a labor-intensive rather than a capital-intensive enterprise. Therein lies the challenge and the hope for a sustainable society.

The promise of modernity is to release families from the burden of poverty. The reality of poverty as a destructive social and psychological force is vivid in Margaret Sanger's account of her work with mothers living on the Lower East Side of Manhattan during the early 1900s:

> Each time I returned to this district, which was becoming a recurrent nightmare, I used to hear that Mrs. Cohen "had been carried to a hospital, but had never come back," or that Mrs. Kelly "had sent the children to a neighbor and had put her head into the gas oven." Day after day such tales were poured into my ears - a baby born dead, great relief - the death of an older child, sorrow but again relief of a sort - the story told a thousand times of death from abortion, children going into institutions. I shuddered with horror as I listened to the details and studied the reasons back of them - destitution linked with excessive childbearing. The waste of life seemed senseless. One by one worried, sad, pensive and aging faces marshalled themselves before me in my dreams, sometimes appealingly, sometimes accusingly.(21)

When life is so impoverished that children are a burden, they tend to further impoverish rather than enrich the quality of life. In our efforts to design a sustainable society centering on the labor-intensive nature of child rearing, we must avoid naive sentimentality about "the good old days." This parallels issues in the economic and technological spheres.(22)

Just how labor-intensive must child rearing be? This is an important issue. Can we substitute money for time and still get well-developed children? If we return to Bronfenbrenner's description of what development is, the answer emerges. For a sustainable society to work, it must be composed of people who have "constructed" an ecologically-sound internal reality to motivate and guide their actions. Children learn the world they experience and then seek to live in that world. If material investment is substituted for psychological and social investment in the rearing of children, the only outcome can be a materialistic construction of reality incompatible with a sustainable society. As Wright made so clear in Islandia, only by establishing an adequate and stable material setting can there be the fullest development and expression of the psychological and social quality of human experience. The essence of development is the child's conception of the world and his or her ability to "discover, sustain, or alter its properties."(23)

A sustainable society requires people who will direct their developing competence toward cultivating renewable, nonpolluting resources. Chief among these "clean" resources is social intercourse. Campbell found that social intercourse, set in the context of enduring relationships, is the primary reliable source of meaningfulness and satisfaction in the human experience. This bodes well for designing a sustainable society. It tells us that such a society is compatible with "human nature," if that society is built on labor-intensive enterprises that generate and sustain a comfortable social web, surrounding, dignifying, and supporting the individual human being. Children and child rearing must stand at the heart of such a web. They are the most reliable "occasion" for knitting people together in mutually satisfying, socially productive work and developmentally enhancing play. They are the perfect vehicle for organizing a sustainable society. All we need do (and, as shall become clear, it is no small task) is to work out the implications of this principle for every aspect of our economic, political, and social life.

The challenge is real and substantial. There are cultural and historical forces working against the necessary psychological and social investment in children. Severe economic stress is a poignant fact of life for at least one in six American children and their parents. The demands of their parents' work socially impoverish many children. The necessary psychological and social investment has been diverted by both poverty and affluence.(24) There is a cultural "poison" in our heritage that makes us suspicious of the child's nature, and belies our claims to be a "child-centered" society. There is growing recognition of this cultural poison, in both popular and professional circles. "The greatest single impediment to our improving the lives of America's children is the myth that we are a child-oriented society already doing all that needs to be done."(25)

The temptation to use material investment as a substitute for psychological investment is real and compelling. The Soviet Union tried creating boarding schools to provide "disadvantaged" children with high-quality, professional child care. They abandoned this compensatory intervention program when they discovered that "you can't pay a woman to do what a mother will do for free."(26) Material investment seems an easy way out of making the necessary labor-intensive investment but is ineffective at best and developmentally damaging at worst. Surveys in the 1950s showed that high on the list of reasons given for purchasing televisions was "to bring the family back together."(27) The result, of course, was physical togetherness but psychological apartness, parallel rather than interactive social experience.

There is a reservoir of support for child rearing and family life, but its potential effects are often blunted by the tantalizing proposition that parents can have their cake and eat it too, invest in their children and do their own thing as well. Unless their "thing" is child rearing, it can't and won't work. And, to do this thing well, parents need a social environment that cares for them as they care for their children. They need a supportive social environment, one that balances nurturance and guidance, consensus and diversity.

FAMILY SUPPORT SYSTEMS

In discussing the relative role of material versus psychological and social investment in child rearing, the concept of "support systems" inevitably arises. In the words of one of the pioneer researchers in this area, support systems are: ". . . continuing social aggregates that provide individuals with opportunities for feedback about themselves and for validation for their expectations about others, which may offset deficiencies in these communications within the larger community context. . . ."(28)

Support systems provide both nurturance and feedback. They provide the individual with warmth and security in addition to guidance and direction. This joint function and meaning of support systems becomes particularly important when considering effective parenthood, where the protective function is particularly salient. Consider Jane Howard's description of her own support system and its ability to soften the hard edges of its members. "But we are numerous enough and connected enough not to let anyone's worst prevail for long. For any given poison, our pooled resources can come up with an antidote."(29) Alternatively, consider the following statement from a young mother interviewed as part of a research project. "Sometimes I just don't know what's going to happen. He gets going and then I get going and then before I know it things are happening. Sometimes I just don't understand what he is doing, or even what I'm doing. There is just the two of us you see."(30)

When it comes to child rearing, support systems are the staff of life. Indeed, the principal factor mediating between the parent-child relationship and the larger society is precisely the family's network of support systems. The richness, diversity, and strength of these support systems contribute to their effectiveness in providing nurturance and feedback to parent-child relationships. This richness is one of the principal environmental determinants of the child's developmental

robustness. In this, the good life for families resembles the
political good life for communities: it is social pluralism that
both protects society from dangerous excesses and provides
diverse and enriching experiences by combining consensus and
diversity.(31)   In all things moderation. Our task is to
design a society to counterbalance those threats that are
universal, and prevent those that are but historical coin-
cidences.

   While most of the public debate concerning the fate of
children centers around the "decline of the American family,"
the issue actually lies outside the family in the family's relation
to the community. Understanding this relationship is a
necessary precondition for looking at the state and future of
American families. The principal challenge of the modern
world to the psychological quality of life is the destruction of
traditional sources of social pluralism. This is the danger of
"social impoverishment" in which the support systems necessary for effective parenthood are undermined. Without these
support systems, the parent-child relationship is thrown into
jeopardy, and it is this jeopardy that is commonly referred to
as "the decline of the American family."

   Social impoverishment springs from a variety of factors.
Among these are geographic mobility, instrumental interpersonal relationships, and the erosion of neighborhoods as arenas
for enduring patterns of behavior among family units. Geographic mobility strains and often breaks the functional
relationships that underlie support systems. While modern
communications permit support systems to function over long
distances, as in the case of the weekly transcontinental phone
call to grandparents, such geographically dispersed social
networks cannot have the same day-to-day significance as more
concentrated, localized ones. Perhaps equally threatening,
however, is the fact that geographic mobility may produce an
adaptive cultural response in which short-term, immediate relationships become desirable in place of the more long-term
"money in the bank" relationships that require day-to-day
contact over an extended period. Geographic mobility may
make it more difficult for children and parents to have a
common history with those in their current support systems,
and to have shared experiences that build trust, understanding, and the motivation to provide nurturance and
feedback. Thus, instrumental interpersonal relationships may
play a larger and larger role. Such relationships are in-
consistent if not incompatible with genuine support systems in
which validating the intrinsic worth of the person is the
essential element.

   The very notion of "designing a sustainable society"
presupposes that we can make alternative arrangements even
though we cannot recapture an idealized past. The promise of
modern life, of course, is to relieve that burden and thus

permit social enrichment to grow out of material adequacy.
Is this Good Life on the horizon?   What does the future hold
for children and parents?

PROSPECTS FOR FUTURE PSYCHOLOGICAL AND
SOCIAL INVESTMENT IN CHILDREN

Just where do we stand on the matter of psycho-social investment in children?   What are the prospects for the future?
The evidence is mixed and often ambiguous.   The challenging
intellectual task of sorting out this evidence is complicated by
the fact that some experts go well beyond their data to reflect
their hunches, their bias, their fears, and even their political
aspirations.   Issues of family and children have become the
leading edge for political ideologues and social activism in the
1970s.(32)   This complicates the task before us because it
demands that we separate enduring patterns of change and
development from transitory and ephemeral politicized "events."
     As was noted earlier, there is a deeply rooted tension –
one might even say conflict – in American life about children.
We hold ourselves up as a child-oriented society, but we
consistently place ourselves at odds with the needs of
children.   We do so because of a kind of cultural poison that
resents children and because of some inevitable realities;
realities that pit children against adults.   As Time magazine
put it (in its own inimitable style), "those who detect a
pervasive, low-grade child aversion in the United States find
it swarming in the air like pollen."(33)   Politically, children
are losers.(34)   The issue is really one of investment; where
do we place that which we value?   I think several important
points can be made on this score.
     First, most Americans retain a fundamental and un-
wavering commitment to parenthood, despite the declining birth
rate.(35)   In a rather extensive review of childlessness in the
United States, Judith Blake reports the results of a nationwide survey of adults dealing with the advantages and disadvantages of childlessness.(36)   She found that adults will not
be priced out of the parenthood market by the high economic
costs of child bearing and child rearing, although they will
decrease the number of children.   People do value children for
their intrinsic worth, and this affirmation is our bedrock for
the future.(37)
     On balance, it seems clear that the primary investment in
children, namely their conception and birth, is still being made
and will continue to be made in the future.   Smaller families
are still families, and tend to be good families at that.(38)
This fundamental commitment to having children, at least to
having one child, saves us from one side of the problem.   It

does not, however, guarantee the future. The quality of
life - that is, the quality of children - in the future is by no
means assured simply by the fact of them being born. The
issue of enduring and appropriate psychological and social
investment remains. In fact, the thrust toward self-gratifica-
tion makes quite real the possibility of adults attempting to
have their cake and eat it too by having children and not
being willing to make the necessary investment. There are
some data to suggest this is a real problem.

A recent study by Bahr(39) offers us a rare opportunity
to compare adolescents' views of their parents in the same
community over a fifty-year span. It should come as no
surprise that teenagers value fathers who spend time with
them. Enough time with one's father is a continuing and
pervasive issue. Thus, in 1924, 63 percent of the females and
62 percent of the males felt that the most desirable attribute in
the father is the fact that he spends time with his children.
In 1977, these figures had risen to 71 percent and 64 percent,
respectively. This change is small and reflects the unchanging nature of father-adolescent relations. What is of real
interest, however, is a significant change occurring in how
much adolescents value their mothers spending time with them.
One presumes that to explicitly value this means that it is
problematic, that it is an issue. In 1924, 34 percent of the
boys and 41 percent of the girls placed a premium on having
their mothers spend time with them. By 1977, the percentages
had risen to 58 percent and 66 percent. Presumably, this
reflects the gradual departure of mothers from the day-to-day
lives of their adolescents over a fifty-year period; a period
that corresponds directly with the tremendous increase in
mothers working outside the home. These data complement
others collected by Bronfenbrenner(40) and his colleagues that
show a continuing decline in the amount of active time spent
by parents with their children. They link this decrease to a
variety of disturbing trends, including impaired social functioning and alienation.

What makes people happy? Happiness lies in what Erik
Erickson calls the issue of one's relation to the future, that of
"generativity vs. despair." It is in psychological and social
investment for the future, for the quality of the future, that
one finds genuine happiness. It is in investment in children,
either directly, as a parent, or indirectly, as one who makes
the world a better place for children. How well does our
society do and how well can it do in the future in making this
investment a productive one, a happy one? The answer is to
be found in the neighborhood and institutional life of adults.

Neighborhoods

Whether or not the intrinsic value of children will triumph over their burdensomeness depends in some measure on how supportive the family's neighborhood is. The quality of neighborhoods as contexts for family life has become a significant issue for students of community and human development. So attractive in principle, neighborhood has proven very difficult to define in operational, concrete, and specific terms. Perhaps one of the best statements of what a good neighborhood is comes from Kromkowski:

> A neighborhood's character is determined by a host of factors, but most significantly by the kinds of relationships that neighbors have with each other. . . . A healthy neighborhood has some sort of cultural and institutional network which manifests itself in pride in the neighborhood, care of homes, security for children, and respect for each other.(41)

When stated this way, the significance of neighborhoods as support systems for families is clear and indisputable. A strong and supportive neighborhood makes the task of parenthood significantly more manageable.

Research on neighborhoods(42) provides some insights into the way a family's social environment can affect the experience of parent-child relationships. Economically and demographically similar settings can present very different social environments, and the quality of life for parents and children can be likewise affected. In a recent study, two neighborhoods were selected on the basis of their economic and demographic similarity and their child maltreatment rates. While wellmatched economically and demographically, one area was particularly high-risk for children while the other was proportionally at lower risk. The rate of child maltreatment differed by a factor of five. When these two settings were examined, it was found that expert informants ranging from elementary school principals to mail carriers saw the low-risk area as a healthy neighborhood and the high-risk area as a socially sick environment. Samples of families drawn from each neighborhood were interviewed. The families identified very different patterns of stresses and supports, different patterns in the use and source of help, differences in the size and quality of family social networks, differences in the use of formal support systems, and differences in parental evaluation of the neighborhood as a setting in which to raise children. Also, parents in the high-risk neighborhood reported high levels of stress in their day-to-day lives, and a general pattern of "social impoverishment." High-risk neighborhoods are areas in which neighbors do not help each other, in which there is suspicion about contact by both parents and children, and in which the norms and behavior increase family weakness.

Creating and maintaining strong neighborhoods for families is one of the principal challenges facing efforts to design a sustainable society. All the elements of quantitative growth work against neighborhoods. Mobility is a threat, of course. Use of motorized transportation to permit bedroom communities and undermine walking communities works against neighborhoods. Restrictive rezoning to produce residental ghettos works against neighborhoods because a functioning neighborhood requires some commercial activity. Within cities, strong neighborhoods resemble strong small towns. The important question is whether or not the seemingly inexorable trends toward the destruction of neighborhoods will be permitted to continue. The answer will come in the public decisions concerning rezoning and mass transportation. The quality of life for children is determined in large part by progress in the institutional life of the community.

The Institutional Life of the Community

The design and delivery of human services, the nature of adult work, and the structure and function of educational institutions all have a significant effect on the quality of life for children. Human services are delivered formally through a variety of public and semi-public institutions. How well can these formal support systems be integrated and balanced with the informal support systems, the "private enterprise system" of human services that offers most help on a day-to-day basis? Models for integrating formal and informal support systems are being developed and, in fact, are in place in some communities.(43)

In the world of work, the issue is whether or not conflicts between the role of parent and the role of worker can be ironed out in favor of the former. The entrance of large numbers of mothers of young children into the work force has made us keenly aware of the need to rationalize the relationship between work and home. The issue of "working mothers" has not been resolved satisfactorily. Providing adequate and developmentally enhancing day care for preschool children is an unresolved and highly charged issue. How we resolve this issue will have a bearing on the quality of life for children and, in fact, on the quality of children for life. When the world of work forces an adult (male or female) to choose between being a good parent and a good worker, children suffer and ultimately the future is impoverished. As we move toward designing a sustainable society we must keep in mind the need to establish norms about the world of work that will reduce its intrusion into family life. Freud said that a well-adjusted person is distinguished by his (or her) ability to work and to love. Similarly, a high quality society will arrange itself so that people can do both and do justice to both.

By and large, children's work is school work. Research on school size suggests that large schools (enrollments greater than 600 in grades 9-12) tend to become psychologically unsustainable.(44) Large schools discourage participation, create elitism, encourage staff inflexibility, and, most insidiously, alienate those students who are already academically marginal. Historical data on school size chronicle the decline of quality of life for children in their primary institutional setting. In this area, perhaps more than any other, we have seen an unthinking policy of growth undermine and destroy socially desirable settings (small schools) on the basis of a warped sense of quantitative progress. The sense that big schools mean power and opportunity directly parallels the notion that an unlimited policy of growth means progress. Depersonalization and a reduction of the effective social pluralism of the child's experience are alarming consequences of large schools. Recent history (the last 30 years) has witnessed a dramatic increase in school size, but the data suggest that a reverse of this trend is possible. Just as escalating energy costs have given pragmatic impetus to "walking neighborhoods," these same forces will increasingly demonstrate the cost effectiveness of small schools. Such schools can now be technology-intensive to permit an academically rich and character-building social environment.

All three areas - family, neighborhood, and the institutional life of the community - are always in influx. Economic and demographic conditions may shift the direction of their influence, sometimes favoring supportive environments, sometimes undermining them, but the constant issue in all these matters is the stance taken by social policy.

A recent crossnational survey of public policy and public services for families concluded that the United States is quite backward in this respect. The study conducted by Sheila Kammerman and Alfred Kahn(45) found that in many respects: "The rhetoric in the U.S. proclaims the value and sanctity of children in family life; reality is something else. We provide nothing like the child care services or cash benefits to protect child and family life that the European countries do." Former director of the Office of Child Development, Edward Zigler echoes Kammerman and Kahn's judgment: "We think we care more than our actions would say."(46)

In any case, public debate in the future must be judged on how well it takes into account the needs of children (and, therefore, their parents) in making decisions. For example, will corporate profit take precedence over the need of workers to have adequate time to care for their children? The essence of ideology is that it permeates all aspects of day-to-day living. Thus, whether or not we develop a suitably pro-child ideology will be revealed not in grand pronouncements or even in master legislation, but in the day-to-day decisions that affect and shape the lives of families. The central position of ideology returns us to the growth policy debate, an essentially ideological discussion.

RELEVANCE OF ISSUES AFFECTING CHILDREN
TO THE GROWTH POLICY RATE

Social impoverishment is a correlate of growth defined by quantitative product irrespective of psychological and social quality. To recapitulate, social impoverishment is the denuding of the individual's environment of those relationships that function as support systems, that provide nurturance and feedback. If we permit the social impoverishment of parent's lives, we undermine the quality of life for children and, thus, in effect, the quality of our future. The quantitative growth ideology undermines children by contributing to social impoverishment. It does so by destroying the social integrity of neighborhoods, by increasing the demographic and social homogeneity of neighborhoods, by devaluing parenthood, by overemphasizing the importance of material productivity as a criterion for personal value, by increasing the instrumentality of social relations, by divorcing work and home, by promoting large schools for their efficiency as mass producers, and by fostering values that emphasize material gratification over social responsibility. The growth policy debate must come to terms with the possibility that conventional thinking (the quantitative product orientation) is not socially sustainable. It is a great temptation to propose a nostalgic, "good old days" solution; but, for a modern rendering of traditional sources of social pluralism to succeed, a restatement of the developmental necessities of life is needed. As individual families struggle with this issue, institutions can make a vital contribution; they will decide how successful most families will be. If institutions are dominated by a quantitative orientation to growth, then families will be swimming against a tide that for most will be irrecusable. The future is a public policy issue. There are at least five areas in which productive action is possible. These topics reflect an intermingling of action and ideology, of cause and effect, of shaping events and shaping minds. To design a sustainable society we must make progress on each of these fronts.

1. National support for the family impact analysis concept:
    The scientific basis for evaluating the impact of change
    - particularly economic growth - is rudimentary. We need
    to make some progress in moving toward a kind of "social
    currency" that can be used to compute the costs and
    benefits to families of various policies and decisions.
    Investment in this area of research and development is a
    high priority item on the agenda for those who would
    design a sustainable society.(47)

2. Neighborhoods as units for analysis and planning: Local
    governments and corporate leaders need to become aware
    of the importance of thinking of neighborhoods - not
    simply individuals and communities - as units of analysis.
    Data collection policies of the U.S. Census Bureau are
    already being changed to reflect this orientation, and in
    many ways adequate data are a precondition for intelligent
    policy. Growth policies must consider how they affect
    existing neighborhoods as well as how socially sustainable
    new residential developments will be.(48) Without such a
    conception at the heart of planning and zoning decisions,
    neighborhoods are doomed to be eroded and new develop-
    ments will not be neighborhoods.

3. Public education: The allure of materialism is great, but
    there are reservoirs of support for the primacy of
    family-related "payoffs" manifest in public opinion
    polls.(49) There is support for family life and there is
    recognition that family stability is a precondition for
    meaningful existence. The pressing need is for public
    articulation of how personal and institutional decisions can
    tap these resources and respect the values they reflect.
    We need to resolve the conflict between home and work.

4. Linking professionals and natural helping networks:
    Natural helping networks provide effective "human
    services" as well as substantial psychic payoffs. A
    socially sustainable society requires that we reduce the
    exclusiveness of professionalized institutions. Also, it
    requires that we do not build up budgetary expectations
    that are a constant economic drain and a periodic political
    liability. Instead, we should encourage greater sharing
    of helping functions with natural helping networks.(50)

IN CONCLUSION

A sustainable society, one that is ecologically sound, should
have children as its focal point because they are labor-
intensive. Children benefit from a "small is beautiful" philosophy. Bending our efforts to produce smaller rather than
larger schools is one concrete step that can serve as a focal

point for efforts to enhance the psychological and social circumstances of childhood and, thus, enrich the quality of human life generally. Directing institutional practice and policy toward families is imperative. This includes everything from giving priority to families in the logistics of travel to offering tax incentives for responsible parenthood. As we look for ways to shift recreational activities away from energy-intensive and materialistic consumption, children and their activities are appealing. Play is both developmentally important and socially enriching. Some have lost sight of this in their efforts to make children's play more professional, as in the proliferation of costly and equipment-intensive sports. Family hikes and other "primitive" activities provide ecologically sound and psychologically satisfying as well as developmentally enhancing alternatives to materialistic, energy-intensive activities. As pointed out earlier, since it is scientifically true that the only thing of real value we have to offer children is our time and interest, it is a pleasant coincidence that such an investment is also a precondition for an ecologically sound and sustainable future society.

NOTES

1. H. Cleveland and T. Wilson, Human Growth: An Essay on Growth, Values, and the Quality of Life (Aspen, Colo.: Institute for Humanistic Studies, 1978).
2. Ibid., p. 24.
3. M.E. Burris, "Food Marketing Institute: State of the Industry," Presentation made in American Marketing Institute Conference, Dallas, Texas, May 7, 1979, Behavior Today (June 4, 1979).
4. Cleveland and Wilson, Human Growth, p. 28-29.
5. "Comments on Kids," APA Monitor 10 (June 1979): 1 ff.
6. A. Emlen, "If You Care About Children, Then Care About Parents" (Address to the Tennessee Association for Young Children, Nashville, Tenn., November 3, 1977).
7. D. Morris, The Human Zoo (New York: Dell, 1970), p. 65.
8. M. Rock, "Gorilla Mothers Need Some Help From Their Friends," Smithsonian 9(4) (1978): 58-63.
9. M. Strauss, R. Gelles, and S. Steinmetz, Behind Closed Doors (New York: Doubleday, 1979).
10. J. Garbarino, "The Human Ecology of Child Maltreatment: A Conceptual Model for Research," Journal of Marriage and The Family 39 (1977): 721-27.
11. L. Harris, "Importance and Satisfaction with Factors of Life," The Harris Survey, November 23, 1978.

12. J. Garbarino and A.C. Garbarino, "Where Are the Children in Utopia?" (Paper presented at the Second National Conference on International Communities, Omaha, Nebraska, October 17, 1978).

13. A. Campbell, "Subjective Measures of Well Being," American Psychologist 31 (1976): 117-24.

14. A.T. Wright, Islandia (New York: Holt, Rinehart and Winston, 1942).

15. Ibid., pp. 84-85.

16. A. Campbell, "Subjective Measures of Well Being."

17. U. Bronfenbrenner, The Ecology of Human Development (Cambridge, Mass.: Harvard University Press, 1979), p. 9.

18. A. Campbell, "Subjective Measures of Well Being," p. 122.

19. Robert Coles, Children of Crisis: Privileged Ones (Boston: Little Brown, in press).

20. National Academy of Sciences, Toward a National Policy for Children and Families (Washington, D.C.: U.S. Government Printing Office, 1979).

21. Margaret Sanger, Margaret Sanger: An Autobiography (New York: W.W. Norton Co., 1938), p. 89.

22. E.F. Schumacher, Small is Beautiful (New York: Harper and Row, 1973).

23. Bronfenbrenner, The Ecology of Human Development, p. 9.

24. U. Bronfenbrenner, "The Origins of Alienation," in Influences on Human Development, edited by U. Bronfenbrenner and M. Mahoney (Hinsdale, Ill.: Dryden Press, 1975).

25. E. Zigler, "The Unmet Needs of America's Children," Children Today (May-June 1976), p. 39.

26. U. Bronfenbrenner, "Who Needs Parent Education?" Teachers College Record 79 (1978): 867-87.

27. J. Garbarino, "A Note on Television Viewing," in Bronfenbrenner and Mahoney Influences on Human Development.

28. G. Caplan, Support Systems and Community Mental Health (New York: Behavioral Publication, 1974), p. 4.

29. J. Howard, Families (New York: Simon and Schuster, 1978), p. 60.

30. From the author's files.

31. J. Garbarino and U. Bronfenbrenner, "The Socialization of Moral Judgment and Behavior in Cross-cultural Perspective," in Moral Development and Behavior, edited by T. Lickona (New York: Holt, Rinehart and Winston, 1976).

32. J. Featherstone, "Family Matters," Harvard Educational Review 49 (1979): 20-56.

33. L. Morrow, "Wondering if Children are Really Necessary," Time (March 5, 1979), p. 42.

34.   Featherstone, "Family Matters"; Zigler, "The Unmet Needs of America's Children."
35.   P. Glick, "The Future of the American Family" (Washington, D.C.: U.S. Government Printing Office, 1979).
36.   J. Blake, "Is Zero Preferred? American Attitudes Toward Childlessness in 1970's," Journal of Marriage and Family 41 (1979): 245-65.
37.   Ibid.
38.   E.J. Lieberman, "Reserving a Womb, 1976: Case for the Small Family," American Journal of Public Health 60 (1970): 87-92.
39.   H. Bahr, "Change in Family Life in Middletown: 1924-1977" (Paper presented at the Annual Meeting of the American Sociological Association, Chicago, August 1978).
40.   U. Bronfenbrenner, Two Worlds of Childhood (New York: Russell Sage Foundation, 1970).
41.   J. Kromkowski, Neighborhood Deterioration and Juvenile Crime (South Bend, Ind.: South Bend Urban Observatory, 1976), p. 228.
42.   J. Garbarino and A. Crouter, "Defining the Community Context of Parent-Child Relations," Child Development 49 (1978): 604-16; and J. Garbarino and D. Sherman, "High-Risk Families and High-Risk Neighborhoods," Child Development 51 (1980): 188-198.
43.   J. Garbarino and S.H. Stocking, eds., Supporting Families and Protecting Children (San Francisco: Jossey-Bass, 1980).
44.   J. Garbarino, "Some Thoughts on School Size and its Effects on Adolescent Development," Journal of Youth and Adolescence 9 (1980): 19-31.
45.   S. Kammerman and A. Kahn, Family Policy in Five Nations (New York: Columbia University Press, 1979).
46.   Zigler, "The Unmet Needs of America's Children."
47.   S. Johnson, Family Impact Seminar, Program Statement, Institute for Educational Leadership, Washington, D.C.: The George Washington University, 1978.
48.   National Commission on Neighborhoods, Final Report of the Commission (Washington, D.C.: U.S. Government Printing Office, 1979).
49.   Cf., Harris, "Importance and Satisfaction with Factors in Life."
50.   Garbarino and Stocking, Supporting Families and Protecting Children.

84¹⁰
7110
7120

8 Feeding the Transitional Society

Anne H. Ehrlich

Imagine a world in which the human population numbers perhaps a billion and remains close to that number for untold centuries. Imagine that everyone in that population has all his or her material needs satisfied - an ample, varied diet, sufficient clothing, comfortable housing, tools and machines to relieve drudgery and enhance life. Suppose everyone has access to education, communications, arts and literature, sports and recreation, travel, and social activities. Every adult can find a useful, socially-valued (and rewarded) job to perform.

There are large cities, which function as centers for large-scale manufacturing and industry, higher education, scientific research, communications, and other specialized activities. A sizable portion of the population lives in small towns, villages, or on farms, however. But with sophisticated communications and efficient transport, rural people are not isolated from urban concerns.

Nations coexist peacefully, trading goods and sharing responsibility for managing the Earth's commons: the atmosphere, oceans and sea life, shared river systems, for instance. A supranational organization exists to settle international disputes and help nations cooperate to improve their citizens' lives. Such assistance could be through dissemination of new technologies, establishment of new trading arrangements, or the fostering of cultural exchanges. Different societies, and individuals within them, have differing lifestyles and standards of living, but there are no gross contrasts of wasteful wealth and appalling poverty.

This idealized society has plenty of energy to support its activities, most of which comes from renewable or for practical purposes inexhaustible sources. Examples of the former would be solar, wind, biogas, perhaps ocean thermal or tidal power;

the latter would include geothermal energy and possible
nuclear fusion. Fossil fuels are regarded as precious commodities and saved for uses for which no substitutes have
been found. Metals and other materials are rigorously recycled. Mining of new materials is permitted only at a level
that will replace the unavoidable losses. Progress is measured
by changes that improve peoples' well-being without increasing
consumption of energy or materials.

Primary renewable resources, which underlie and sustain
the production of food, fibers, forest products, sea foods, and
other biological products, are carefully protected, preserved,
and, where possible, even improved. These primary resources
include croplands, grazing land, forests, and their soils; fresh
water, underground or on the surface; the biological resources
of natural ecological systems, aquatic or terrestrial; and the
genetic resources of both the natural systems and domestic
plants and animals. This civilization is deeply conscious of its
obligation to preserve these essential resources for future
generations.

High on the list of priorities is insurance of a dependable
and adequate food supply, which is dependent, in turn, on
the primary renewable resources and climatic stability. Famine
for any area is a remote threat because the system is resilient
enough - through storage of surpluses, avoidance of over-
dependence on monocultures, maintenance of genetic variability
in crops to confer resistance to pests and weather stress, and
a well-developed trade network - to cope with failures when
they occur. Both quality and quantity are important considerations in both agriculture and marketing so that everyone
has access to a wide variety of foods. This provides both
good nutrition and pleasure (good food is, after all, one of
life's delights).

Just described is one vision of a "sustainable society" - one
that can be maintained indefinitely into the future; forever, in
essence. Is such a utopian world possible? It may be. The
really crucial question is whether humanity can make the long
and difficult transition from today's predicament to such a
sustainable world without, along the way, undermining or
destroying the resource base that must support both the
transitional and eventual sustainable societies.

Leaving aside the possibility of thermonuclear war (by no
means a negligible risk), failure to make the transition successfully is most likely to come from a massive failure in the
global food production system. Avoidance of such a vast
tragedy and putting the world's food system on a sound,
dependable basis must be a centerpiece of any strategy for
making the transition. This is no easy task.

THE FOOD SITUATION TODAY

Analyses of world food production almost always are confined to a short-term outlook - a decade or two at most. Usually they are projections based on past performances. Recent studies, however, have expressed concern about the feasibility of maintaining global food supplies for the expanding human population even for the remainder of this century. Even though it appears that, worldwide, growth has slowed slightly, population is expected to increase by nearly two billion - or almost 50 percent - between 1980 and 2000. Accommodating that increase alone is a tough assignment since the food production system is already showing unmistakable signs of stress.(1) Since 1970, global food production has risen rather unsteadily and at a lower average rate than in the previous two decades. Meanwhile, the population has continued to grow at 1.7 percent per year or more. Despite a slight slowdown in the population growth rate, average food production per capita has increased only marginally in the past decade.

Average figures of course can, and do, conceal great differences between regions and income groups. Much of the per capita increase in food supplies during the 1970s occurred in the already well-fed rich countries. Most of the less-developed world fared less well, and many of the poorest countries lost ground.(2) A substantial portion, perhaps as much as 25 percent, of the human population today is poorly fed and roughly half of those, approaching 500 million during the 1970s, have been designated by the United Nations Food and Agriculture Organization as seriously undernourished. Most vulnerable are infants, young children, and mothers of poor families. By contrast, the most affluent quarter of the population, mainly in the developed countries, is, if anything, overfed.

The world food system today is characterized by gross inequities in the distribution of available food, misallocation of priorities, inefficiency, lack of coordination of food policies between nations, wastefulness in some areas, inadequate supporting technology in others, and poor or even destructive management of such primary resources as land, soil, forests, water, and fisheries stocks.(3)

Maldistribution allows a substantial portion of humanity to exist on the edge of starvation while another large portion fattens cattle with crops that could feed people. Many developing countries have emphasized industrial development to the neglect of their agricultural sectors and rural areas. It is doubtless no accident that among the most "successful" developing countries, measured in terms of reducing both poverty and birthrates and attaining a degree of affluence, are several that have given rural development and food production high priority. Among these are Taiwan, South Korea, Costa Rica, and, most spectacularly, China. But for many less-developed countries, "rural development" has meant supporting large-scale agriculture for cash crops, often for export, at the expense of crops produced for local consumption. Credit, irrigation water, access to green-revolution inputs to increase yields are often available to large farmers but not to small farmers.

Unexpected declines in total worldwide food production in 1972 and 1974 (in the face of continued population growth) stimulated some efforts to establish a nationally held, global grain reserve and a small UN-administered emergency reserve. But renewed good harvests have fostered complacency since then, and reserves are still inadequate to cushion two bad years in a row.

Perhaps the most alarming and least noticed trend of all is the undermining of primary resources on which food production is utterly dependent. Nor is the destruction limited to developing countries. A surprising share goes on in one of the world's breadbaskets: the United States. Vast tracts of cropland are threatened by high rates of soil erosion in the United States and elsewhere.(4) Desertification and salinization are serious problems in arid and semi-arid regions around the world. The UN Conference on Desertification concluded in 1977 that nearly a fifth of the world's cropland is being degraded at a rate intolerable for the long term and has already suffered an average 25 percent reduction in productivity.(5) The prospects for opening much new land for cultivation in coming decades are dim. What remains unexploited would require enormously costly development before it could be made productive; primarily, clearing and irrigation. Most of it is of poor quality compared to what is being lost.

Deforestation is proceeding rapidly throughout the tropics and subtropical regions as expanding populations clear the forests for fuel and land to grow food. The loss far outweighs the gain. Tropical forests may be the richest and most complex of ecosystems on the planet. Their disappearance means the irreplaceable loss of a wealth, not yet even assessed, of biological resources that could be potential sources of new foods, drugs, fibers, or other materials.

Large-scale deforestation also destabilizes watersheds and local climates and accelerates soil erosion. Farmland adjacent to deforested hills is far more subject to both drought and flood than land where forests are maintained. Removal of a forest also removes an essential source of fuel, construction materials, and other benefits to local people. Finally, especially in the humid tropics, forest soil is often too thin and poor to support permanent cultivation.(6)

Deforestation indeed is only one, relatively obvious aspect of the general destruction of natural ecosystems everywhere in the wake of "development" and expansion of agriculture. The results go far beyond the aesthetic loss of wildlife. Ecosystems perform many irreplaceable functions on which human beings, like other organisms, utterly depend. Most of these services directly or indirectly benefit and support agriculture, a man-made ecosystem itself, commonly called an "agroecosystem." Natural systems maintain the quality of the atmosphere, regulate and moderate the hydrological cycle (and thus strongly influence local climate and weather), recycle nutrients (including those in agriculture), break down wastes, build and replenish soils, and control the overwhelming majority of agricultural pests and vectors of diseases of both people and their crops and livestock. When these services are disrupted or lost, civilization is the loser. Mostly, humanity is incapable of replacing them adequately; what compensation is possible is usually very costly and less than satisfactory.

Increased water resources are essential for raising crop yields where they are still relatively low, mainly in developing countries. Yet competition for those resources from other activities such as energy development, industry, and urban expansion is rising. In many regions, such as the U.S. high plains, intensive irrigation is depleting "fossil" groundwater supplies. That is, water that accumulated in aquifers over millennia is being pumped out within decades.

Food from the sea, once thought a panacea for increasing protein supplies for poor countries, clearly offers little hope as an expandable food source. World fisheries yields reached a peak in 1976, but per capita yields have declined since 1970.(7) Most fisheries have suffered from overexploitation, but pollution and habitat destruction of estuarine nurseries have doubtless played a part. There is hope, however, that aquaculture could make a significant contribution to protein supplies in developing countries if pollution from farm chemicals can be controlled or prevented.

This dismal series of trends does not inspire confidence in the world's ability to continue increasing food production. Unless the trends can be reversed, it may not be possible to maintain even the present level of food supply per person for even a few decades. Just struggling through another decade or two, lurching from crisis to crisis, is an insufficient goal for humanity. What is needed is a clearly defined goal such as the concept of a sustainable society as previously described. Then it becomes possible to find the right path within the limits dictated by demography and available resources.

Toward the Transition

If population growth could be halted this year, the task of converting the present food system to one adequate to support today's population over an indefinitely long term would still be enormous. Unfortunately, the world population is demographically committed to continued growth for a century or more and to at least a doubling of its present size - unless, as sadly seems quite possible, some large-scale catastrophe intervenes to reduce numbers sharply in major regions of the world.

A sustainable society can be established only with an essentially stationary population - neither growing nor shrinking significantly. The human population must thus pass through the end of its growth phase and, because of resource restraints, enter into a period of shrinkage before reaching a long-term sustainable level. That level, unless a very low average standard of living prevails, must almost certainly be well below today's population of over 4 billion. The peak population has been projected as likely to fall between 8 and 12 billion.(8) A major priority must be to hold that peak as low as possible through vigorous population control efforts. The other chief priority is to find a way to support the human population, including producing enough food, during this long transition (perhaps two centuries or more) toward equilibrium. And this must be accomplished without destroying the primary resources that are the foundations of agriculture.

There will, of course, be substantial differences between regions or nations in how soon their populations can be stabilized at sustainable levels and in the lifestyles and levels of living chosen. Part of one's lifestyle, naturally, is the selection of foods that may be available. This, in turn, influences the size of the population that can be supported in a particular area. In general (though there are exceptions governed by such factors as terrain, soil, and climate), a larger, mainly vegetarian, population can be supported more easily than a mainly meat-eating population. Lifestyles and food preferences are heavily based on tradition and this, too, will play its part in determining each society's food system.

The range and quality of a society's food supply depend not only on such obvious factors as land quality, climate, water supply, and buffering natural systems, but also on how these resources are utilized and protected and on the size of the population being supported. They further depend on the efficiency of production methods and whether those are aimed at maximizing yields for the long or the short term. Finally, they depend on such factors as supply, along with meeting other basic human requirements for the poorest quarter, or even half, of the human population. To accomplish this, the richest quarter may have to sacrifice something in the quality of its overrich, wasteful food supply, at least for part of the

transitional period. Eating less red meat, especially beef,
which is the least efficient conversion of grain to meat, would
release substantial quantities of grain for hungry people and
land to grow other nutritious foods such as legumes. Such
an exchange would benefit the health of both groups of
people.
     Since the problems of managing the transitional food
supply are quite different for the developed and less-
developed countries, it is useful to consider them separately.

Developed Countries

The populations of most industrialized nations are expected to
reach their peak sizes and begin slowly declining within the
next few decades.(9)   Some have already begun their declines.
Demographers do not presently foresee any significant reversal
of the long-established trend toward low birthrates in developed countries.   These societies, however, are now consuming
by far the greatest share of the world's resources (particularly nonrenewable ones) and doing the heaviest amount of
environmental damage.
     Developed   nations   also   have   technologically   highly
developed agricultural systems, depending for their productivity on large inputs of fossil-fuel energy.   Crops commonly
are raised in extensive monocultures, which renders them more
vulnerable to pests and diseases and tends to erode the
genetic variability of crops.   Such variability in seed stocks is
essential for breeding new varieties with desired characteristics, such as higher yield or resistance to pests.   Heavily
mechanized farming methods and an agribusiness orientation
toward short-term profits rather than long-term land husbandry often lead to unnecessarily high rates of soil erosion
and general environmental deterioration.(10)
     Because most of the available technologies for increasing
yields are already in place in developed countries, substantial
increases in productivity are relatively unlikely to be made in
the foreseeable future.   Further increases await new breakthroughs, such as developing nitrogen-fixing symbionts for
grains, higher yields from DNA manipulation, or some method
of increasing photosynthetic efficiency, which may or may not
be successful.(11)   Yet it is to some of these countries,
especially the United States, that the world looks for surplus
food.   In the coming decade, even greater demands for food
will be made.   The fact that the populations of industrialized
nations may soon stop growing is one of the most encouraging
of present trends.   Because their standards of living are
already high, these countries may soon by making their transition to steady-state economics.(12)   Indeed, many developed
societies may soon have to <u>reduce</u> their per capita consumption

of some resources, particularly nonrenewable ones already depleted or becoming environmentally costly to obtain (petroleum being an obvious example). Such reductions in consumption are imperative in a context of long-term sustainability. The losses, however, can be largely compensated by greater efficiency of use (which has the additional advantage of reducing environmental impact) or by substitution of other, more abundant materials or energy sources. All this has been discussed in detail elsewhere;(13) the concern here is with the implications for agriculture.

In recent years, with the growth in awareness of environmental and nutritional considerations related to agriculture and of impending resource constraints, the need for changes in the food system has become evident. These will be discussed in the context of the United States, but the following considerations also apply to other countries.

Land tenure and use

The long-established trend toward larger farms and fewer farmers in the United States may now have gone too far.(14) The shift in pattern from owner-operated farms to absentee ownership for investment or speculation is a particular cause for concern. A family farm is measurably more efficient and productive, despite the fiscal efficiency of corporation ownership. Over the long haul, especially, family farmers demonstrably put more effort into protecting and caring not only for crops but also soil and other resources.(15) New land-tax, zoning, and other policies are needed in the United States, and other countries, to discourage absentee ownership and to support family farmers and help them stay in business.

Another aspect of land use in the United States that needs examination is the low priority accorded to agricultural land as reflected in land values, tax rates, and zoning laws. For almost any other use, land has a higher value. Thus, farmers are squeezed off good farmland, which is gobbled up by speculators and developers for subdivisions, airports, highways, strip mines, or water projects.(16) Clearly, preservation of high-quality land for production of food must become a matter of high priority for all nations.

Soil protection

Farmland must also be protected against overintensive use such as continuous cultivation of marginal lands that should be kept fallow or in pasture part of the time, or uncontrolled grazing on rangeland. In 1973, the U.S. Department of Agriculture abolished the Soil Bank, a program that paid farmers subsidies to hold part of their land out of production. The Soil Bank ensured that each farmer's poorest land was kept fallow much of the time and thus protected against overuse and erosion. Its abolition led farmers to plant fence-to-fence continuously, discouraged conservation measures such as crop rotation, and led to destruction of natural buffer zones and windbreaks. Although other factors such as bad weather were involved, the results included increased soil erosion and reduced per-hectare yields; although total production rose slightly. In 1978, a new "set-aside" program was established (a soil bank by another name), but, in the face of tighter food supplies following the 1979 harvest (some 4 percent below the 1978 worldwide total), it may prove short-lived.(17)

Abolition of the Soil Bank reflected the enormous pressure being put on American farmers to produce, both for the export market (to offset oil imports) and just to make a living in a time of depressed grain prices. With the consequent neglect of soil conservation practices, soil erosion rates rose to equal those of the 1930s Dust Bowl era. Apart from the loss of precious soil - and cost - the soil, with accompanying farm chemicals, pollutes waterways, clogs ditches, and silts up reservoirs.(18)

Reinstatement of long-established conservation methods such as contour plowing, strip planting, crop rotation, and windbreaks should certainly be made a high priority policy for American agriculture. In addition, experimentation with and deployment, where suitable, of newer methods could be encouraged. Minimum tillage, for instance, substantially reduces erosion.(19) Unfortunately, it also encourages weeds and pests, but there may be ways to mitigate this disadvantage without resorting to heavy use of pesticides.

Energy

Farms in the United States today operate largely on petroleum.(20) Oil shortages and escalating prices make it clear that this situation must soon change. Alternative energy options for many farming operations exist, however. Solar energy is suitable for heating, cooling, and drying of crops; wind energy can provide electricity and pump water; and biogas can be used for heating and cooking. Most of these have so far been promoted mainly for developing countries,(21) but there is no reason that they cannot be used in developed countries as well.

Substituting for liquid fuels to run farm machinery and vehicles is not yet feasible, but consumption certainly could be reduced. Huge farm machines are not only gas-consumptive, they are incompatible with some soil-conservation measures. And the high degree of mechanization on most American farms may not really be necessary for high productivity. A recent analysis of the methods of Amish farmers, whose religion discourages use of machinery, indicates that a considerable reduction in use of machines is possible for many crops without loss of productivity.(22) Experience in countries such as Taiwan and Japan, where farms are relatively tiny and machinery kept small-scale, confirms this. Using smaller and less machinery would both protect soil and require less energy.

While reduction of fossil-fuel consumption on the farm should be adopted as an immediate goal in developed countries, a more distant goal must be their complete replacement with renewable energy sources.(23) This alone could force a virtual revolution in farming methods, though it would be reinforced by environmental and other resource pressures. The sooner new agricultural methods that work within emerging constraints can be developed, the more smoothly and quickly the transitional process will go.

Fertilizers

Heavy dependence on artificial fertilizers for high productivity is another mainstay of present-day agriculture that may have to change, for several reasons.(24) One is that nitrogen fertilizers in particular consume so much fossil-fuel energy, accounting for nearly a third of what goes into agriculture. Fertilizers of all three major types - nitrogen, phosphates, and potassium - are serious pollutants, especially of waterways where they lead to eutrophication. Phosphates also threaten to be in short supply within a few decades. Finally, nitrogen fertilizers may, like fluorocarbons, pose a danger to the atmospheric ozone layer.

Extensive artificial fertilizing produces high yields for the short term, but does not add to soil structure or contribute other nutrients. Progressive soil erosion and impoverishment can be masked for awhile by fertilizers, but the end result, unless organic materials are also added, is serious, perhaps causing irreversible damage to soil.

There are, of course, well-known substitutes for inorganic fertilizers - namely, natural fertilizers such as manure, crop residues, and even sewage. The first two have been used traditionally everywhere and still are used extensively in developing countries. American farmers still use crop residues, but since livestock were moved to feedlots, manure has been little used. Treated sewage sludge, however, is increasingly being used even in many developed countries. Feedlot and human sewage, however, are largely wasted in the United States. Both are simply discarded to pollute rivers and oceans.

There are problems with using human sewage; there is some danger of cycling disease organisms, and urban sludge often contains toxic industrial contaminants such as heavy metals which may be taken up by crops. But there is reason to believe that these problems can be overcome.(25)   There is less excuse for wasting feedlot manure, which is already concentrated and needs only to be treated and distributed. The advantages of preserving and recycling the nutrients within the agroecosystem, improving soils, reducing the need for inorganic fertilizers, and preventing pollution elsewhere surely would justify the effort in both cases.   Of course, all three sources of organic fertilizer are potential energy sources as well.   After fermentation for biogas (which also kills most transmissible disease organisms), they retain full value as fertilizers.

Looking further ahead, recycled wastes probably cannot entirely compensate for inorganic fertilizers.   But there is hope that, eventually, enhanced nitrogen fixation by symbionts of some crops can help; when nitrogen is added to soil this way, less is lost to become a pollutant.

Pest control

The present chemical-based system of controlling pests and crop diseases has widely come to be recognized as an ecological disaster and a failure at solving pest problems to boot.(26) An alternative system, known as "integrated control," based in ecological principles, is demonstrably superior in several respects, but there are many social and economic barriers to its adoption.   Integrated control employs a variety of methods to discourage pests, including cultivation methods (such as crop rotation, interdropping, mixed crops, and careful timing of planting and harvesting), biological controls (encouragement or introduction of pest predators), natural buffer zones (which can harbor the predators and provide barriers between fields), genetic resistance bred into crops, and, if all else fails, chemical poisons.(27)

Many of these methods, of course, have been practiced for centuries and, in many developing countries, are not yet lost arts (though threatened).   China, lacking pesticides, has consciously and successfully cultivated nonchemical pest controls.   They have also been practiced and refined through experimentation in several developed countries by "organic farmers," who use no chemicals at all; pesticides or inorganic fertilizers.   It is commonly assumed that these inputs are essential for high productivity, yet organic farmers roughly match conventional farmers in yields, costs, and profits. Interestingly, their energy consumption is well under half that of conventional farmers.(28)

In modern high-yield agriculture, resistance to common diseases is one characteristic plant breeders try to include in new varieties.   But pests and diseases are in a coevolutionary race against the breeders; sooner or later the pest evolves a way around the crop's defenses.(29)   This is inevitable when crops are grown in a monoculture; acres of land planted with thousands of genetically identical plants, which usually have only one or two defensive traits against a given disease. But research shows that superior protection, as well as resistance to other environmental stresses, can be gained by developing "polygenic" plants with diverse resistance abilities. Perhaps more can be gained if planting heterogenetic crops (that is, individual plants of varying genetic makeup) together.(30) The latter tactic most closely resembles the way wild plant populations apparently defend themselves against their predators through an array of defenses, often chemical, and through individual variation in the expression of those defenses.

To build such genetically variable crops requires a rich breeding stock which is essential for future breeding programs anyway.(31) But the advantage, besides reducing monocultural susceptibility to pests and diseases, is that a reservoir of broad genetic variability would be constantly preserved in the best possible way; grown in large populations in farmers' fields.

The greatest drawback to integrated pest control is that it requires considerably more sophistication and some willingness to experiment on the part of the farmer. Switching will be difficult, since past heavy use of pesticides has devastated many populations of potential pest predators, which are inherently more susceptible. Suddenly stopping the spray program could bring on huge pest outbreaks. Natural buffer zones, which have disappeared in large areas of the U.S. agricultural belt, will have to be restored. Modern agriculture has become specialized; mixed farming is a foreign concept to most American farmers. Yet, it clearly would provide a more stable agroecosystem and would be more efficient in terms of energy and fertilizers, if livestock were included. Moreover, farmers would be less vulnerable to market fluctuations.

Difficult as it may be, agriculture in the United States and other developed countries will have to switch to more ecologically sound methods of controlling pests. The environmental and human health costs of present methods are too high to be sustained, especially when more benign approaches are available.

Developed countries are not staring starvation in the face, but they have some serious problems to solve in their food system if it is to maintain high productivity indefinitely. Indeed, a small sacrifice in productivity may be necessary in order to make the system sustainable. The world's food supply can be expected to become progressively tighter in future decades, which doubtless will lead to continued inflation in food prices for the rich countries, many of which are heavy importers. The magnitude of the pressure felt in rich

countries will depend not only on their success in converting
their systems to sustainability, but on how successful the
developing world is in raising its food production and lowering
birthrates, and on how willing the rich are to share their
surplus food.

Developing Countries

In sharp contrast to developed nations, populations in developing countries are still growing rapidly. All major regions
except East Asia and temperate South America still have growth
rates above 2 percent per year. Most of these populations are
projected to double or even triple before growth ends, even
under the most optimistic assumptions.(32) The task of
meeting the food needs of this unavoidable population surge is
staggering, given the resource and agricultural conditions
prevailing in many countries.

Considerable effort in coming decades will have to go into
correcting past mistakes.(33) First must come recognition of
the fundamental importance to every nation of a soundly-based
food system. In countries where agricultural and rural
development have been neglected, they should be given high
priority. Where rural development has concentrated on cash
crops for export, the value of the foreign exchange thus
earned should be weighed against using the land to grow more
crops for domestic consumption. Domestic food production
should be accorded at least as much support and assistance
as export crops. In many developing countries, there are
various institutional hindrances to agricultural development,
such as food price controls, subsidized food imports, restrictions on land tenure and farm credit, and export controls and
taxes, which discourage farmers from increasing food production.(34) Removing such disincentives could be a first step
to boosting output.

In the best and most effective sense, rural development
means ensuring that people's basic needs, including education,
health services, housing, potable water, and sanitation, are
met. It also implies direct benefits to farmers: availability of
seeds, fertilizers, fuel, and other needed materials; credit to
obtain them; plus development of roads, irrigation works, and
other infrastructure.(35) In many countries, land reform or
some system for employment of the landless poor will be an
important element of rural development. There is considerable
evidence that this "bottom-up" kind of development, besides
increasing food supplies and the well-being of rural people,
effectively motivates them toward smaller families.(36)

Another essential part of rural development must be a
serious effort to halt rural environmental deterioration,
especially desertification and wholesale deforestation. Given

the pressures on the land in many regions, reversing the downward trend will not be easy. But failure even to try will quickly lead to destruction of the land's ability to support people at all; successful restoration offers hope of enhanced productivity in the future.

Agricultural assistance from developed countries has mostly been an attempt to transfer their highly mechanized, chemical-based technology directly to developing countries, whether or not it fit the new social and environmental setting. Unfortunately, if often did not.(37) While the "green revolution" succeeded in increasing grain harvests, there were unanticipated economic and environmental side-effects.

The lesson is sinking in that a technological package developed in one setting is not necessarily appropriate to another; temperate-zone agricultural techniques, for example, are ill-suited to conditions in the tropics. Indeed, as discussed earlier, many aspects of American-style agriculture are inappropriate in their own setting and clearly incompatible with long-term sustainability. But the problems and disadvantages of chemical pest control, overmechanization, and intensive inorganic fertilization become acutely obvious in developing countries, especially tropical ones.

This certainly is not to say that high-yield production cannot be established in developing countries. It surely can be and must be, but in a different form. Previously recommended changes for American agriculture apply even more strongly here. Small-scale and minimal mechanization make sense where farms are small, labor abundant, and energy scarce and costly. Chemical pest control and monocultures invite environmental disaster and famine where the growing season is year-round and potential pests are abundant. Inorganic fertilizers quickly deplete thin tropical soils and cause environmental problems, unless natural fertilizers are added. Both pesticides and fertilizers will be needed, of course, but in small quantities, judiciously applied.

Developing countries have one advantage. They can implement ecologically-sound farming procedures in the beginning rather than having to overhaul an existing technology. Indeed, many changes previously suggested would simply be extensions of traditional methods: using natural fertilizers, controlling pests through mixed cropping, rotation, genetic resistance, and biological controls. A new technology is likeliest to succeed if it is based upon and adapted to indigenous farming practices which, after all, are the product of centuries of experience with local conditions and crops. The best agricultural research being conducted for and in developing countries today operates on this principle.

It must be borne in mind that, difficult as the problems are in developing countries to protect and restore the environment and primary resources while establishing population

control and enormously expanding food production for the next
century or two, the potential for greatly increased food production does exist. Most farmers get very low yields compared
to what would be possible if they had improved crop strains,
sufficient water and fertilizer, protection from pests and
diseases, and incentive to produce. What they need is encouragement and intelligent, appropriate assistance.

THE PROSPECTS

It all sounds very simple. But implementing these suggestions
in many countries will be extremely difficult, especially where
a major reordering of priorities is required. Vested interests,
industrial sectors accustomed to receiving a government's first
attention; landowners threatened by attempts at land reform;
international corporations seeking profits, not equity or environmental protection, will strongly oppose bottom-up rural
development. So will government officials who are unable to
see beyond the next election, or coup.

There will also be obstruction and opposition in developed
countries. Any erosion of living standards, even to help the
world's poor, will not be easily tolerated by the rich. Leaders
in developed countries have demonstrated no greater talent for
long-range planning than those in poor countries who literally
must live hand-to-mouth. Possibly, the human resource in
shortest supply is wisdom.

But people of broader vision can be found. It remains
for them to convince the short-sighted in both the developed
and developing worlds that taking the long view not only
brightens the prospects for their great-grandchildren, but will
enhance their own well-being in the relatively short term as
well. If a new conservation, sustainable ethic is to be established, it must be soon. Time is growing very short.

NOTES

(1) U.N. Food and Agriculture Organization (referred to
hereafter as FAO 1978), State of Food and Agriculture,
1977 (Rome: FAO, 1978); Lester R. Brown, "Resource
Trends and Population Policy: A Time for Reassessment,"
Worldwatch Paper 29, Worldwatch Institute, Washington,
D.C., 1979.
(2) FAO 1978; U.S. Department of Agriculture, World Agriculture Situation (WAS-18), December 1978.
(3) United Nations, Assessment of the World Food Situation,
Present and Future (Rome: World Food Conference,

1974); Erik Eckholm, Losing Ground: Environmental Stress and World Food Prospects (New York: Norton, 1976); Lester R. Brown, "The Worldwide Loss of Cropland," Worldwatch Paper 24, Worldwatch Institute, Washington, D.C., 1978; Council on Environmental Quality, The Global 2000 Report to the President: Entering the Twenty-first Century (Washington, D.C.: Government Printing Office, 1979) (hereafter referred to as The Global 2000 Report); David Pimentel et al., "Energy and Land Constraints in Food Protein Production," Science 190 (1975): 754-62.

(4) Brown, "The Worldwide Loss of Cropland"; The Global 2000 Report; D. Pimentel et al., "Land Degradation: Effects on Food and Energy Resources," Science 194 (1976): 149-55; Luther J. Carter, "Soil Erosion: The Problem Persists Despite the Billions Spent on it," Science 196 (1977): 407-11.

(5) U.N. Conference on Desertification, "Economic and Financial Aspects of the Plan of Action to Combat Desertification." (Nairobi: United Nations, 1977).

(6) The Global 2000 Report; Eckholm, Losing Ground; Erik Eckholm, "Planting for the Future: Forestry for Human Needs," Worldwatch Paper 26, Worldwatch Institute, Washington, D.C., 1979; Paul R. Ehrlich, Anne H. Ehrlich and John P. Holdren, Ecoscience: Population, Resources, Environment (San Francisco: W.H. Freeman, 1977).

(7) Brown, "Resource Trends and Population Policy."

(8) United Nations, A Concise Report on the World Population Situation, 1970-1975, and Its Long-Range Implications. (New York: United Nations, 1974) (hereafter referred to as The World Population Situation).

(9) Charles F. Westoff, "Marriage and Fertility in the Developed Countries," Scientific American (December 1978): 51-57.

(10) Carter, "Soil Erosion"; James Risser, "Soil Erosion Creates a Problem Down on the Farm," Conservation Foundation Letter, Conservation Foundation, Washington, D.C., 1978; General Accounting Office, To Protect Tomorrow's Food Supply, Soil Conservation Needs Priority Attention (Washington, D.C.: Government Printing Office, 1977); Peter Barnes, "The Corporate Invasion," New Ecologist, no. 6 (Nov./Dec. 1978): 197-99.; Pimentel et al., "Land Degradation"; Edward Groth III, Food Production, Population Growth, and Environmental Quality, Caltech Population Program Occasional Papers, Series 1, no. 7 (Pasadena, 1973).

(11) Neal F. Jensen, "Limits to Growth in World Food Production," Science 201 (1978): 317-20; S. H. Wittwer, "The Next Generation of Agricultural Research," Science 199 (1978): 375; Richard Radmer and Bessel Kok,

"Photosynthesis: Limited Yields, Unlimited Dreams," BioScience 27 (9) (1977): 599-605; James A. Bassham, "Increasing Crop Production Through More Controlled Photosynthesis," Science 197 (1977): 630-38; Sylvan H. Wittwer, "Nitrogen Fixation and Agricultural Productivity," BioScience 28 (9) (1978): 555.

(12) Herman Daly, Steady State Economics: The Economics of Biophysical Equilibrium and Moral Growth (San Francisco: W. H. Freeman, 1977).

(13) Donella H. Meadows et al., The Limits to Growth (Washington, D.C.: Universe Books, 1972); Dennis C. Pirages, ed., The Sustainable Society: Social and Political Implications (New York: Praeger, 1977); The Global 2000 Report; Lester R. Brown, The Twenty-ninth Day: Accommodating Human Needs and Numbers to the Earth's Resources (New York: W. W. Norton, 1978); Ehrlich et al., Ecoscience.

(14) "The New American Farmer," Time (Nov. 6, 1978); Barnes, "The Corporate Invasion." See also Robert G. Healy, "Rural Land: Private Choices, Public Interests," Conservation Foundation Letter (August 1977).

(15) Bruce Stokes, "Local Responses to Global Problems: A Key to Meeting Basic Human Needs." Worldwatch Paper 17, Worldwatch Institute, Washington, D.C., 1978.

(16) Brown, "The Worldwide Loss of Cropland."

(17) U.S. Dept. of Agriculture, Foreign Agricultural Service, "World Crop Production," Foreign Agricultural Circular (WCP-2-79), Aug. 10, 1979.

(18) Risser, "Soil Erosion,"; William Lockeretz, "The Lessons of the Dust Bowl," American Scientist 66 (1978): 560-70.

(19) Glover B. Triplett, Jr. and David M. Van Doren, Jr., "Agriculture Without Tillage," Scientific American (January 1977): 28-33.

(20) Groth, "Food Production"; David Pimentel et al., "Land Degradation."

(21) Arjun Makhijani and A. Poole, Energy and Agriculture in the Third World (Cambridge, Mass.: Ballinger, 1975); Ehrlich et al., Ecoscience.

(22) Warren A. Johnson, Victor Stoltzfus, and Peter Craumer, "Energy Conservation in Amish Agriculture," Science 198 (1977): 373-78.

(23) W. J. Chancellor and J. R. Goss, "Balancing Energy and Food Production, 1975-2000," Science 192 (1976): 213-18; Brian Pain and Richard Phipps, "The Energy to Grow Maize," New Scientist (May 15, 1975): 394-96.

(24) S.H. Wittwer, "The Next Generation"; National Research Council, Nitrates: An Environmental Assessment, (Washington, D.C.: National Academy of Sciences, 1978); Ehrlich et al., Ecoscience.

(25)   George M. Woodwell, "Recycling Sewage through Plant
       Communities," American Scientist 65 (1977):   556-62.
(26)   Robert van den Bosch, The Pesticide Conspiracy (New
       York: Doubleday, 1978); Ehrlich et al., Ecoscience.
(27)   Edward H. Glass and H. David Thurston, "Traditional
       and Modern Crop Protection in Perspective," BioScience
       28 (2) (1978):   109-14.
(28)   William Lockeretz et al., A Comparison of the Production,
       Energy Returns, and Energy Intensiveness of Corn
       Belt Farms that Do and Do Not Use Inorganic Fer-
       tilizers and Pesticides (St. Louis, Missouri: Center for
       the Biology of Natural Systems, Washington University,
       1975).
(29)   Ehrlich et al., Ecoscience.
(30)   J. Artie Browning, "Relevance of Knowledge about
       Natural Ecosystems to Development of Pest Management
       Programs for Agro-Ecosystems," Proceedings of the Amer-
       ican Phytopathological Society 1 (1975):   191-99; Graham
       Harvey, "The Cambridge Strategy," New Scientist, (Feb-
       ruary 16, 1978): 428-39; P. M. Dolinger, P.R. Ehrlich,
       W. Fitch, and D. Breedlove, "Alkaloid and Predation
       Patterns in Colorado Lupine Population," Oecologia 13
       (1973):   191-204.
(31)   O. H. Frankel and E. Bennett, Genetic Resources in
       Plants: Their Exploration and Conservation (Philadelphia:
       F.A. Davis, 1970).
(32)   United Nations, The World Population Situation; The
       Global 2000 Report.
(33)   Kenneth A. Dahlberg, Beyond the Green Revolution: The
       Ecology and Politics of Global Agricultural Development
       (New York: Plenum Press, 1979).
(34)   Abdullah A. Saleh and O. Halbert Goolsby, "Institutional
       Disincentives to Agricultural Production in Developing
       Countries," Foreign Agriculture, Supplement, August
       1977, U.S. Dept. of Agriculture, Washington, D.C.
(35)   James E. Kocher, "Rural Development, Income Distribu-
       tion, and Fertility Decline," Population Council Occasional
       Paper, New York, 1973.
(36)   Ibid.
(37)   Dahlberg, Beyond the Green Revolution; Nicholas Wade,
       "Green Revolution (I):   A Just Technology, Often Unjust
       in Use," and "Green Revolution (II):   Problems of
       Adapting a Western Technology," Science, 186 (1974):
       1093-96, 1186-92; Daniel H. Janzen, "Tropical Agroeco-
       systems," Science 182 (1973):   1212.

III
INSTITUTIONAL MODIFICATIONS FOR A SUSTAINABLE SOCIETY

9 World Politics and Sustainable Growth: A Structural Model of the World System
George Modelski

EXPLAINING THE WORLD PROBLEMATIQUE

Past studies and criticisms of the world process have demonstrated the facts and figures, but not the nature, of excessive growth. They have shown the dangers lurking in the continuance of the exponential trends in such fields as world population, industrial production, raw materials extraction, energy use, and pollution. They have convincingly demonstrated that these are not just isolated global problems but a whole world problèmatique.

But, even though the trends depicted are striking and the projections frequently alarming, it is also fair to say that these facts alone, in and of themselves, give us insufficient understanding because they do not tell us enough about the reasons for the growth: they do not explain the problèmatique. It is, in fact, surprising how little attention has been paid, in the past few years, to this basic question: why is it that the world has experienced unsustainable growth? One of the reasons for the heated debate on growth is a lack of a broad-gauge theory of sustainability.

Explanations of the world problèmatique are most often couched in terms of "beliefs" in continuous growth. It is held, for instance, that the main historical root of the ecological crisis is religion, and it is asserted that "Christianity bears a huge burden of guilt" because of the Judeo-Christian tradition of "man's charge to subdue the earth,"(1) and yet Christianity alone antedates the modern world by more than a millenium. Or sometimes the onus is laid on the "Baconian" tendencies of modern science for which "knowledge is power," a means of establishing the "dominion" of the human race "over the universe of things,"(2) and yet science has certainly had

145

more than one tradition. Most generally, reference is made to
the overriding belief in unremitting growth as a variant of the
faith in universal progress fueled by science and technology –
the inseparable and desirable features of the contemporary
world. It is not really surprising that religion and science
figure so prominently in these explanations because the questions raised bear directly on the place of humankind in the
universe and verge on those of cosmology. But beliefs, as
such, are an incomplete; they are a basically unsatisfactory
explanation of such a powerful process as the world problèmatique, and we need to go beyond them.

THE NATION-STATE AND CONTROLS ON GROWTH

The most obvious and also the most basic reason for seeking a
good explanation is the design of controls; for, to manage a
problem, one ought to, in the best of possible worlds, fully
comprehend it. That is not to say that control is impossible
without full understanding. On the contrary, the record of
every society abounds with policies and prohibitions that are
no more than hit-or-miss techniques for solving serious problems. Indeed, the problems may sometimes yield to Draconian
measures of barbaric cruelty or severity. But for lasting,
effective, acceptable controls that can be convincingly advocated and defended, a theoretically sound model is the only
reliable foundation.
    An understanding of the world problèmatique is partic-
ularly necessary for the design of macrocontrols on growth,
for it is now widely recognized that macrocontrols are superior
to microrestrictions;(3) and, if macrocontrols are preferred,
then the most effective must be those that operate at the
global level. But, to have the necessary confidence to institute and apply such controls, we need a reliable model of
the structure and operation of the world system and of the
ways in which controls on growth might feed back upon that
structure.
    While the Meadows' original study of the limits to growth
was boldly cast in a world perspective, the projects that have
followed it have tended to narrow their scope and to cultivate
sensitivity to regional and sectoral particularities. At the
same time, the conviction has been gaining ground that, in the
matter of controls, the nation-state alone can be expected to
be effective: "only the nation-state seems to have the authority to impose those necessary restraints; no world authority
with sufficient power exists"(4); "solutions seem most likely to
come only on the national level."(5) The most drastic version
of that position may well be that of Ophuls,(6) for whom the
only escape from "oblivion" seems to be the strong author-
itarian state: clearly a counsel of despair.

But there are, in fact, serious reasons for doubting the efficacy of the nation-state as an instrument for limiting the growth process. All of them have to do with the long-term, global and holistic nature of the problèmatique, but the most direct and obvious doubts arise from the difficulty of ensuring that a large enough proportion of states act in the desired manner and in a coordinated fashion. For if they do not, the effect of their behavior on the world system is likely to be inconsequential. States that, at one point, decide to limit growth may, at another, take the opposite stand and reverse their course. Yet others might do no more than engineer a shift of their own problems elsewhere, e.g., through the export of polluting industries; and the net effect may be self-canceling. Unless structures (including norms) change at the international level, the experience and the efforts of some countries will be no more than idiosyncratic.

Secondly, national growth rates affect a state's position in world politics. In the past, countries experiencing low and/or declining growth rates or diminishing populations have been those states whose status (hence, also, capacity to influence world politics and shape the world system) has been shrinking. Such was the case of France, whose stationary population in the first half of the twentieth century was widely adjudged to be a sign of weakness (if not "decadence"); or Great Britain, whose European position after 1945 deteriorated significantly in relation to France and West Germany, both buoyed by strong economies. Toward the close of the nineteenth century, Britain's growth rates, lower than those of the United States or Germany, were widely seen as putting into question her world position and paving the way for World War I. More recently, Japan's spectacular performance in the growth league put her in the position of a "superstate."

A special case is the position of a world power such as the United States since at least 1945. It is arguable that measures taken in a country that, in important respects, serves as a role model for the entire world will, over time, be transmitted through emulation and encouragement (e.g., through aid measures) to most, if not all, parts of the world. This could, indeed, be a significant process if conditions in the world system were ripe for it, but are they?

World power position is an accrued function of the exercise of leadership during and following a period of global war (such as that between 1914 and 1945); it is based on military and economic strength, both of which are posited upon growth. Hence, growth limitation undercuts world leadership and, in the logic of the modern world system, the ability to lead by example. What is more, world power position, on past experience, has turned out to be far from permanent; it has been unstable and generally prone to gradual erosion. The world position of the United States depends on both military

and economic strength; that is why lagging growth in productivity and in exports shrinks the world role of the American
economy and increases the sacrifice required in allocating
attention and resources to international and to military purposes. Limited growth policies, by the United States alone,
would, therefore, tend to weaken not only its role as model
but also the structure of world order that rests upon it,
including the relationship to nuclear deterrence.

Believers in the nation-state seem to regard it as a
neutral instrument that might be used for efficiently carrying
out any policy it is instructed to perform. They forget that
the nation-state is the dominant organization in the world
today precisely because it has been an essential part of the
growth process. The nation-state has grown and proliferated
so that, at the present time, it consumes a major portion (up
to a third, and, at times, up to half or more of global warfare) of the output of world economy, and a significant part of
the output of culture. By every count, the nation-state's
interest is vested in growth: the state can hardly become, all
of a sudden, the trusted guardian of limits. Thus, even at
the most general level, doubts are in order about the suitability of nation-states as the political framework of a sustainable
society. All considerations point directly to solutions located
at the global level.

A STRUCTURAL ANALYSIS OF THE WORLD SYSTEM

The present study explores the problem of sustainability with
the help of a structural model of the world system. The world
system is composed of three elements: polity, economy, and
culture.(7) The clear identification of these elements calls for
a fair degree of social differentiation, but, conceptually, we
might define polity as referring to the order, justice, and
security-maintaining apparatus; economy, as the productive
machinery and the market exchange system; and culture, as
the stock of norms, values, and knowledge, and the arrangements for preserving, transmitting, and enriching these. All
three have their human and material components, and they all
interact with each other and with the environment.

We shall define structure as a relatively invariant ag-
gregate of ratios and relations characterizing a concrete
system.(8) The structure of the world system concerns the
ratios and relations of its elements. In this structural analysis, therefore, emphasis will be laid on the characteristics
of elements and on their interrelationships, as well as on the
transformability of the relational set thus established. The
theoretical problem starts with a model of the system and, in
the manner of Claude Levi-Strauss,(9) embodies the question:

to what extent do empirical world systems conform with the theoretically possible transformations of that structure?

Thus, it is the working hypothesis of this study that unsustainable growth is the product, or the result, of the way in which the world is organized, not just economically but in its totality, as an ongoing system with certain specific political, economic, and cultural dimensions. It is asserted, in other words, that growth is not merely or solely an economic process, that it cannot be divorced from politics or culture as though these were extraneous circumstances, and that politics must be seen not only as part of the solution (as a regulatory instrumentality) but also very much as part of the initial problem. The basic relationship postulated in this analysis is shown in figure 9.1, and our purpose is to investigate this basic linkage and its associated feedback loop.

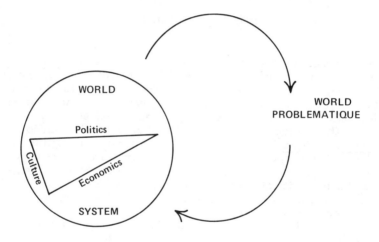

Fig. 9.1.

Three axioms govern this analysis: (1) the elements of a structure are mutually interdependent, hence, change in one will have repercussions on the others; (2) for any structure there is some set of ratios or relations that is optimal; this set shall be called the balanced set. The notion of balance inheres, in fact, in the notion of structure viewed as ratios or relations and it expresses the likelihood that one set of ratios or relations may create a more appropriate (that is, a more pleasing, more stress-resistant, more stable) system than another. Thus (3), a balanced system is a stable system.

The general concept of balance is, of course, of ancient lineage. It was prominent in classical Greek thought, and has

been current in more recent social thought in a variety of
applications. In a manner similar to that used here, the need
for balance underlies, for instance, discussions of the proper
scope and role of the public sector (that is to say, the relations, broadly speaking, between the polity on the one hand,
and the economy and culture, on the other), the governing
idea being the need for maintaining an appropriate ratio between elements of a social system.(10)

Unsustainable growth may now be identified as the attribute of a distinct structural configuration of the world
system. In fact, unsustainable growth, as a form of systemic
stress, may be regarded as the product of imbalance in the
structure of the world system, hence, of its instability. Sustainable growth, then, is growth in a stable society; unbalanced social structures bring about unsustainable growth.

THE MODERN WORLD SYSTEM

Critics of modern life commonly assume the world problematique
to be a feature of the industrial age, of the period that
opened with the introduction of steam power into the English
factory system in about 1750. In their view, the sustainable
society must be, by contrast, a postindustrial society.

In the present analysis, this "industrial" conception of
the problematique is unduly restrictive for two reasons: (1) it
singles out for special attention a certain form of economic and
technical organization and, because of this "economism," ig-
nores basic political and cultural factors; and (2) it directs
attention to the upward-thrusting portion of the growth curve,
and neglects to ask questions about the slowly-rising segment,
and, hence also, about the fundamental conditions of the
process.(11)

We assume here, on the other hand, that the system we
are observing has experienced exponential growth over its
entire life span. Thus, for any process doubling in size
every 50 or 75 years, the first 200-300 years would have
shown significant but not unduly alarming growth. The
system then would have been riding the slowly-rising segment
of the curve, the A-sector in figure 9.2. "During all that
time growth would have been desirable and unhampered by
physical limitations."(12) Then, quite rapidly, the growth
curve thrusts upward and becomes dizzyingly vertical. On
this view, those who single out the industrial age as posing
problems of sustainability fix too much attention on the B-
sector, on the vertical portion of the curve and fail to search
for the "law of growth" governing the entire process. For
that, we might as well go back to the beginning, however
modest these beginnings, because the underlying law of this
growth has remained unchanged throughout.

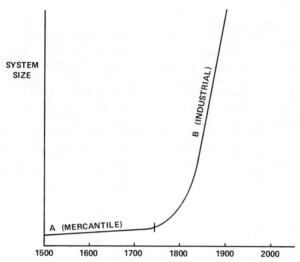

Fig. 9.2.   The Modern World System

        This analysis places the onset of the present-day world
system some five centuries ago, at about 1500 A.D. (or, if we
need greater precision, between 1492 and 1500) and calls it the
modern world system.(13)   In 1500, the dispersed and weakly
structured world system of low-saliency economics, and lower
and close to zero politics and culture transformed itself into
the modern form.
        For those who prefer an economic classification, we might
distinguish between the "mercantile" era (from 1500 to 1750),
when the thrust of growth was in long-distance trade, and the
"industrial" era, from 1750 onward.   In doing so, we would
adhere to the convention attributing the birth of the Industrial
Revolution to developments in England soon after 1750, even
while being aware that the essentials of the industrial system
(large-scale factory organization, power-driven machinery)
were already much in evidence in Renaissance Italy three to
four centuries earlier (particularly noteworthy being the
Arsenal of Venice, with its industrial assembly of ships) and
were further refined and consolidated in the low countries from
the sixteenth century onward.   But in any event we recognize
these as one system passing through two stages, exhibiting
the same law of growth throughout the span of life.
        The creation of the modern world system ca. 1500 (or,
more precisely, the passing of the world system at that point
from one structural form to another) may be attributed to
certain crucial political processes with strong economic and
cultural overtones.   The political processes were the opening
of the Cape-route between Europe and Asia through naval

expeditions. These expeditions were organized by the King of
Portugal for the purpose of breaking the monopoly of Venice
by developing new trade routes and outflanking Islam in
continuation of centuries-old conflicts, and also the explor-
ations of the Americas by Portugal and Spain. These operations broke up the established Moslem trading system in Asia
and created the first coherent and unified political system at
the global level and, within it, a network of intercontinental
economic relations.

    Had a world system not been established at that time
through the political decisions primarily of Portugal, but also
of Spain, and had the world remained without an over-arching
political framework of intercontinental proportions, most probably there would have been no system to exhibit high growth
because the area of high growth (already in evidence in Italy
in the previous two to three centuries) might have remained
restricted to Europe and, failing to expand, could have
reached a stationary state. Had another type of world system
become established in the sixteenth century, for instance
through the Ottoman conquest of Europe (in 1480 the Ottomans
established a beachhead in Italy and in 1529 they besieged
Vienna) and of Persia and India, yet another and probably a
nongrowth system would have taken shape.

    In sum, the high growth system of contemporary ex-
perience has its origins in the beginnings of the modern age,
and its laws of growth must be assumed to have been the same
throughout. Another glance at figure 9.2 helps resolve the
paradox of how both progress and nonsustainability can be the
features of one and the same system. What in the eighteenth
and nineteenth centuries appeared as proof of humanity's
inexorable march forward became, in the steeply rising B-
segment of the exponential growth curve in the twentieth
century, the rapidly approaching threat to survival.

STRUCTURE IN THE MODERN WORLD SYSTEM

The structure of the modern world system has three characteristic elements:

1. high-saliency politics;
2. high-saliency economics, in double bond with politics, and
3. low-saliency culture at the global level.

    The high growth experience of the past five centuries has
been intimately associated with this particular configuration of
the world system.

High-Saliency Politics

High-saliency politics is the most characteristic feature of the modern world. The state, its wars, and its revolutions have held the center of the world stage, mesmerizing the world's attention. At first, all the action was on the sealanes, at the global level; then it spread to certain regions, especially Europe, and now it holds the entire world in thrall.

Upon reflection, this centrality of politics is not really surprising. In the past half-millenium, the world has experienced astonishing changes in its political organization: continents have been settled and politically organized; established political structures have been destroyed or disrupted all over the globe; the nation-state has become the standard political unit; and, above all, the world has, for the first time, been brought together at the global level in one coherent political organization. Spectacular bursts of violence, major wars have been fought over the question: by whom and how shall the world be organized; this has become the constitutive process of world politics. Such wars occurred with surprising regularity and in each century and lasted approximately one generation (in reverse chronological order, the World Wars of the twentieth century; the Wars of the French Revolution and of Napoleon; the Wars of Louis XIV; the Wars of Dutch Independence; and the Italian Wars at the turn of the sixteenth century). Each time, their ending brought into being a substantial, though temporary, degree of international order.

In the modern world system, answers to the question by whom and how shall the world be organized has so far been given by successive "world powers." These were states emerging victorious from each bout of global warfare; again, in reverse order, the United States, Great Britain (twice); the Netherlands, and Portugal (their early Mediterranean prototypes being fifteenth century Venice, and fifth century B.C. Athens). These states gave leadership, especially coalition-leadership, at times of global war and, generally, supplied the public goods of security and organization at the global level (e.g., on exploration, security of shipping routes, of supplies, and of world communications). In their times, they were the hub of the world's attention structure and gave it identity and coherence. Their position attracted universal admiration but, in short order, also envy, and attempts at emulation. These latter challenges, and the ensuing competition, eventually brought about conditions of new conflict, thus propelling a powerful, if long, cycle of global politics.(14)

It should by now be evident that world politics in the modern period have been exceptionally unstable. The global political system (the world powers, their competitors, and other states) has been profoundly unstable in several ways because of (1) the rapid succession rate among the world

powers (four in five centuries), attended by large-scale warfare; (2) the persistent and unsettling degree of structural
change in each century, the result of continuous change in
power distributions (from unipolar to multipolar arrangements
and back); and (3) the destabilizing effects of innovation in
military technology and in techniques of mobility and of information.

Inherent instability at the systemic level has been reinforced by another process generated by world politics and,
in fact, a necessary complement to it; the formation of nation-
states. In 1500, there were only a few nation-states in existence (Portugal being one of them). Today, they have
proliferated to more than 150. Their growth rate in the period
also approximates an exponential process, hence they, too, can
be regarded as a product of world system growth. All world
powers have been nation-states; world-power status advan-
taged and strengthened these particular nation-states over all
other competing organizations. Other states, cooperating with
them, or competing against them, imitated their successes as a
matter of dire need and as the best form of protection against
the anxieties and uncertainties of the modern world, so that,
by now, this form of organization (the nation-state) is de
rigeur for the entire globe. The political growth process has
been spectacular and powerful, but its price has been another
worldwide capital investment process of unprecedented scope
going by the name of nation-building.

World politics has been highly salient because it has been
unstable. This instability, however, is not inherent in it but,
rather, is the characteristic of this particular period. That
is why Wagner's Law, according to which state functions and
public expenditures constantly expand with the progress of
civilization and in accordance with which the size of the public expenditures is, at present, positively correlated with
GNP,(15) can only be expressive of conditions in the modern
world system. It cannot be a universal law of politics. State
functions cannot keep rising indefinitely until they end up
absorbing the entire social product. But as long as they do,
they signify the continued high saliency of politics.

The Double Bond of Economics and Politics

The evolution of the world system, however, is a story not just
of world politics nor (as Wallerstein(16) would have it) just a
story of world economy alone but, rather, that of world
politics in close tandem with the world economy.

The world economy has had high saliency, too. Never
before in human history has wealth and plenty been so close to
the center of the attention of mankind. At first the Portuguese and then the Spaniards launched the world on its long

quest for gold, with striking success. But then thoughtful minds elsewhere began to ask why it was that all that gold and silver did the Iberian countries so little good in the long run and left them unprotected from their industrious challengers to the North. Out of such reflections grew new practices of economic policy and theories of the "wealth of nations," wherein political economists designed ways of maximizing power as well as plenty. By the nineteenth century, economic development was firmly on the world's agenda and, in the twentieth, a universal goal. Some see the essence of the modern system as being "capitalism," that is, a system of property relations, while others see it as primarily political. Although a balanced judgment might give an edge to politics, the equally high saliency of economics as the leading point of change is beyond doubt, too; it has remade society and it is futile to try to diminish that role.

What is crucial, however, is the close linkage between these two near-equally salient processes, for which linkage the term "double bond" is used here. The central feature is the close interrelationship between world power and high growth. At the height of its political role, each successive world power (the United States, Britain, the Netherlands, Portugal) also was a "dominant economy" and (in Francois Perroux's terminology) an economically "active unit," that is, a zone exercising asymmetrical and irreversible influence over the rest of the world both in the matter of trading relations and in its industrial and technological strength. Each world power was, at the same time and in its own time, leader in the world growth league. Thus, in more than a coincidence, Britain also served as the birthplace of the Industrial Revolution.

How do we explain this critical conjunction? Obviously, there is reciprocal dependence: growth flourishes within a powerful and positive political framework and world power, in turn, depends upon and finds support in resources generated by growth. Hence, parenthetically, the function of growth has been not only to ease redistributional problems but also to help with problems of international disorder by supplying the wherewithal of global operations.

Growth derived two-fold benefits from world power: (1) The nation-state, in each case the political base of world power, also served as the unified and secure framework for economic development.(17) Within it, innovation could confidently be encouraged and leading industrial sectors be launched, e.g., shipping and exploration in Portugal, or electronics, aviation, and space in the United States. (2) The world power provided the rules and the framework for international economic relations, world trade, finance, banking, and also for transnational enterprises. The great surges of world economic activity have been those occurring under the protective shelter of world powers, such as the great free trade boom of mid-nineteenth century and the trade expansion of 1945-1973. Growth of a world power produces wealth, while its weakening threatens depression.

The relationship also is reciprocal. The exercise of world power is expensive and cannot be managed on an empty treasury. Historically, the chief instrument of this function, navies, has always been more expensive (and capital-intensive) than land armies; today's strategic nuclear forces (and the heavy investment in R&D they call for) are in a class apart from conventional units. Hence, world power needs the steady support of an expanding economy and a surplus in its transactions with the rest of the world. An expanding economy is legitimizing, marking the world power as a rich and progressive country and a model of development. Thus, power is also the product of wealth.

The concrete embodiment of the double bond is the characteristic alliance between the state and business (later to be recognized, in a slightly narrower sense, as the military-industrial complex). Equally significant is the position of science, as supportive of that bond, as well as the alignment between political and urban interests, fostering city growth (or conurbation) at the heart of each world power, with the city the privileged sector at the center of each nation-state.

The double bond of economics and politics is thus complex, self-reinforcing, and cumulative in its effects; not just powerful but excessive and unbalancing. That is also why the economy is a source of additional instabilities for the system: (1) its growth is unequal, being concentrated, as shown, in the world power and then diffusing in a pattern of competitive emulation; (2) its growth center (or pole of development) being the world power, steadily shifts its position in a politico-economic macroprocess that is linked to global wars. Thus the "core" of the world system (the key concept of dependency theory) does not remain fixed but, rather, moves steadily to areas previously part of the "periphery" in step with movements of world politics from Northern Italy, through Iberia, to Northwest Europe, to the United States.

Such basic instabilities have been accompanied by a succession of economic cycles of various kinds including long-range fluctuations (the Kondratieffs) by migrations, and by great bouts of inflation (historically the most famous being the price revolution of the sixteenth century). In short, growth and its excesses have been as much the result of the political process as the object of its regulations and restrictions. Because political power is unstable, so also must be the economic process; the latter does not lack its own instabilities either, and these feed back too.

Low-Saliency Culture at the Global Level

A necessary complement of the double bond of politics and economics has been the low saliency of the issues and concerns of culture and value, identity and solidarity at the global level. By contrast with the standard configuration of medieval Europe (high culture, low politics and economics), the modern world has embraced value relativity and has implicitly declared matters of culture to be irrelevant to problems of world organization. The Portuguese were the only world power to include (without giving it maximum priority) a religious mission in their posture (the most interesting aspect of that being the attempt to Christianize China late in the sixteenth century). But as the Reformation broke up the religious unity of Europe, the impetus of that drive slowed, and all succeeding world orders kept the religious element in low key. The common criticism of world powers has portrayed them as preoccupied solely with political, and especially with economic, matters ("a nation of shop-keepers," "perfidious Albion"; "economic imperialists,"), and cast doubt on their common humanity.

The low saliency of culture at the global level has had a profound impact on the structure of the world system.

1. The nation-state has become the principal locus of culture, at first for the world powers and then for most other states. This came easiest in countries that are islands, or semi-islands; their geographic insularity transforming without difficulty into psychological insularity that characterizes the nation-state configuration. Nation-states evolved elements of civic religion; they turned it into the chief source of solidarity for their members, and became organizers of great public ceremonies. The structure of the world system has reinforced the other processes strengthening the nation-state but, inevitably, subverted the fabric of global interdependencies making them appear to be instrumental and manipulative.

2. Lacking the substratum of values and solidarities, the world system has developed little capacity for placing restraints or setting limits on national or any other action. Thus the extraordinary growth of politics and economics has become possible through the lack of restraints on global action. The weaknesses of global solidarity made any appeal to the world public interest appear "unrealistic." But it also made enduring cooperation and stable political arrangements improbable and has brought in train political and economic instability.

3. The most general characteristic of low-saliency culture is the prevalence, throughout the modern period and in the key areas, of what Pitirim Sorokin has described as "sensate culture": a cultural configuration whose aims and needs are mainly physical and whose maximum satisfactions are sought through the modification and exploitation of the external

world.(18)   This has been the dominant value pattern of the
modern world according fully with conditions of high growth
but hardly supportive of initiatives of collective solidarity
either at the global level or even at that of the state, hence
also responsible for the transience of world power status.

IMPLICATIONS FOR POLICY

The Syndrome of Instability

A structural analysis shows the modern world system to be an
unbalanced system. If a balanced system is one that exhibits
a harmonious development, one in which political and economic
concerns are constrained and compensated by considerations of
value and of solidarity, then the modern world fails that test
in respect of global organization.   Its politics and its economics have forged ahead at unprecedented rates, but its
culture and its coherence have lagged far behind. The result
is a syndrome of instability, and high growth is one of its
principal manifestations In turn, high economic growth is
inextricably linked to high politics.(19)   Structural imbalance
explains the world problêmatique.
     Using a term that goes back to the formative stage of the
American party system, we might say that our world comes
close to being Hamiltonian: one of strong, centralized, "energetic" nation-states, joined with powerful and enterprising
industries, fully alive to global interactions, and actively
involved in mastering them.   What Alexander Hamilton advocated for the newly constituted United States is now a model
for the whole world, but its instabilities, so well revealed in
debates with Thomas Jefferson in 1793-1800, are now also a
matter of world record.

The Nation-State

As this analysis has shown, the nation-state is a principal
institutional achievement of the modern system; it has proved
itself as the seedbed of economic growth and the launching pad
for global political competition.   On its past record, it is an
implausible base for policies of growth limitation.   Growth
being an attribute of the world system, its effective limitations
must also be a global enterprise, even if, in practice, the
problem must be disaggregated to take account of the several
levels of world organization (global, national, or regional).
Saddling the nation-state alone with growth controls would only
add to the load of politics and its consequent instabilities.

For those who would seek escape from a Hamiltonian world, the nation-state is no refuge. The Jeffersonian state is one where free peoples, enlightened and well-educated, could govern themselves in decentralized communities: "the best government being that what governs least" and one that is separate from church. Jefferson's conditions are closer to a sustainable society than those of Hamilton, but the element absent from his thought, though not from his statesmanship, was the relationship with the world system. It may be that the age of sensate culture is now passing into a Jeffersonian world, but the conditions of that passing need more systematic specification.

Conditions of Stability

This analysis suggests that a stable world system, hence a sustainable "post-modern" world system, needs to satisfy the following three conditions (these are also the three dimensions of the problem, and the conditions for the macrocontrol of growth):

1. De-emphasize politics. Reduce the saliency of politics (in a sort of world-wide Proposition 13), specifically by evolving an institutionalized solution to the question of world power. Without such a solution, the world system will drift into decay, hence into conflicts and successive crises, threatening the maximum instability of global war and the destruction of the environment. The reason for thinking this possible is that world politics is approaching its limits set by the destructive potential of nuclear weapons and, in another dimension, by the approaching completion of the worldwide process of nation-building. The heroic age of world politics is over; soon there will be no more nation-states to build and it will be time to settle down and preserve what has been accomplished. In such an age, the tasks of the world power would also be more limited. Without such stabilization it is difficult to look forward to any kind of future.

2. De-emphasize economics, and separate from politics. Reduce the saliency of economics, hence also the compulsive drive to growth, especially attenuating the double bond (if not affecting the complete separation) between economics and politics. The primary need is to dissolve the link between growth and world power. If growth were not needed to support world status, powerful pressures for it would be eliminated. The reason for thinking it possible is the fact that economic growth, too, is running into limits for all the well-known reasons; the economy would be more sensitive to those limits if the political compulsions to grow were removed. This cannot be achieved without the simultaneous resolution of the question of world power.

3. Vitalize world culture. Stability of the world system requires the vitalization of culture at the global level or, as Lewis Mumford once put it, the "re-moralization of society." Lesser priorities for politics and economics need compensation through increased attention to what are essentially religious questions at the global level: the rise of a new ethic of limits, and of new values, the most important of them being those of universal solidarity. If we accept Emile Durkheim's definition of religion as "a unified system of beliefs and practices relative to sacred things, that is to say, things set apart and forbidden - beliefs and practices which unite into one single moral community called a church, all those who adhere to them,"(20) then it becomes clear that the third basic condition of world stability is the solution of a fundamentally religious problem.

For the problem of the sustainable society is one of limits: limits that cannot be transgressed, hence limits that are sacred. But the maintenance of these limits also requires a unified moral community, one whose observance of the limits is made possible by the joint celebration of the sacred. For, if there are limits beyond which mankind courts catastrophe (on nuclear warfare, on resources and the environment, on population), then those limits ought to be sacred. If they are sacred, then their protection goes to the very heart of a world structure, to its supremely "entrenched clauses," whereby any threat to the sacredness of limits would promptly trigger the response of an outraged community. This is no "macroautocracy" but, rather, the constitutional basis for a stable community. The common recognition of limits and membership in that community also become a source of common identity needed as lubricant for world organization and the seedbed of solutions to political and economic problems. Since the recognition of limits must be based on a rational act of knowledge, it also posits a coherent view of the world system.

CONCLUSION

The two-fold object of this study has been to establish an empirical association between the world problematique and the world system, and, to demonstrate that high growth has been the characteristic of the entire "modern" era; and to suggest that this association might have a theoretical basis, namely, that structural imbalance leads to instability, hence to excessive growth.

The operative term in both instances is "association." Our knowledge of so large, complex, and long-lasting a system as the modern world is too imperfect to assert at this stage more than linkages. We need to resist the temptation of seeing simple causal chains (hence, clear solutions). But an association is also a feedback loop wherein influences are likely to move in both directions and wherein some of these might be subject to control. This analysis is, therefore, also an invitation to asking questions that might otherwise have been overlooked.

Given the relative invariance of structures over time, structural analysis inevitably turns to the long run; it may, in fact, be the only sound basis for such an analysis. But the feedback loop also suggests that structural change can occur and may be reinforced and channeled by deliberate policy, or else may occur as the unanticipated consequence of social change. Direct policies of growth limitation might help stability in the world system: applied on a large enough scale, population or resource controls or measures of redistribution may help moderate pressures of political competition and economic expansion. (Though this still begs the question: what are the structural conditions of the world system most likely to be conducive to such policies?) On the other hand, the continued growth of the world system is also generating forces that, in favorable circumstances, might bring about a realignment of the social structure: the much-heralded growth of education and of the knowledge industries (possibly curtailing their role as handmaidens of politics and economics); the rise of the professions, the arts, and the sciences; conceivably the equalization of the sexes. They might provide the social basis for the "remoralization of society" and, through it, the recognition of the need for limits.

Our analysis yields a set of general parameters within which a structural balance in a postmodern world system may be struck, though it contains no specific policy recommendations. Its contribution, it is hoped, has been to bring out the interdependency of the elements of the world system as an antidote to the predominantly technical and economic solutions so frequently offered, and to underscore the crucial role of world politics at the global level as an especially unstable and, therefore, dominant subsystem - the rogue elephant at large without whose containment techniques of growth limitation will likely miss the target. On those grounds, too, this is an antidote to the prescriptions of those who would approach the sustainable society with a yet larger dose of politics, the erection of still more powerful national or global leviathans. More politics is not the road out of oblivion and, yet, without resolving the problem of world politics, there is likely to be no stable system.

NOTES

(1) Lynn White, "The Historical Roots of Our Ecological Crisis," Science 155 (March 10, 1967): 1206.

(2) Lewis Mumford, The Pentagon of Power (New York: Harcourt Brace Jovanovich, Inc., 1970), p. 118.

(3) "Micro-freedom makes macro-control less onerous; while macro-control makes micro-restrictions less necessary," Herman Daly, "On Limiting Economic Growth," in Alternatives to Growth I, edited by D. L. Meadows. (Cambridge: Ballinger Publishing Co., 1977), p. 158.

(4) Ibid., p. 157; see also Harlan Cleveland and Thomas W. Wilson, Jr., Humangrowth (Palo Alto: Aspen Institute Publications, 1978), p. 37: "National governments will still be the basic building blocks of world order. . . . "

(5) Jay Forrester, "New Perspectives on Economic Growth" in Meadows, Alternatives to Growth I, p. 109.

(6) William Ophuls, "Leviathan or Oblivion?" in Toward a Steady-State Economy, edited by Herman Daly (San Francisco: W. H. Freeman & Co., 1973); his preference is for "macro-autocracy to give us a maximum of micro-democracy" (p. 227.).

(7) Cf. Figure 12-1, "Societal Subsystems" in Joan Davis and Samuel March, "Strategies for Societal Development" in Meadows, Alternatives to Growth I, p. 224.

(8) F. Perroux, Unites Actives et Mathématiques Nouvelles (Paris: Dunod, 1975), p. 14.

(9) Edmund Leach, Totemism (Methuen, 1963) p. 16; Claude Levi-Strauss, rev. ed. (Baltimore: Penguin Books, 1974) p. 20 ff.

(10) See, for example, Richard Musgrave, Fiscal Systems (New Haven: Yale University Press, 1969), esp. chs. 2, 3; James M. Buchanan and M. R. Flowers, The Public Finances 4th ed. (Homewood, Ill.: Richard D. Irwin, 1975), ch. 6, "Reasons for Growth in the Public Sector."

(11) For these reasons it also tends to narrow the vision of the future as, e.g., in Daniel Bell's Coming of the Post-Industrial Society (New York: Basic Books, Inc., 1973) which focuses on economics and technology but altogether leaves out politics.

(12) Jay W. Forrester, World Dynamics (Boston: MIT Press, 1971), p. 4.

(13) This means that we are more demanding in terms of a historical perspective than, e.g., Elise Boulding's two-century framework in "Education for Inventing the Future," Meadows, Alternatives to Growth I, p. 304.

(14) George Modelski, "The Long Cycle of Global Politics and the Nation-State," Comparative Studies in Society and History 20, no. 2 (April 1978): 214-235.

(15) Walt W. Rostow, The World Economy (Austin: University of Texas Press, 1978), p. 58.

(16) Immanuel Wallerstein, The Modern World-System I (New York: Academy Press, Inc., 1978).

(17) On the linkage of an effective nation-state and the demands of modern economic growth, see Simon Kuznets, Economic Growth of Nations (Cambridge: Harvard University Press, 1971), pp. 345-48.

(18) Pitirim Sorokin, Social and Cultural Dynamics (Extending Horizon Series, Sargent Publishing, 1971), pp. 27-28.

(19) Entailing the not-so-paradoxical conclusion that high economic growth cannot be had without high politics; growth advocates please note.

(20) Emile Durkheim, The Elementary Forms of the Religious Life, Joseph W. Swain translation (New York: Free Press, 1954), p. 47.

10 Business Organizations in the Sustainable Society
Dillard B. Tinsley

Successful transition to a sustainable society will require meaningful participation by all segments of society. If the varied talents and resources of the business community are to be effectively mobilized in this transition, business managers must be given a clear picture of how businesses will operate in a sustainable society. It is not enough to assert that the economy as a whole will be structured in a particular manner or that resources will be allocated according to certain priorities. Business managers desire to know how the values, goals, and operations of their organizations will be affected. How will business interact with its customers? What will be the roles of managers and other employees? What will be the criteria for judging employee performance? Business managers will very likely resist transition to a sustainable society, at least until such questions are answered.

At present, the limited models of business operations in a sustainable society do not address these questions regarding specific employee and customer interactions. Therefore, the purpose of this study is to characterize the operations of the business organization in a sustainable society. The objective is a realistic characterization that reflects modern business thought and society's trends which have implications for business. Because satisfaction of human needs is the ultimate goal of any organization, the challenge is to develop business organizations that meet the needs of employees and customers for quality life in an environment of limited resources. This is an ecological view of the organization.

164

THE RESPONSE OF BUSINESS TO SOCIETY'S NEEDS

There is an immediate question as to why society should retain businesses as an acceptable form of economic organization. One important reasons for doing so is the fact that, although socialist countries have shown that they can achieve significant success in capital-intensive industries, they have encountered problems in producing consumer products.(1) Further development of the socialist system may be necessary before American consumers will accept its performance as satisfying them.

A second important reason for characterizing business organizations in a sustainable society is the strength of the business community for resisting radical change. Even if business organizations are to play no role in the ultimate structure of a sustainable society, there will be a transition period in which they will be allocated some role in order to reduce the business community's resistance to change. A complete collapse of the "American system" is probably the only thing that would allow a radical restructuring of America's economic system.

Beyond this, business has shown extreme flexibility in its contributions to the success of the United States. There is reason to think that the correct combination of business, high technology, research, and government policy can effectively address society's problems.(2) Business executives at both the top management level and the operating level are accepting social responsibility as a legitimate requirement of business operations.(3) Scarcity of resources and development of a sustainable society are integral parts of this social responsibility of business to address society's problems. We can utilize business recognition of social responsibility requirements in moving to a sustainable society, but there are certain problems in doing so.

Large business corporations - that perform the bulk of economic activity in the United States - increasingly assign social responsibility concerns to some specific social responsibility office which may be comprised of individuals, committees, or departments within their organizational structures.(4) This social responsibility office faces a wide spectrum of issues that could be addressed by company action. In this spectrum of issues, unfortunately, the problems of scarcity and conservation are not usually given the highest ranking in concern.(5)

Recent developments regarding energy may rectify this low ranking to some degree for energy resources. Also, there is an increasing concern in business about the possibility of long-range problems in the supply of metals available to American industry.(6) However, business awareness does not mean that the resulting responses will move America toward a sustainable society. The responses may involve deliberate or mistaken policies that provide short-range maximization of profits, yet have long-range detrimental effects on resources and the environment. To prevent such effects, there is need to identify and characterize the business techniques that will move business organizations toward a sustainable society.

As resource-responsible business techniques are characterized, the existence of social responsibility offices becomes more important. Existence of these offices means that business is considering its long-range impact on society, and that there is a specific office where efforts to educate business organizations on the need for a sustainable society can be focused. This office is also an appropriate place where resource-responsible techniques can be introduced into business organizations. In other words, the mechanism for business analyses and responses to a sustainable society is increasingly accepted and instituted within organizational structures.

BUSINESS CHARACTERISTICS AND
RESOURCE LIMITATIONS

Operations of the social responsibility office will vary from company to company. Each office will monitor and analyze social responsibility issues with respect to its own company's individual talents, resources, missions, and concerns. Selection of social responsibility issues for company actions can be expected to reflect each company's particular characteristics - especially when high levels of cost vulnerability or profit opportunity exist.(7) Because all organizations are not involved to the same degree with physical resources, conservation of resources will tend to affect some companies more than others. This tendency is confirmed in a recent survey which ranks the intensity of industry participation in resource conservation to be as follows, going from highest to lowest: (1) oil, gas, mining; (2) transportation, communication, utilities; (3) manufacturing; (4) wholesale and retail; and (5) finance, insurance, real estate.(8)

Although the intensity of effort in resource conservation and a sustainable society will vary according to company characteristics, generalized guidelines for such efforts can be developed. In this guideline development the following simple model of an organization aids in visualizing the areas of interest:

INPUTS - TRANSFORMATION - OUTPUTS

The model simply says that organizations acquire inputs and transform them into outputs. Inputs include materials, ma-

BUSINESS ORGANIZATIONS   167

chinery, and human beings as workers. Outputs include
goods and services, which are referred to by the general term
"products." Outputs also include the rewards to owners and
employees - both financial rewards and personal satisfactions.
Transformation processes include the facilities, equipment, and
techniques of production.

In considering a sustainable society, this study concen-
trates on the transformation and output processes, given an
environment of resource scarcity for inputs. Guidance for the
social responsibility office regarding transformation and output
processes is a key to business participation in a sustainable
society because of the possibilities that business has to control
them. Of the three types of organizational processes, organizations can exercise the most control over transformation
processes. As will be shown, organizational influence over the
output processes can be considerable.

Transformation Processes

Transformation processes are obvious candidates for techniques
which conserve scarce resources. Production efficiency and
cost reduction are permanent goals for most companies. As
the nation moves toward a sustainable society, the limitations
in resource supplies and the increasing prices of the scarce
resources will pressure business to practice conservation in
transformation processes. Scientists, engineers, and managers
will develop processes and techniques that conserve scarce
resources. For example, companies faced with metals shortages are presently (1) studying substitutes for scarce resources, (2) seeking ways to recycle used metals, and (3)
utilizing special techniques for saving materials, e.g., powder
metallurgy and computer design of die layout.(9)

A problem often arises in development of such processes
in that efficiency analyses usually are based on resource cost,
rather than resource scarcity. Often, scarcity is only assumed to be included in the analysis through its effect on
cost. Such an assumption is not always correct, especially in
a time of price controls or rationing. To overcome this problem in energy input analyses, some companies are presently
utilizing "net energy analysis," which attempts to include both
costs and scarcity when considering production processes.
For example, Dow Chemical Company keeps records on precisely how much energy is consumed in producing each of its
finished products.(10) This allows Dow to decrease production
on high energy products during energy shortages, and Dow
also is alerted to which processes are candidates for improved
techniques. Surprisingly though, energy analysis is under
considerable criticism by the "conventional wisdom" of certain
economists and government officials who think that prices will
adequately reflect the effects of scarcity.

The growth of net energy analysis indicates that business is responding with sophisticated analyses to scarcity problems in transformation processes. American industry should be especially concerned with such analyses because American industry developed its present structure in an environment of plentiful resources and cheap energy. In fact, the development of net energy analyses is extremely timely because there exists a significant opportunity to move American manufacturing processes toward a sustainable society over the next decade.

Starting in the early 1970s, there has been a slowdown of business investment for production facilities in the United States. This aging of the American industrial plant plays a significant role in the slowing growth of American productivity. This slowing productivity complicates efforts to deal with such problems as environmental protection, stagflation, and maintenance of living standards. In part, erosion of the dollar is due to competition from modernized manufacturing plants in many foreign countries. Improving productivity will improve the nation's ability to cope with these challenging concerns. Therefore, improvement and replacement of business transformation processes is increasingly critical for American society.(11)

Movement toward a sustainable society will occur if productivity is improved by replacing these outmoded transformation processes with energy-efficient processes. One study estimates that as much as 25 percent of the American industrial energy demand projected for 1985 could be saved by installation of energy-efficient processing equipment.(12) Society must grasp this opportunity to move beyond mere economic efficiency in replacing its aging transformation processes. The specific processes selected to conserve scarce resources will vary from industry to industry. Their selection will involve highly-technical analyses based on the present and future availability of appropriate technology. Business organizations presently conduct analyses of such improvements as continuing effort; however, they concentrate on economic efficiency because businesses are basically economic organizations. How can they be induced to also consider processes which involve a loss of economic efficiency to gain a saving of scarce resources?

Governmental restrictions may be required to limit the amounts of specific scarce resources that are allocated to certain industries. Joint financing of research to develop resource-responsible processes may be required, involving government, industry associations, and research organizations. Once such processes are developed, government regulations may be required to mandate their use by business organizations. There are many other possibilities which may be considered. Those which involve lowering economic efficiency can be expected to present problems of acceptance by business managers.

Acceptance and effective use of the resource-responsible transformation processes form real barriers to moving business into a sustainable society. People resist improvement because it may involve changes in their habits, power bases, rewards, or problems. Uncertainty is an unpleasant feeling for many people, and unexpected results are often feared. Introducing changes into business organizations is an art - a discipline in itself with its own special techniques. People form a major barrier of resistance that is common to all organizations.

Instead of investigating specific technical aspects of transformation processes which may be valid for only a few industries, this study will consider the behavioral problems involved in changes which move business toward a sustainable society. These problems reveal themselves in the output processes (satisfactions and rewards) involving business employees, so their resolution will be considered. First, however, the output processes which involve customer satisfaction will be considered because movement toward a sustainable society requires that employee changes also occur in these processes. Guidelines for resolution of resistance by all types of employees can then be developed for companies in general.

Output Processes - Customer Satisfaction

The satisfaction of customers requires business organizations to adjust their outputs to customer demands. Scarce inputs imply scarce outputs, and there is already a growing body of literature regarding business techniques for allocating scarce outputs among customers without offending them.(13) However, present approaches to allocation do not really move business organizations toward a fully developed sustainable society, which is this study's interest. Present approaches generally attempt to spread shortages among customers without really trying to find a way to develop arrangements for permanent satisfactions in view of permanent scarcity. Therefore, business concepts which involve output processes and facilitate a sustainable society will now be considered.

The "marketing concept" is a philosophy for developing customer satisfaction that is increasingly accepted by business managers.(14) It can also be the vehicle for guiding business outputs in a sustainable society by expansion of its present characterization, which falls into the following three parts:

1. Customer Orientation - This means that a business should research the needs of potential customers before it develops products. Pro-

ducts are then designed to fulfill specific
needs, which facilitates their acceptance by
customers and increases satisfaction.

2.   Integrated Efforts - The activities of all segments of the organization are evaluated for
their impact on customers, and anything that
can help fulfill customer needs is integrated
into marketing programs.

3.   Exchange Satisfaction - Each sale by a business
should satisfy the business, the customer, and
society.(15)

The key to the marketing concept's use lies in customer
orientation, which asserts that products should be designed to
fulfill customer needs. Business organizations must realize
that a given set of customer needs may be fulfilled in a
number of different ways. In a sustainable society, products
would be designed to fulfill customer needs without requiring
significant usage of scarce resources in the construction or
consumption of products. This is an obvious requirement, but
it presents difficulties.

Design of new products is an uncertain process - often
with high costs and failure rates. The requirement that new
products conserve certain resources can be expected to increase the uncertainty, difficulties, and costs of new product
development. An appropriate package of governmental policies, regulations, laws, and financial encouragement may be
required to move business toward the uncertainty and risks in
development of new, resource-responsible products.

To facilitate acceptance of resource-responsible products
by consumers, consumer products should be designed to fit
into consumer life-styles. A life-style consists of the total
pattern of product selection and usage by an individual.
Products are selected and used because they complement and
reinforce the benefits, satisfactions, and symbolic aspects of
each other. New products will be accepted more readily if
they fit into present life-styles.

Identification of consumer life-styles is in a state of
development, but researchers are gaining a clearer view. For
example, one recent study identified the following life-styles in
America: self-made businessman, successful professional,
contented housewife, retiring homebody, devoted family man,
militant mother, traditionalist, elegant socialite, and frustrated
factory worker.(16) These different groups of consumers
exhibit different patterns of product selection and use, sug-
gesting that each group will prefer different types of resource-responsible products. Selecting the right products and
inducing the consumers to fit them into existing life-styles will
be difficult, but other problems may be even more troublesome. For example, major changes in existing life-styles or

entirely new life-styles can be expected as a sustainable
society develops. Governmental restrictions on the production
or sale of certain wasteful products may be required in cases
such as the following:

1. Customers prefer existing, wasteful products over new,
    resource-responsible products.
2. Development of resource-responsible products to replace
    certain wasteful products may not be technically possible;
    therefore, customers must give up the old products
    without any new products to substitute for them.

The second part of the marketing concept should also be
modified to explicitly consider the sustainable society. All
segments of the organization will be evaluated for their influence on resource-responsible customer behavior. Employees
will be instilled with the idea of commitment to resource responsibility as a continuing objective of company management.
This causes both employees and company to act as responsible
members of society, actively working for its improvement.
The third part of the marketing concept involves the
satisfaction of business, customers, and society with the
products that business offers. Society as a whole should be
satisfied if the products supplied to customers are resource-
responsible. However, there is still the question of customer
acceptance of resource-responsible products, which was discussed previously. Even if such products are designed to
fulfill customer needs, customers may not accept them as
adequate substitutes for older, wasteful products. How can
customers be moved toward acceptance of resource-responsible
products in the face of resistance to change?
All of society's segments and organizations have a responsibility for inducing the populace to accept resource-
responsible products and to practice conservation. The
experience of business organizations in developing and using
promotional techniques should be a valuable asset in helping all
organizations to influence society toward responsibility. One
possible form of help would be the temporary loan of business
executives with advertising expertise to governmental and
public service organizations. During a one- or two-year
assignment, these executives could provide valuable assistance
in developing the advertising programs used by such institutions to educate people about a sustainable society's benefits
and requirements. These executives could draw on company
records as well as their own experience.
One of the most fruitful approaches to promoting a
sustainable society should lie in the techniques now being
developed under the banner of "customer education." Customer education means that promotional efforts should be
dominated by product facts as they relate to customer needs.

An educative approach is already required to some extent when one business sells to another business because most business needs are identified by technical specialties. This situation causes business purchases to be guided to some extent by rational organizational requirements. In such situations, resource-responsibility will be an increasingly important selling point. However, in a sustainable society, the most important application of consumer education may be in educating consumers in resource-responsible consumption.

In general, consumers are characterized by (1) a lack of technical knowledge about product performance characteristics, and (2) a significant psychological element in purchase decisions. To overcome these problems, consumer education should be directed toward helping each consumer to develop a resource-responsible life-style. The goal is to show the consumer a life-centered approach to consumption that leads to a satisfying life-style.(17) Manufacturers, distributors, and retailers can all become involved in promotional efforts for consumer education regarding their products. Companies which do not directly deal with consumer products could promote resource-responsible life-styles. Such promotional efforts would obviously be enhanced if the promoted products reflect the responsibility requirements discussed regarding the customer orientation segment of the marketing concept.

The consumer-education approach to promotion is somewhat controversial. For example, some retailers are presently developing such programs while other retailers think that consumers should be offered only what they want.(18) As resources become more limited, however, society must take an increasing interest in what consumers desire. Because promotion can affect which products will be desired and chosen by consumers, society may be best served by educational promotion that supports a sustainable society. The ultimate choice is between (1) satisfied consumers in spite of limited resources, and (2) dissatisfied consumers because of limited resources.

As in the design of resource-responsible products, participation problems may arise; but some attempts at voluntary cooperation already exist. Industry-wide cooperative programs which set product and promotional standards have been advanced as devices for voluntary participation in social responsibility in the appliance industry.(19) For full cooperation in a significant number of industries, governmental action in the form of subsidies for educative promotion or of legal restrictions on other types of promotion may ultimately be required.

Output Processes - Employee Rewards

The rewards that employees draw from participation in a business organization are vital outputs of that organization. Financial rewards are obviously important; but psychological rewards, such as prestige of the job or recognition from supervisors, are also important. Different employees require different amounts of each type of reward; however, some mixture of rewards must be provided to motivate effective employee participation in the organization on a continuing basis.

Several significant problems regarding employee rewards exist for business organizations in the sustainable society. One is that efforts to conserve scarce resources may cause a company to have fewer economic rewards to divide among its employees. Another problem lies in the fact that conservation is not the primary mission of business organizations. This means that employees exerting their efforts in conservation may not be rewarded with adequate recognition, raises, or promotions. The first problem causes employees to resist conservation on the group level - union officials or managers responsible for overall company performance are especially affected. The second problem causes employees to resist expending their personal efforts in conservation - preferring to expend efforts where rewards and advancement are largest and surest. To cope with these problems, the social responsibility office must induce employees to accept conservation efforts, even when employee financial rewards decline; and assure that the specific rewards for conservation efforts will be sufficient to motivate effective employee participation in this area.

To aid in addressing these problems, there is no general philosophy in management that corresponds to the marketing concept in sales. However, there is increasing interest in a group of concepts that are referred to as "human resource" concepts.(20) The human resource approach generally attempts to make employees more satisfied and more productive. This may be accomplished by giving responsibility and recognition to employees. It also involves structuring jobs to be challenging and interesting. A common thread that runs through these efforts is participation - employees are given certain rights in determining how, when, or where their jobs will be performed. This increases their commitment to job goals and their motivation to reach them.

Unfortunately, there are many job factors that complicate usage of the human resource approach. One problem is that a satisfied employee is not always productive, e.g., an employee can be satisfied because he does not have to work hard. Other employees may be hard workers, but they may not want to use their time to help decide how their job is to be done.

Some employees prefer to be told exactly what to do in order to place full responsibility for any problems on their managers. In fact, a recent survey shows a growing gap in work satisfaction between managerial and hourly employees. Employees in general expect more satisfaction from their jobs than they are receiving, and their discontent with their jobs is growing.(21) Another survey which was made in 1977 revealed ". . . that 36% of American workers feel that their skills are underutilized, 32% believe that they are 'overeducated' for their jobs, and more than 50% complain about a lack of control over the days they work and their job assignment."(22)

Unfortunately, working conditions may be made even worse by company movement toward a sustainable society. A company structuring its jobs for resource conservation may have to make these jobs less interesting. Employees may become more constrained in how and when they perform their jobs. How can employees be induced to accept such developments and maintain their motivation in such jobs?

First of all, top management must establish a clear company commitment to resource conservation and to moving toward a sustainable society. This, in itself, should improve employee commitment because it gives employees an opportunity for pride in their company's efforts to address the great problems of society. Talcott Parsons notes that an organization must first justify itself to the society that nurtures it, and secondly to its members.(23) However, other steps must be taken to gain employee motivation. Movement toward a sustainable society must be implemented in the organization's day-to-day operations.

Employees who work in less satisfying conservation jobs might be given recognition and extra rewards for being productive under adverse circumstances. Because conservation of scarce resources may result in inefficient use of plentiful resources, employees in such jobs should not be rewarded only on the criterion of economic efficiency. Rewarding employees on bases other than economic efficiency will present new problems for management in recognition and evaluation of employee performance. A space for "Conservation Performance" might be added to all forms for evaluating employee performance.

Evaluating an employee's capabilities for the purpose of promotion to a higher-level position may prove difficult if the employee has been involved in low efficiency jobs, which are structured for conservation. One way to combat this problem would be to rotate all employees between such jobs and jobs with more traditional structures.

Special problems arise for executives who are loaned to other organizations, such as government agencies or public service institutions, in order to assist in promoting or explaining a sustainable society. These executives will be

separated from their home company and its operations for a
significant period of time. Other employees may grasp the
loaned executive's advancement opportunities that arise in the
home company during the loan period. How can the home
company evaluate the loaned executive for merit raises -
especially since the work is performed for a different organization?

One of the most difficult tasks will be to determine the
importance of conservation efforts relative to other employee
efforts. Advancement through company ranks must be possible
for employees who concentrate on the company's efforts regarding the sustainable society. Such employees must not be
concentrated in social responsiblity offices because commitment
to a sustainable society must run throughout the company.
The second part of the marketing concept must be implemented
to evaluate the efforts of all parts of the company to influence
resource-responsible consumer behavior.

There are encouraging signs that business will be able to
develop procedures that fairly evaluate its employees on their
contributions to a sustainable society. For example, the
International Paper Company has developed a method for
evaluating the performance of its executives in some of their
social responsibility efforts by setting special goals which are
called:

> . . . "Budgeted Nonfinancial Objectives" or
> BNFOS - "budgeted" because they are an integral
> part of the short- and long-term planning and
> review process, "nonfinancial" because they need not
> be measured in financial terms but still require
> action. . . . At International Paper in 1975, ap-
> proximately 50% of the individual managers' Incentive
> Compensation Award was based on performance on
> BNFOS. (24)

Even with such measures, employee resistance to a sustainable
society may be high, especially if the result will be decreased
income for employees. To overcome this situation, business
may have to draw on employee needs to participate in directing
their own destinies. Allowing employees some degree of
participation in determining their own goals, activities, and
production techniques is a common idea in modern management
thought. Specific techniques for actual application of this idea
include management by objectives, job enrichment, and "flex-
time" - a practice which allows the employee to select the
hours worked each day. A notable success of production
worker participation in structuring jobs has been achieved by
General Motors and the United Auto Workers Union at the
Tarrytown, New York, production facility. (25)

The American success with employee participation is encouraging, but such techniques are primarily limited to individual job goals and structure of work. Moving business toward a sustainable society may prove so difficult that more significant forms of employee participation may be required. Fortunately, reasonably successful patterns of such employee participation do exist. Business organizations in Europe have established several different patterns of employee participation in which lower-level employees, such as those on the production line, play a role in top managerial decisions. Topics considered include company objectives, policies, and allocation of resources. Union representatives may even be members of a company's board of directors.(26) Problems do exist in the operation of such joint decision-making.(27) Also, some observers feel that the special circumstances that allow such high-level participation are unique to Europe and that it cannot work well in the United States.(28) American labor leaders have consistently denied any interest in such forms of participation. However, these unique forms of business-labor cooperation were developed in Europe after World War II when a widespread threat of unemployment existed.(29) The United States now must face a threat of like magnitude in shortages of resources and increasing competition from other nations for these resources. A sustainable society may call for a new concept of employee functioning within American business organizations. If employees offer significant resistance to management's efforts to move a company toward a sustainable society, employee participation in top management decisions may be an appropriate method to enlist employee support for this movement.

In any case, a sustainable society means that the training capabilities of personnel departments must be improved. Employees must be trained to incorporate resource-responsibility into all their planning and efforts. Resource-responsible production and management techniques must be devised and inculcated into employees. They must learn how to recognize and to correct wastage of scarce resources. If employees are shifted between their regular jobs and conservation-oriented jobs, an obvious need exists for training and retraining. Employees will also need training in appropriate ways to conduct themselves during involvement in participative management - especially if it is to be used at top management levels.

The suggestions given above show that there are specific steps that businesses can take to move their employees toward a sustainable society. The limiting factor to all of these suggestions is the desire of business organizations to make such a move.

INDUCING BUSINESS PARTICIPATION

Full commitment of business to a sustainable society will probably come only when employees and owners incorporate resource responsibility into their own value systems. In other words, an ecological view of business organizations must become incorporated into American value systems.

Value systems are recognized as organizational foundations. They are the generalized ideological justifications and aspirations of a business organization, underlying its norms and the roles of its members.(30) This means that an organization's structure holds together only when the members share some common set of values. To develop these values, business and society must support the idea of a sustainable society with appropriate education, rewards, and justifications. Education of the general populace means that employees will have an ecologically sound value system when they enter business organizations, and consumers will accept - perhaps even demand - products that contribute to a sustainable society.

Society's acceptance of ecological values implies that the owners of business organizations will incorporate ecological goals into their own value systems. Smaller economic returns from business investments might be accepted because greater intrinsic rewards may come from the satisfaction offered from fulfilling society's needs, as guided by ecological values. Such an attitude should improve the cooperation between business, government, and the rest of society.

Inculcation of this ecological view into the value systems of Americans will take time. In the meantime, some business organizations are responding to shortages and price pressures. However, there are certain problems in waiting for improvements in America's value system. One problem is assuring that present business responses will move America toward a sustainable society instead of away from it. Another problem is motivating business organizations to take a preventive approach to resource problems that have not yet developed. Also, some coordination between efforts of different organizations - both business and nonbusiness - should increase the overall effectiveness of society's responses. Piecemeal movement that meets only immediate pressures is inadequate because delays allow correctable waste to continue and savable resources to be squandered.

The severity of these problems is such that comprehensive government regulations must be considered as a real possibility. However, comprehensive government regulations will most likely be resented and resisted by business. Implementation of other approaches may be accepted more readily, causing businesses to commit themselves to a sustainable society with enthusiasm instead of hostility. What can government do while the needs for regulation are analyzed and needed implementations take place?

One immediate function for governmental action, with or without regulation, should be the gathering of statistics on resource quantities and their rates of usage. This would identify which resources are presently or potentially limited in supply. Business organizations cannot react rationally without such identification; however, the United States presently

> . . . has no mechanism to calculate the extent of the nation's mineral supply needs and problems or to assess how other U. S. policies - economic, environmental, and social - affect the mineral industries. And because no metal is defined as economically critical, there is no system to signal or respond to shortages or cutoffs. (31)

Metal resources are obvious candidates for governmental identification action. Revelation of impending scarcity in various metals may well act as a catalyst for business action. Some business leaders are already calling for a national materials policy. Government and business cooperation in developing this policy should assure that other policies will move business toward a sustainable society. For example, there is an immediate need for legislation that encourages the recycling of scarce resources, replacing the present federal policies which actually discourage recycling. (32)

Development of a metals policy may serve as a catalyst for business actions. Another possibility is joint cooperation between multinational corporations (MNCs) and governmental agencies in moving toward a sustainable society. There is a worldwide trend for national environmental policies to be (1) integrated with other resources, energy, and social policies; (2) oriented to problem prevention rather than cure; and (3) catalyzed and coordinated through regional and international governmental organizations. (33) Those MNCs operating in Europe are increasingly concerned with corporate social reporting, which ". . . calls for including non-economic elements in the planning, information, and accounting systems of corporations. (34) In other words, MNCs are increasingly required to cooperate and coordinate with national governments on noneconomic issues. The resulting techniques and modes of operation to address these noneconomic issues may well be suited for coping with scarcity.

Will business respond to governmental encouragement before comprehensive regulation becomes necessary? This study has already given suggestions for several basic regulatory steps that might be taken. The need for further regulation becomes pressing as other approaches fail or problems intensify. The willingness to wait for voluntary business action is weakened by evidence that some business organizations still regard social responsibility as a constraint on business rather than a goal.(35)

Institution of comprehensive regulations must be approached with caution. In addition to the resistance of business organizations, failures in past regulatory processes are many. For example, major weaknesses in government legislation or regulations to solve consumerism problems include the following: (1) lack of technical know-how in regulatory agencies; (2) lack of uniformity in enforcement; (3) enforcement limited to trivia; (4) lack of realistic theories of buyer behavior; and (5) the ability of industry lobbies to weaken regulatory requirements.(36)

Business regulation that involves scarcity problems should take an approach which induces voluntary business efforts and which is supportive of these efforts. Stringent regulation should be reserved for usage when cooperative efforts are thwarted. After all, business organizations cannot evade scarcity problems in the same manner that they can circumvent other social responsibility concerns. Scarcity is a fact with unavoidable impact on actual resource availability, rather than a set of legal requirements whose impact is felt by the organization primarily when government takes specific actions. Business must respond and cope with scarcity, whether it wishes to or not. The purpose of regulation is to assure that these business responses lead to sustainable society.

CONCLUSION

Scarcity of energy has made a significant impact on America, and scarcity of metals is recognized as an impending problem. Lessons being learned in the energy crisis may provide guidance on the correct approaches for society to cope with scarcity in other resources. In the movement to a sustainable society, fundamental changes can be expected in the structure and the functioning of many of society's institutions.

To cope most effectively with scarcity, businesses must make appropriate modifications in their organizational structures, employee relations, and customer interactions. This study has suggested specific steps in this direction. Governmental legislation that requires these steps is possible, but mandated requirements are likely to be resented - perhaps resisted - by business. Governmental activities that induce voluntary business efforts are preferable. Voluntary commitment will reduce business opposition to a sustainable society and may well result in more efficient implementation of the efforts necessary to move toward it.

The declining state of America's manufacturing capabilities can make business movement toward a sustainable society especially effective at this time, if the replacements selected are energy-efficient and resource-responsible. Will business voluntarily confront this challenge? Must government mandate business response? Regulation imposes extra burdens on society - financial costs and restriction of freedom.

A massive bureaucracy is already seen by some to be the primary threat to "human striving" under every major modern government - socialist or free enterprise.(37) This may be the ultimate reason for business organizations to voluntarily support a sustainable society. There are limits on what governmental guidance and participation can accomplish. The goal should be self-guiding citizens and self-guiding organizations who see a sustainable society as being in their own self-interest.

NOTES

(1) Otto Eckstein, "Will U. S. Capitalism Survive?" Business and Society Review/Innovation 10 (Summer 1974): 5-7.

(2) Louis Banks, "The Mission of Our Business Society," Harvard Business Review 53 (May-June 1975): 57-65.

(3) Lyman E. Ostlund, "Attitudes of Managers Toward Corporate Social Response," California Management Review 19 (4) (Summer 1977): 35-49.

(4) Sandra L. Holmes, "Adopting Corporate Structure for Social Responsiveness," California Management Review 21 (1) (Fall 1978): 47-54.

(5) Ostlund, "Attitudes of Managers"; Sandra L. Holmes, "Corporate Social Performance: Past and Present Areas of Commitment," Academy of Management Journal 20 (3) (September 1977): 433-38.

(6) "Now the Squeeze on Metals," Business Week (July 2, 1979): 46-51.

(7) Terry McAdam, "How to Put Corporate Responsibility into Practice," Business and Society Review/Innovation, 6 (Summer 1973): 8-16.

(8) Holmes, "Corporate Social Performance."

(9) "Now the Squeeze on Metals."

(10) Peter B. Roche "Energy - Costly Energy Is Wasting Resources, Some Analysts Worry," The Wall Street Journal (May 3, 1979): 1ff.

(11) Burton G. Malkiel, "Productivity - The Problem Behind the Headlines," Harvard Business Review 57 (3) (May-June 1979): 81-91.

BUSINESS ORGANIZATIONS   181

(12) G. N. Hatsopoulos, E. P. Gyftopoulos, R. W. Sant, and T. F. Widmer, "Capital Investment to Save Energy," Harvard Business Review 56 (2) (March-April 1979): 111-22.

(13) Philip Kotler, "Marketing During Periods of Shortage," Journal of Marketing 38 (3) (July 1974): 20-29.

(14) "Marketers Equipped to Meet Challenges of '80," Marketing News 12 (26) (June 29, 1979): 1ff.

(15) Martin Bell and C. William Emory, "The Faltering Marketing Concept," Journal of Marketing 35 (4) (October 1971): 37-42.

(16) Peter W. Bernstein, "Psychographics Is Still An Issue on Madison Avenue," Fortune (January 16, 1978): 80-84.

(17) Gerhard Scherf, "Consumer Education As a Means of Alleviating Dissatisfaction," Journal of Consumer Behavior 8 (1) (Summer 1974): 61-75.

(18) Larry J. Rosenberg, "Retailers' Responses to Consumerism," Business Horizons 18 (5) (October 1975): 37-44.

(19) Guenther Baumgart, "Industry Cooperation for Consumer Affairs," California Management Review 16 (3) (Spring 1974): 52-57.

(20) Ted Mills, "Human Resources - Why The New Concern?" Harvard Business Review 53 (2) (March-April 1975): 120-34.

(21) Michael Cooper, Brian Morgan, Patricia Foley, and Leon Kaplan, "Changing Employee Values: Deepening Discontent," Harvard Business Review 57 (1) (January-February 1979): 117-25.

(22) John Hoerr, "A Warning That Worker Discontent Is Rising," Business Week (June 4, 1979): 152.

(23) Talcott Parsons, Structure and Process in Modern Societies (Glencoe, Illinois: The Free Press, 1960), pp. 20-21.

(24) Donald P. Brennan, "Establishing and Measuring Management's Nonfinancial Employment: Contemporary Perspectives in International Business (Chicago: Rand McNally, 1979), pp. 115-16.

(25) Robert H. Guest, "Quality of Working Life - Learning from Tarrytown," Harvard Business Review 57 (4) (July-August 1979): 76-87.

(26) Renato Mazzolini, "The Influence of European Workers Over Corporate Strategy," Sloan Management Review 19 (3) (Spring 1978): 59-81.

(27) "The Worker Dissidents in Opel's Boardroom," Business Week (July 23, 1979): 79.

(28) Nancy Foy and Herman Gadon, "Worker Participation: Contracts in Three Countries," Harvard Business Review 54 (3) (May-June 1976): 71-83.

(29) George S. McIssac, "What's Coming in Labor Relations?" Harvard Business Review 55 (5) (September-October 1977): 22-36 ff.

182   QUEST FOR A SUSTAINABLE SOCIETY

(30) Daniel Katz and Robert Kahn, The Social Psychology of Organizations (New York: John Wiley, 1966).
(31) "Now the Squeeze on Metals," p. 47.
(32) M. J. Mighdoll and Peter D. Weisse, "We Need a National Materials Policy," Harvard Business Review 54 (5) (September-October 1976): 143-51.
(33) Thomas N. Gladwin, "Environmental Policy Trends Facing Multinationals," California Management Review 20 (2) (Winter 1977): 81-93.
(34) Meinolf Dierkes and Rob Coppock, "Europe Tries the Corporate Social Report," Business and Society Review 25 (Spring 1978): 21.
(35) Gerald D. Keim, "Managerial Behavior and the Social Responsibility Debate: Goals Versus Constraints," Academy of Management Review 21 (1) (March 1978): 57-68.
(36) Jagdish N. Sheth and Nicholas J. Mammana, "Recent Failures in Consumer Protection," California Management Review 16 (3) (Spring 1974): 64-72.
(37) William NcNeill, The Rise of the West (Chicago: The University of Chicago Press, 1963), p. 804.

11 Ecosystem Education: A Strategy for Social Change
Edward T. Clark, Jr.
W. John Coletta

RATIONALE AND CONTEXT FOR ECOSYSTEM EDUCATION

Education is like putting together a jigsaw puzzle. The child upon entering school begins to collect pieces of the puzzle. He learns to identify and sometimes memorize the pieces, occasionally fitting a few together, and dutifully stuffing as many as he can into his pockets. By the time he graduates, each of his pockets bears a label (math, history, art), and is filled with odd bits of the puzzle. He still occasionally plays with the pieces trying to find fits where he can, but now he is too busy earning a living to spend much time on the puzzle.

Through his school career, in most cases, he would have had only a few hints as to what the whole picture might look like. His knowledge is fragmented, discrete, and atomistic. Without some sense of the coherent structure which underlies the curriculum he studied, his "world view" is often distorted and based on false assumptions concerning the nature of the world in which he lives.

There are two world views which are competing for dominance in modern societies, each representing a philosophical perspective concerning the nature of the world. One is the <u>technological world view</u>. It is an analytical, reductionist perspective dating from Descartes and Newton. Mechanistic, linear, logical, and atomistic, it made possible modern science and technology. It is the perspective of the scientific method which posits Man, the subject, outside and apart from the object of his study, that is, the world in which he lives. This linear, technological world view is explicitly taught in our educational systems today; and the values reflected in this world view represent the dominant values of our society. These values include individualism, nationalism, free enter-

183

prise, unlimited growth and progress, and competitive achievement.

A second perspective, which shall be called the ecological
world view, is implicit in the intuitive wisdom of primitive man.
In its more rigorous form, it dates from Darwin and Wallace,
the first of our modern scientific era to recognize the holistic
nature of life on the planet. This systemic world view is
implicit in much of science today, but has gained virtually no
acceptance in education and has had limited impact on social
decisions. There are values implicit in the ecological perspective which reflect what might be called "ecosystem values."
Interdependence, diversity, cooperation, equilibrium, and
limits are not new values but have their roots deep in human
culture. For example, folk wisdom such as "don't put all your
eggs in one basket" reflects the ecological principle of diversity.

While these two philosophical perspectives are not mutually exclusive, and while each provides important information
about the world in which we live, the analytical and technological perspective as a world view, along with its concomitant
social values, must be subsumed within the context of the more
comprehensive systemic and ecological perspective with its
concomitant ecosystem values.

We live in a jigsaw puzzle world. Ecosystem Education,
by encouraging ecological literacy concerning the nature of the
earth ecosystem and humankind's relationship to it, will result
in new insights which suggest at least the outline or border of
our jigsaw puzzle. At one level of "putting it all together,"
establishing the outer limits, the border will be determined by
the limits of the Earth's ecosystem. At a more personal level,
establishing the inner limits, each individual will define the
borders of his or her puzzle by the conscious value choices
which are made.

GOALS AND STRATEGY OF ECOSYSTEM EDUCATION

Ecosystem Education has four goals, each identified with one
phase of a progressive four-phase strategy: Ecoliteracy,
Ecollage, Ecologic and Ecoresponse.

Goal one: To increase ecological literacy
Phase one: Ecoliteracy

Ecological literacy, "understanding the connectedness of
things," involves an understanding of how the Earth's ecosystem functions as a system, and the relationship of the
human species to that system. Just as one does not have to
be a doctor to understand the basic functional relationships of

a human body necessary to maintain body health, one need not be a scientist to understand the basic functional relationships of the ecosystem necessary to maintain ecosystem health. Ecosystem Education seeks to explain these functional relationships by describing how the major components of the Earth's ecosystem act as a functional whole. Within this whole, the parts are understood in relationship to each other, and thus in context. This ecosystem context is basic to relevant decision making.

Ecological literacy is primary to all subsequent phases because all other systems, natural and cultural, are perceived as subsystems of the Earth's ecosystem. Thus, ecological literacy is necessary to the successful understanding and maintenance of all other systems.

Goal two: To apply ecological literacy to cultural systems
Phase two: Ecollage

Ecollage is "putting it all together" in an ecological context. Based on an understanding of how the Earth's ecosystem functions (ecoliteracy), and using general systems theory which emphasizes the similarities between ecological and cultural systems, Ecollage leads to increased insights concerning humankind's social systems and how they can function, and increased understanding of the relationships between the natural sciences and social sciences and their joint impact on social decision making.

General systems theory provides the philosophical rationale for studying cultural systems as natural subsystems of the Earth's ecosystem, subject to the same operating principles. From a general systems perspective, all systems - atomic, organic, and cultural - are recognized as ecological systems, functionally interdependent and mutually defining each other.(1) As a result of Ecollage, the context within which any issue is perceived is further expanded.

The more abstract principles of general systems theory make most sense when introduced in an ecological, "natural" context. By learning how general systems principles operate in an outdoor, hands-on, experiential milieu, these principles can more readily be understood and applies to cultural systems.

Goal three: To utilize ecological thinking
Phase three: Ecologic

Ecologic, or "systemic thinking," is the thought process which goes beyond both analysis and holism, and applies the rigors of systems theory to the organization of thoughts and ideas in a kind of ecology of mind,(2) effectively expanding the context for decision making beyond linear, either/or alternatives. While providing important and necessary information, traditional logic alone no longer provides a broad enough context within which effective cultural decisions can be made.

Ecologic may be likened to the process of thinking in a second language, when one readily takes information from the first language (linear logic) and translates it conceptually into a second language (systems logic). Ecologic integrates the subjective mode of knowing into the entire thinking process. Einstein demonstrated that things can only be understood subjectively and in relationship. Thus, Ecologic, incorporating both objective and subjective knowledge, provides a comprehensive "gestalt" as the context within which better decisions can be made.

At the earlier, Ecollage phase, people are discovering the relationship and similarity in structure that exist between organic and cultural systems. They consciously make comparisons and extrapolations and think about systems. Ecologic represents the next, more complex task where the act of thinking about systems evolves to the act of thinking systemically, that is, utilizing systems logic. The ability to think systemically, like a second language, has become internalized.

Goal four: To bring about value shifts necessary for effective cultural decision making

Phase four: Ecoresponse

By describing the comprehensive context within which decisions are made, Ecologic sets the stage for value shifts to occur. For example, when an environmental issue such as the pollution of the Mediterranean Sea is perceived only in a national context, values, and thus decisions, tend toward national concerns. When the context of the problem is expanded to an ecosystem context, the issue becomes an integral part of regional and global concerns, out of which a new set of alternatives emerges.

When people recognize the comprehensive nature of the context within which all social decisions take place, ecological values will begin to take precedence over traditional values. When we recognize our dependence upon the ecological life support system in a manner similar to the scuba diver's recognition of his dependence on the life support system he carries on his back, rational and intelligent decisions will result. These decisions, perceived as being in enlightened self-interest, will be based on the operating principles of the Earth's ecosystem and will lead to global awareness of and national adaptations to both steady-state systems and social systems limits.

THE CONTEXT FOR DECISION MAKING

Cultural decision making always takes place within the context of the prevailing "world view" and its concomitant social values. Indeed, decisions are largely determined by that context, although the assumptions and values implicit in the world view are seldom identified and are generally taken for granted.

There are four contextual dimensions that are basic to any world view and that define the context within which decision making takes place. Ecoresponse can only occur when these four dimensions become an integral part of the decision making process.

The Ecosystem Context	– the outer limits within which decision making occurs.
The Time Context	– the implications of the past and the future on present decision making.
The Information Context	– the minimum amount of relevant data necessary for decision making.
The Subjective Context	– the inner limits, represented by the personal and social values held by those participating in decision making.

By understanding the structure of a world view, we can more readily identify the assumptions and values implicit therein.

The Ecosystem Context

The technological world view is predicated on a belief in unlimited resources with ultimate dependence on the "technological fix." Historically, from this perspective, the ecosystem context was considered as a component in decision making only in terms of available resources and cost of extraction. In contrast, the ecological world view gives major importance to the ecosystem concept of limits. The ecosystem context is primary because it represents the physical life support system upon which humankind is inextricably dependent. It also affords an "objective given" against which environmental decisions must be measured. Thus, the ecosystem context is seen as a crucial perspective necessary for the training of decision makers and problem solvers. While the ecosystem context describes limits, it does not prescribe approaches or solutions. Indeed, by describing limits, it often suggests previously unconsidered options.

The Informational Context

The technological world view places reliance upon increased amounts of information to ensure better decisions. In contrast, the ecological world view treats information differently. In the midst of our current knowledge explosion, emphasis must be given to discovering the minimum amount of appropriate information necessary to effectively understand a given topic. Ecosystem education and its tools provide a framework within which appropriate information can more easily be identified. These tools provide a way of organizing information about a topic, issue, or problem that enables laymen as well as professionals to better understand the basic structure or nature of that topic. Focus is on the organization of information rather than the accumulation of information. Traditional ways of organizing information stress polarization of thinking and lead to polarized behavior. By organizing information in a more systemic way, polarization disappears so that a minimal amount of appropriate information may be far more useful than the overabundance of linear information.

The Time Context

Although society, with its technological world view, has depended heavily on the historical perspective as a primary context within which decisions are made, there has been almost no effective utilization of the future as a context for decision making. In addition to past trends and present tendencies, future potential adds a major new perspective. For example, in a historical context, the answer to the question, "How much energy does the United States need?" would be an extrapolation of past trends and present tendencies. When the future is considered as context, the question must be rephrased to be, "What kind of energy future is possible?" Decision making in the context of future planning can become a powerful tool to serve long-range social needs.

The Subjective Context

The technological world view has an explicit commitment to "objectivity" in information gathering and decision making. An ecological perspective recognizes that in the decision-making process, a subjective context is created by the values which each participant brings to the decision. Often consciously ignored in the name of "objectivity," this context exerts a powerful influence which must be recognized and integrated into our decision making processes. At the present time, there is obvious tension between traditional, socially dominant values (individualism, nationalism, unlimited growth) and ecologically realistic values (interdependence, global perspectives, equilibrium within limits). Only by recognizing the impact of the subjective context can decision makers learn to creatively resolve these tensions.

Ecosystem Education seeks to expand the context of personal and social decision making by expanding the socially dominant technological perspective into an ecological perspective in order to bring about value shifts necessary for societal acceptance of ecological values.

IMPLEMENTATION

Systems Training Workshop

Ecosystem Education is most effectively introduced in the context of a Systems Training Workshop. This workshop model is a functional strategy which provides an integrative and systemic learning experience utilizing cognitive, affective, and psychomotor learnings. Because first hand experience with the Earth's ecosystem should be a fundamental part of everyone's experience base, utilization of the ecosystem as a "hands-on," multisensory, experiential milieu provides a highly effective learning experience. Here, the medium is the message, and the ecological and systemic content becomes both the process that leads to increased understanding, and the context within which systemic thinking can take place.

The Systems Training Workshop utilizes the four phase strategy described above and includes the following:

1. an introduction to the systemic nature of the Earth's ecosystem and how that ecosystem functions;
2. the application of ecosystem principles to cultural systems;
3. the utilization of systems logic; and
4. the implications of ecosystem values for cultural decision making.

Ideally, the Systems Training Workshop is utilized as an integral part of the decision making process, bringing together decision makers for several days to consider specific issues. These issues are then considered within the context of the four-phase strategy.

Specific educational tools have been developed to implement each stage of this strategy. Each of these tools has been used experimentally with one or more groups and their effectiveness has been demonstrated.

Phase one: Ecoliteracy

1. Ecological Model
    Function of Model:
    Models such as the Ecological Model perform two functions:
    a. They order concepts, and in so doing facilitate the recognition of the structure and organization inherent in any body of knowledge; and
    b. They direct thinking by encouraging questions about relationships between particulars of various bodies of knowledge, thus expanding the traditional boundaries as new questions are raised.

By ordering ecological concepts, the Model directs one to determine how any particular object or phenomenon is related to the ecosystem as a whole.

From the Parts to the Whole:
The ecosystem can be divided into two primary functions: the flow of energy and the cycle of materials. Energy flow from the sun powers the cycling of materials throughout the system. Because energy flows in "one direction," it cannot be recycled. For example, while the materials out of which an automobile is made can be recycled, the energy from the gasoline used to power the automobile cannot.

All of the hundreds of biogeochemical cycles that operate in the Earth's ecosystem can be subsumed within four fundamental cycles, each of which is primarily concerned with one of the four basic materials necessary for life: rock, water, air, and food.

The rock cycle (figure 11.1): Essentially, the rock cycle is a process whereby big rocks are ground up into little rocks (sediments), and the little rocks, through heat and pressure, are built up into big rocks.

The water cycle (figure 11.2): Water is evaporated into water vapor which condenses and precipitates as rain, snow, etc., and flows over the surface of the earth, and through living things and is evaporated, and so on.

The nutrient cycle (figure 11.3): Essentially, nutrients as food travel in circular food chains or webs through the biosphere. Plants (producers) take nutrients from the soil and the atmosphere and make food. Animals (consumers) eat the plants and, through death and decay (decomposition), the nutrients are released to the soil and atmosphere again to be used by plants, and so on.

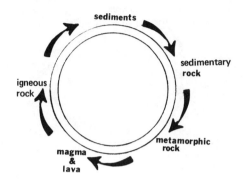

Fig. 11.1.   The Rock Cycle.

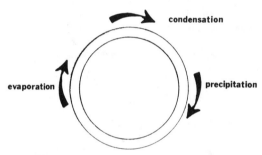

Fig. 11.2.   The Water Cycle.

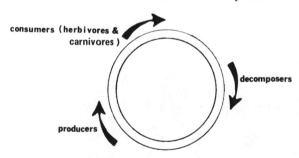

Fig. 11.3.   The Nutrient Cycle.

The CO_2/O_2 cycle   (figure   11.4):   Essentially,   carbon
dioxide (CO_2) is used by plants to make food.   They give off
oxygen (O_2) which, in turn, is used by animals to break down
the food produced by the plants.   The animals give off carbon
dioxide for use by plants again, and so on.

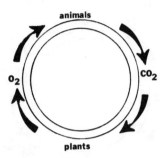

Fig. 11.4.   The CO_2/O_2 Cycle.

By visualizing these four fundamental cycles working together as a dynamic, integrated whole, one can better understand how these cycles function as subsystems to maintain life, and the relationship between these cycles and the flow of energy from the sun (figure 11.5).

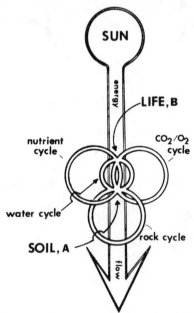

Fig. 11.5.   Ecological Model.

There are two major interfaces (Power Points A and B in fig. 11.5) that mediate the circuitous flow of all these materials within the Earth's ecosystem.   These coordinating interfaces represent soil (A) and life (B).   Soil and life, as the two most highly organized aspects of the Earth's ecosystem, link together all of the earth's cycles. As such, they are powerful agents of change in the system as well as indicators of the system's health.   Any action taken upon soil or by life is amplified throughout the entire ecosystem.

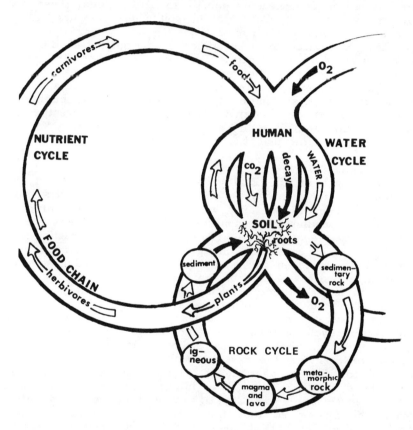

Fig. 11.6.   Detail – Ecological Model.

Figure 11.6 will aid in visualizing how the four funda-mental cycles interact to support <u>human</u> life. The function of the <u>rock cycle</u> is to bring the raw materials necessary for life to the soil.   The physical process of this cycle breaks down rock into fine sediments that are easily acted upon by the chemically and biologically active soil.   The soil, with the aid

of the water cycle mediates the flow of raw materials into the
nutrient cycle. Suspended in water, these raw materials enter
the roots of plants which anchor the nutrient cycle into the
soil. The raw materials then become integrated into the living
tissue of the plants. If pesticides happen to be in the soil
water, they would also become integrated into the living tissue
of the plant. Humans eventually "eat rocks" (and pesticides)
when they consume these plants or the animals that ate these
plants. Oxygen from the CO_2/O_2 cycle breaks down this food
into raw materials, releasing energy for life. Thus, these raw
materials are made available to the soil where they may enter
into the same or another cycle.

The Ecological Model graphically demonstrates that no
cycle can exist independently. For example, without the water
cycle, both soil and the nutrient cycle would break down.
The model further demonstrates how humankind is literally tied
to the Earth's ecosystem by the cycles that run through us.
The food we eat, the water we drink, the air we breathe are
seen as components of a life support system necessary for all
living things on this planet.

A Systems View:
Each part of the Earth's ecosystem as depicted in the
Ecological Model represents certain systemic functions that
relate to the ecosystem as a whole. Soil (A) as the primary
life support medium represents the function of the system's
order and maintenance. Life (B) represents the direction and
creative edge of ecosystem change. Humankind, as the most
powerful life force on the planet stands at the cutting edge of
the change process. Each of the four cyclical subsystems also
represents major functions within the Earth's ecosystem as a
whole. The rock cycle functions as the base of the system,
providing the. raw materials necessary for system functioning.
The water cycle fulfills the function of unity within the
system. Water, the universal solvent, is the only medium
capable of carrying the raw materials necessary for life from
the soil to life and back again, circulating through all four
subsystems uniting them by intermixing materials. The
nutrient cycle and the CO_2/O_2 cycle function as dualities
within the system so that they stand in a unique dynamic
tension. The making of food is balanced by the breaking
down of food. This balance is made possible by the reciprocal
relationship between these two cycles.

The Ecological Model and Decision-Making
Both implicit and explicit in the model are concepts which
have significant implications for cultural decision making.
While the insights themselves are not new, the Ecological Model
provides a context within which they can be more easily
understood and thus utilized.

The concept of cycles as represented in the model can help one to visualize that there is no such thing as an "away" to throw things. All pollutants continue to cycle through all four spheres of the system with various ecological consequences, usually tending to accumulate in living things or in the soil, where they do the most damage. Ecological literacy would provide a strong basis for discontinuing tax incentives which encourage planned obsolesence and for building a tax structure which encourages the recycling of materials.

When perceived in an ecosystem context, the nonrenewable nature of fossil fuels is more clearly understood. While materials can be recycled, energy cannot. Even the fission process, utilizing uranium as a fuel, can be understood as only a temporary alternative, since eventually all of the uranium can potentially be converted to energy. Ultimately, the sun is viewed as our only certain long-term source of energy.

Until recently the soil has acted as an effective filter for water. However as the model shows, as pollutants are injected into the system they eventually enter the soil, so that the filter can no longer effectively handle the load. We currently spend millions of dollars in water purification plants to do the job that the ecosystem once did naturally.

The Ecological Model graphically depicts several loci within the ecosystem that are most sensitive to humankind's tampering, and that serve as efficient indicators of the general health of the ecosystem. They are:

1. The water cycle. Since the water cycle unifies the system, the water itself always contains "information" from throughout the whole system. Tests of water often provide the most information in the shortest time. (This is analogous to the use of a urinalysis or a blood test to determine overall body health.)

2. The soil (A). The model shows that soil coordinates and orders the many processes necessary for the maintenance of life. Thus, soil quality should be an indication of the quality of life. In this light, the increase of "hardpan" soil through the Midwest farm region should provide a serious warning to an ecologically literate people of the health of that regional ecosystem. Instead, the primary result has been to increase the size of the farm equipment necessary to cut deeper into the soil.

3. Life (B). Because living things interface with many subsystems, they can provide, often immediately, useful information about the ecosystem as a whole. The presence or absence of a single living "indicator" species can often indicate the quality of the system without the need for scientific testing. For example, if stone fly or may fly nyads are found in a stream ecosystem, it is an

indication of a healthy system. Conversely, the absence
of these species indicates just the opposite.

The Ecological Model is an aid in training people to be able to
"read" their life support system more effectively. Instead of
dials and meters they must become sensitive to soils and
cycles.

2. Ecological Concepts

Basic ecological concepts play an important function in an
understanding of the Earth's ecosystem. Implicit in the
Ecological Model, these concepts are: interdependence, carrying capacity, adaptation/evolution, diversity, change, niche/
community, competition/cooperation, cycles, energy flow, and
patterns. Each of these concepts represents a particular
perspective into how the entire ecosystem functions and is
taught by using "Concept Building Activities" developed
especially for this purpose. These activities combine cognitive, affective, and psychomotor learning and afford an
excellent introduction to an experiential understanding of the
Earth's ecosystem.
These concepts, common to all living systems, are like
facets of a crystal. Each presents a different way of perceiving an ecosystem and reflects a different characteristic of
that system. These concepts seem to be universal and may be
identified in both the microcosm and the macrocosm.

Phase two: Ecollage

The educational tools that are described below are utilized in
both the Ecollage and the Ecologic phases of Ecosystem Education. The theoretical nature of these tools is described in this
section and their application to cultural decision making is
described in phase three.
1. The Systems Schema
The Ecological Model is based on a Systems Schema
(figure 11.7), the characteristics of which reflect the basic
principles of general systems theory. This Schema is an
essential tool for use in the Ecollage phase of Ecosystem
Education.
The systems schema, by its organizational characteristics,
orders knowledge in a manner that directs inquiry toward the
identification of basic isomorphic functions common to all living
systems - organic and cultural. It serves as a guide for
determining the minimum relevant information necessary to
understand an issue (the informal context).
Base represents the resources of the system whose
function it is to provide the raw materials. Unity represents
the integrative, homeostatic principle the function of which is

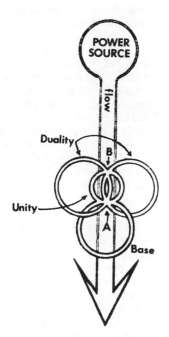

Fig. 11.7. The Systems Schema.

to provide system equilibrium. Duality represents a basic
principle in the universe that is present in all natural systems, "an explicit duality expressing an implicit unity."(3)
The whole system, an integrated functional unity that is
greater than the sum of its parts, provides the effective
boundaries of the system. Coordinating interfaces represent
functional relationships that provide order and maintenance (A)
and direction (B) for the whole system. The circular loops
represent the function of feedback for the system as a whole.
Energy flow powers the system. In cultural systems this is
identified as information flow, i.e,. knowledge is energy "information."

2. Systems Concepts
       Ecology, standing at the heart of Ecosystem Education,
provides ecological concepts with which an integrated view of
the world can be built. Extended through the principles of
general systems theory to apply to all living systems, organic
and cultural alike, these concepts may be considered to be
Systems Concepts. As such, they are particularly appropriate
for use in problem solving. By identifying a problem as a

sytems problem, it may be studied in the context of a whole system, rather than as an isolated problem. The following identifies the functional representations of concepts in systems terms.

Interdependence:	Defines the mode of relationship that exists between the parts of a system.
Diversity:	Defines the basic mode of system maintenance which insures system stability.
Change:	Defines the process of a system as dynamic and not static, and identifies time as a relevant dimension for any system.
Pattern:	Defines the organizational structures of a system.
Adaptation/Evolution:	Describes the mode of system change and creativity suggesting directionality.
Energy Flow:	Describes the way the system is powered.
Cycle:	Delineates the pattern for feedback that is fundamental to all systems.
Carrying Capacity:	Defines the limits of the system.
Competition/Cooperation:	Defines patterns of interaction by which living systems are regulated.
Niche/Community:	Defines the relationship of the individual (subsystem) to the system as a whole.

The following is an illustration of how these Systems Concepts may provide useful insights when utilized in problem solving for cultural systems, using our economic system as an example.

Diversity, as expressed in ecology, states that in general the greater the diversity, the more stable the system. Applied to the economic system, this Systems Concept suggests that economic stability is also dependent upon diversity, and that stability is increasingly threatened by economies of scale such as regional power units each operating in a functionally interdependent manner.

Adaptation and evolution as Systems Concepts represent the creative response of a system to its changing environment. These concepts suggest that all systems change over time in an evolutionary manner. When applied to the national economic system, these concepts suggest that such changes should be anticipated and recognized so that it can be utilized creatively. To understand that such change is a natural process is a first step toward controlling the direction and impact of change.

3. Contextual Map
    A contextual Map can be utilized to generate information
and/or ideas necessary for "putting it all together." The use
of the map ensures that each of the four contexts are represented, thus keeping both the "outer limits" and "inner limits"
in focus when considering an issue. Systems Concepts are
integrated into the map to provide a general systems framework. The task is to fill in the "cells" with information
relating to the topic under consideration, thus adding rigor to
brainstorming.
    The tools of Ecosystem Education are most effective when
utilized within the comprehensive context provided by the
Contextual Map (figure 11.8).

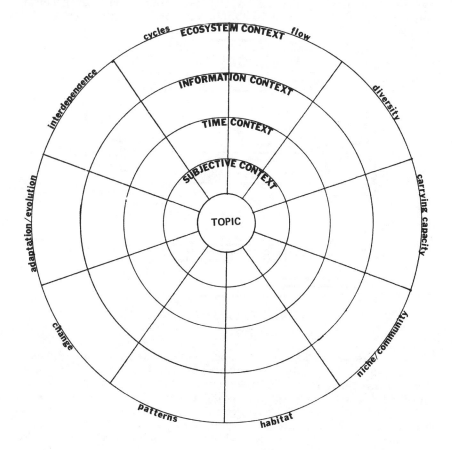

Fig.11.8.   Contextual Map.

Phase three: Ecologic

The process of <u>ecological thinking</u> as applied to cultural decision making is encouraged by the use of the educational tools described below. The major focus of Ecologic is the utilization of these tools to introduce the use of systems logic in cultural decision making. The ideas that follow are representative of the kinds of ideas which can be generated by the use of these tools.

1. The Systems Schema
    The Systems Schema provides significantly different information than that provided by traditional reductionist systems models. Figure 11.9 describes the fundamental dynamics of the societal system in traditional reductionist terms.

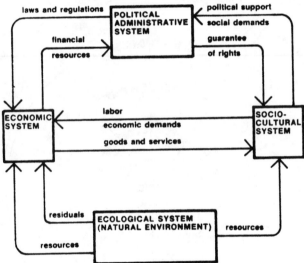

Fig. 11.9.   Reductionist Model.(4)

Depicted is a sociogram of social subsystems whose primary relationships can only be defined in terms of specified linear trade-offs between the subsystems. The model implies that all subsystems are separate but equal in their relationship to each other and to the whole. It provides little information as to the specific, differentiated role that each system plays in producing a functioning whole which is greater than the sum of its parts.
    When the same subsystems are placed in the Systems Schema, different information occurs. By utilizing the rigor of the mathematical model, these same subsystems are placed in

the schema based on their functional relationship to the whole system (Figure 11.10).

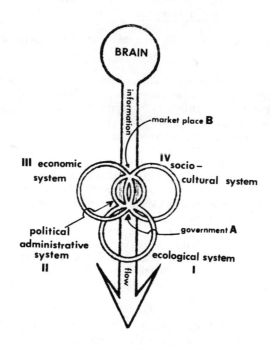

Fig. 11.10.   Societal System Model.

The ecological system provides the resource base and raw materials upon which the entire societal system depends for survival.   This ecological system is finite with many resources of a nonrenewable nature.   The function of unity in any societal system is the primary responsibility of the political-administrative system of which government is but one part. One way this has been accomplished in our political-administrative system has been through the distribution of wealth (resources).   The functional duality in our societal system is expressed in the dynamic tension that exists between the economic and the socio-cultural systems.   This relationship is most easily identified with the classic duality of supply (producer) and demand (consumer).   Energy flow represents the information available to the system for its use.

In this configuration one is forced to deal with the question of total system organization and the functional relationships between the subsystems.   In order to understand

these organizational relationships, it is necessary to understand
the functioning of power points A (government) and B (market
place) where subsystems interface. The point at which all
subsystems intersect represents the twin function of whole
system order and maintenance. These two functions are the
legitimate and primary functions of government. In a complex
system, effective order and maintenance is dependent upon two
factors:

1. The Law of System Maintenance. When controls (limits)
    are applied to a system as a whole, subsystems tend
    toward self-regulated, dynamic equilibrium. When
    controls (limits) are applied to individual subsystems as
    isolated units, the system as a whole tends toward dis-
    equilibrium and disorder.
2. The Resource Base. The resource base (I) is the
    ultimate determining factor in the success of the system.
    Whole system order must occur within the limits estab-
    lished by resource availability over the duration of the
    expected life of that system.

Representing the cutting edge of the system, the function of
growth (creativity and direction), in our societal system has
been traditionally assigned to the "free" market place. Effective system direction and creativity is dependent upon two
factors:

1. The successful maintenance of whole system limits within
    which whole system growth takes place, and
2. Fully functioning subsystems. Once whole system limits
    become effective, subsystems can function with a great
    deal of autonomy within those outer limits established by
    the system as a whole.

Application to Cultural Systems
    When viewing our present societal system in the context
of an "ideal" system, certain anomolies appear. At present:
system controls established by the government (A) are
primarily in the form of detailed regulations aimed at controlling individual subsystems perceived as discrete units.
Rather than increasing autonomy of subsystems and the
freedom of the market place (B), this approach to social
system limits has increased centralized authority and is
becoming increasingly counterproductive.
    Resource control is primarily a function of the market
place (B) rather than government (A). With an insatiable
appetite, the market place will always utilize as many resources
as are immediately available, regardless of long-range consequences. The consumer (socio-cultural system) no longer
exerts an effective counterbalance to the producer (economic

system). Because wealth tends to accumulate more rapidly in the economic or production section, and because of increased centralization and concomitant power, the producer is so strong that the consumer can no longer exert effective power in the market place. The government (A) by increasing its consumer function has increasingly subsumed the role traditionally played by the consumer in the free market place so that the dynamic tension now exists between the producers and the government (A) as they compete for control of the market place. This misplaced tension can eventually destroy the system unless corrective measures are taken. One such measure would be to return the consumer to greater power in the market place by a more equitable distribution of income. Distribution of income is one of the major responsibilities of the political/administrative system of any nation as it fulfills its systemic function of unification.

2. Systems Concepts

Ecological concepts, when applied as systems concepts, provide useful information as to how cultural systems function. The concept of cycles, when applied to our economic system, provides a context within which one might interpret the major fluctuating modes of economic behavior long recognized in economic literature; three-to-seven-year business cycles, intermediate-term (15 to 25 years) investment or Kuznets cycles, and long-wave or Kondratieff cycles spanning some 45 to 60 years. This concept suggests that these cycles represent natural rhythms common to any system. Thus, it should be possible to organize the economy in a way which could fully utilize these cycles and optimize their impact. At the present, most efforts are aimed at eliminating these fluctuations.

Heretofore, our economic system has been interpreted from the perspective of a pendulum (i.e., from less government control to greater and back to less control) rather than from an evolutionary perspective implicit in systems logic.

Initially, the capitalistic economic system was perceived as a natural system subject to natural laws expressed in the free market place. Any attempt at social control of the economy was seen as interference with nature's "invisible hand." However, the exigencies of the Great Depression required adaptive measures in the form of federal "pump priming."(5) From this initial adaptation, the system has evolved to a highly complex one in which the federal role in the market place has increased to a point where it is now counterproductive to a "free" market place. Appropriate adaptive measures are again required which will enable the economic system to evolve toward greater effectiveness. The law of system maintenance suggests that a necessary adaptation would be for the government to withdraw as a primary competitor in the market place and resume its primary function of order and maintenance. By

establishing whole system limits, it will enable the market place
to again function effectively and "freely."

Phase four: Ecoresponse

In order to effectively identify and understand the subjective
context which is present in a given decision-making process,
additional models will be utilized.

1.   Hierarchy of Values.
       There seem to be four sources of values.   Some values
are biologically determined (food), some are personally essential (security, friendship), some are socially ordained (job,
success), and others are ecologically necessary (limits).(6)
These sources represent a hierarchy of values that function in
a way similar to Maslow's "hierarchy of needs" (figure 11.11).

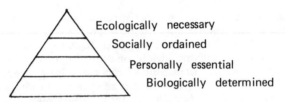

Fig. 11.11.   Hierarchy of Values.

       It has already been determined that the decisions which
an individual makes are influenced by the "breadth and depth"
of the context within which the issue is perceived.   In addition, decisions are also influenced by where the individual is
within this hierarchy of values.   One cannot expect a person
who is threatened with the loss of a job (security, success) to
be concerned about ecologically-sound decisions which may
contribute to a jobless possibility.

2.   Values Model
       A Values Model (figure 11.12) is used to introduce the
function of values in decision making.   This model depicts an
"anatomy of values system."   As such, it takes the hierarchy
of values described earlier one step further.
       Any individual's value system is made up of subsystems
which impinge on the decision-making process.   One, two, or
all of the subsystems may be functioning at the time any particular decision is made.   Rational decisions in today's world
require a full "set of values."   Before the limits of our Earth's
ecosystem had been reached, rational choices were made without paying heed to ecologically necessary values.   This is no
longer the case.   By directing studies to the role of values in

decision making, decision makers will be able to explore their own "set of values" and their relationship to personal decision making. Values clarification, in this context, becomes a significant tool whereby the decision maker can evaluate his or her own value system in the light of the different influences that impinge upon a particular decision.

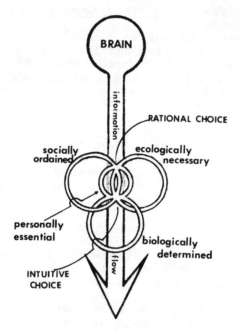

Fig. 11.12.   Values Model.

The Values Model highlights certain functional relationships: (a) the dynamic tension between socially ordained and ecologically necessary values, and (b) the centrality of the personally essential value in any decision.

The relationship of values to decision making, utilizing the two highlighted relationships above, can be illustrated in the debate concerning whether or not to hold the 1980 Winter Olympics within the Adirondack Park at Lake Placid, New York. On the one hand, the Adirondack Park Agency, set up to keep the park "forever wild," argued that the Olympics would upset their ecologically necessary guidelines. In tension with this perspective, the New York State Department of Environmental Conservation was primarily concerned with optimizing socially ordained values, such as integrated, multiple-use of recreation, wildlife, timber, aesthetics, and monetary gain. The final decision was heavily influenced by

the people living within the Park. Their response was primarily motivated by personally essential values such as
economic security, represented by new jobs and better incomes. Their decision stands in contrast with that reached by
the people of Colorado when faced with a similar issue surrounding the 1976 Olympics. Because the Adirondack Park is,
in essence, a "depressed area," the citizens were not "free" to
choose the "higher," ecologically necessary value as did the
citizens of Colorado.

The Values Model and the Hierarchy of Values are useful
tools with which to understand the subjective context that
subsumes all of the above points of view. By identifying the
dynamics of the value structure which underlies an issue
quickly and without bias, a more effective resolution of conflict
can occur. This often results in more appropriate decisions.

3. Values and Responsiblity.

Cultural values always reflect the operating principles of
the perceived life-support system. For example, if survival is
perceived as depending on the success of a particular economic
system, cultural values will reflect the operating principles
necessary for the continuity of that system. As decision
makers begin to understand how survival depends on the
Earth's ecosystem, and as they begin to understand how that
ecosystem functions, they will discover that implicit in its
principles are a set of what might be called "ecological
values." Values such as diversity, interdependence, change,
and carrying capacity are as relevant for cultural as for
natural systems.

As decision makers recognize that the successful functioning of our cultural system will depend upon the cultural
acceptance of ecological values, they will seek to provide the
prerequisites necessary to make that acceptance possible. One
prerequisite is ecological literacy. A second is ecological
responsibility. However, as the Adirondack Park example
illustrates, if ecological responsiblity is to result, people must
be "free" to accept those values necessary for cultural survival. These two prerequisites provide the outer and the
inner limits which define the borders of our jigsaw puzzle
world.

Ecosystem Education is a program to train decision
makers, by providing them with a basic strategy which encourages the values shifts necessary for societal acceptance of
steady-state systems and social system limits.

NOTES

(1)   Ervin   Laszlo,   A Systems View of the World   (New   York:
       Gearge Braziller, 1972).
(2)   Gregory   Bateson,   Steps to an Ecology of Mind   (New
       York: Ballantine, 1972).
(3)   Alan   Watts,   Tao,   The Watercourse Way   (New   York:
       Pantheon, 1975), p. 26.
(4)   Joan   Davis   and   Samuel   Mauch,   "Strategies   for   Societal
       Development," Alternatives to Growth I,   edited   by   D. L.
       Meadows   (Cambridge, Mass: Ballinger, 1977), p. 244.
(5)   Robert Heilbroner, The Worldly Philosophers (New York:
       Simon & Schuster, 1967), pp. 262 ff.
(6)   F.   Robert   Steiger   (Unpublished   address   to   the   George
       Williams faculty, September 1975).

IV

CONSEQUENCES OF SUSTAINABLE GROWTH: TWO CASE STUDIES

12 Nature's Technology
David Hopcraft

DESERTIFICATION AND HUMAN SYSTEMS

A great deal has been said in recent times about the population "time bomb," and the urgent need for stabilizing this trend. Only much more recently have we begun to realize the existence of a more serious threat to our future, namely, the survival of our land and vegetational resources. If these are destroyed, we have no future on this planet. The greater threat is posed in the lower-rainfall areas of the world - the grasslands, bush, prairie, plains, pampas, or veld.

A new word has been introduced into our language - desertification. As a world community, we have acknowledged the process defined by this word in a recent Desertification Conference in Nairobi, Kenya, sponsored by the United Nations. Information given at the conference disclosed the alarming fact that the world now loses at least 14 million acres a year to desert. The process is insidious: a gradual deterioration of grasslands over the years, loss of vegetation, followed by wind and rain erosion, until nothing but rocks or sand remain. The disruption of human societies following the loss of this primary resource, the terrible loss in lives and the suffering that accompanies it, and the enormous cost in international resources are only some of the effects of this process, recently demonstrated by the Sahelian experience.

The Sahel is a strip of land stretching 4,000 miles from Mauritania in West Africa to the Sudan, following a line south of the Sahara. Here, land deterioration has reached the point of disaster, with nothing left for the stock to eat. After the drought of 1968-73, in Mali alone nine out of ten animals died, along with at least 250,000 people. This same "desertification" process is happening all across Africa, and now affects nearly two-thirds of countries in our world.

As a teen-ager in Kenya, I watched the first dust storm ever recorded in our farming area. I was shocked to tour the region and find that the land to the north of us was completely bare. Some African families were still living there, starved, bewildered, and refusing to leave their home territories. Children with bloated bellies and matchstick legs stared at me through uncomprehending eyes. A few skeleton cattle remained eating bark off the trees. I later learned this same land had been rolling grasslands only 25 years before. I was thoroughly horrified and resolved to find out what had happened.

I was told this was the result of overgrazing and, at the time, accepted this assessment. In subsequent studies, I found this experience was by no means unique. It was as universal as it was tragic. There were, however, areas within these low-rainfall zones that were still in excellent condition. It was soon apparent that these were the areas that man had not touched, where nature continued her long-tried and stabile systems. As I began to document this information and compare these lands with deteriorated regions, there was always the same basic difference. In every case, the land deterioration and destruction followed human substitution of domestic stock for indigenous animals. In other words, the only other physical fact along with range destruction was this animal switch. This began to change my whole line of thought. Was it possible that the introduction of man's favored animals might, in fact, be responsible? Man had been placed in a carefully balanced and viable ecosystem, and changed it. I saw this as an amputation. Removing the indigenous animals is like cutting off a part of the living body. The rest soon deteriorates and dies. We were now seeing the results - land degradation and desert formation.

A STUDY OF A NATURAL SYSTEM

In thinking about these things, it appeared that if the theory was correct, then to return to utilizing indigenous animals would reverse the destructive process. But, could these animals be used as a viable resource; for meat and hides, like cattle? Could the natural system be as productive as cattle ranching? I hoped that perhaps it would come close. But I was totally unprepared for the findings that I now relate: a view of a land-use system many times more productive than cattle ranching, a system that offers a viable alternative to our present destructive systems.

I had, by now, obtained a Master's Degree in Animal and Wildlife Science from Cornell University and approached the National Science Foundation for research funds. It was time to put my theory to the test. Would utilization of a natural system complete with indigenous animals be nondestructive and yet productive in comparison to usage of imported stock? I proposed to set up an experiment to compare cattle with an indigenous species, to monitor the comparative effects on grasslands, and measure the off-take of meat and hides. The National Science Foundation was impressed with the concept and backed the project, thus enabling work to begin. A uniform, 300-acre plot of dry land in Kenya was fenced off and then divided down the middle. One side was then stocked with cattle, and the other with gazelle.

Stocking the area with cattle was not difficult, but catching the gazelle was quite a problem. We tried many different systems - nets, traps, dart guns, and spotlights at night. Catching a few was easy, but we needed nearly three hundred for the experimental project, and it proved extremely difficult. We finally settled on a night system using a special type of spotlight with a covered bulb which gave a narrow beam of light. Success was achieved only on dark nights, using a fast approach with a bush vehicle, and finally jumping out and catching by hand. Ant bear holes and thorn trees caused many a drama, but we finally filled our quota.

Matching of stocking rates was the next problem, entailing a series of trials to make sure that the two areas were stocked similarly, so that grazing potential was equal. Predators had to be controlled, including jackal and hyena which were living down ant bear holes, and even a leopard found his way in before we modified the fence. We further discovered that Martials Eagles, huge white-chested birds, were making off with baby gazelles. A day guard was posted at the experimental area.

Eventually, the problems were overcome and stocking rates matched. Over the next three years, controlled culling took place and data was collected to provide answers to the many questions in our minds. These could be split into three categories: (1) Ecological - comparative effects on the range of the two species; (2) Yield - comparative quantities and qualities of meat and hides produced; and (3) Financial - comparative gross and net returns.

Ecological Effects

Though the experimental area was homogeneous to start with, the effects on the range of the two species were totally dissimilar. This confirmed the pattern of events occurring in many parts of Africa.

Clearly, cattle were adversely affecting this semi arid rangeland. They are water-dependent animals and must walk daily

Table 12.1.   Range Results

Item Measured	Cattle Enclosure	Gazelle Enclosure
Grass Cover	Significantly reduced	32% more cover than in cattle enclosure
Grass Species	Reduction in climax vegetation	100% more climax species than found in cattle enclosure
Tracking	Significant and serious, especially to water hole	None
Devastation around Water Hole	Serious and extensive	None

to water, trampling vegetation under foot, compacting and tracking the delicate soils.   Indigenous animals require very little water or, in some cases, none at all.   Cattle have a specific food preference, and cannot possibly utilize the vegetation evenly as do a variety of game animals.   Certain grass species are eaten out, therefore, while other, nonpreferred species become entrenched.   A series of changes in species composition, and a loss of vegetational cover result, reducing the productive quality of the whole.   Each year the situation becomes worse where cattle are used, and in many African countries this same deleterious progression has led, and is continuing to lead, to the point of land disaster, followed by starvation and death of the stock and the owners.

Yield

Cropping was carried out regularly, making sure that stocking rates were maintained.   The natural increase of weight within each of the enclosures was carefully tabulated.   Carcass and lean-meat measurements were taken.

Table 12.2.   Lean Meat: Pounds per Acre per Year

Experimental Gazelle _____/14.6 lbs.

Experimental Cattle _____/7.9 lbs.

Ranch Cattle _____/4 lbs.

Nomadic Cattle ___/1 lb.

Apart from being more efficient animals, <u>within their home
environment</u>, there are two reasons for the high level of lean
meat obtainable with gazelles.   First, game animals have a
higher ratio of useable carcass to live weight than do cattle,
thus providing 20 percent heavier useable carcass.   Second,
game animals have very little fat, usually only 1 percent, as
opposed to more than 20 percent fat in cattle.   Lean meat was
thus 47 percent of the gazelle and only 32 percent of the
cattle carcass.   No saturated fats exist in game meat, a factor
of great importance to health.

These data give an indication of the potential of even one
animal species within its natural area, and show that adaptation to environment is a very important factor.   An indigenous
animal spends far less energy than an imported beast in
overcoming the harsh environmental conditions such as disease,
weather, and vegetation.   Thus, more energy becomes available for growth.

The above results were quite unbelievable to me, raised
as I was on a cattle farm.   I asked other scientists to verify
the results.   What a shock to find that indigenous animals,
which have in the past been regarded either as a nuisance or
a curiosity, could be so much more productive than cattle in
this low-rainfall environment.

Financial Returns

In assessing the income from the two areas under comparison,
I took into consideration income from meat prices for such
wildlife as has been cropped have been higher than beef.   In
West Africa, this price is consistently almost double.   However, even taken at equivalent prices, we can count on 50 to
100 percent more meat to sell per acre.   Hides command a very
good price and are likely to do so for the foreseeable future.
During the trials, a gazelle hide was fetching $5, where a
cowhide brought in less than $4.   A ten-acre area was needed
per cow, and it took three years to produce a hide.   Eight
gazelles were turned over per year in the same area, giving 24
hides.   Thus, the income was $120 to $4.   This high income
level, obtained from only one animal species, is likely to be
increased through the utilization of a whole spectrum of game
species.   Each of these has evolved to fill a specific niche
within the system, making full use of the whole.

Without looking at costs, we would see a substantially
higher gross income from the indigenous animal.   Costs in-
curred with these animals, however, are negligible.   No
dipping, inoculations, water supplies, or night enclosures are
required.   Table 12.3 gives an indication of our present
estimates, with costs on a cattle ranch at about 66 percent and
on a game ranch at only 20 percent of income.

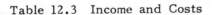
Table 12.3   Income and Costs

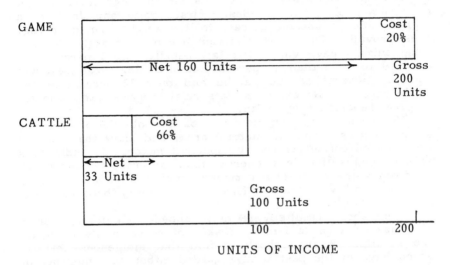

UNITS OF INCOME

Apart from the above results, some fascinating facts were
discovered about the gazelles, which give us insight as to how
beautifully nature has ordered and arranged her webs of life
and which confirm the idea that we should take more seriously
her systems. They were able to live without water. They
have a beautifully arranged life style, with territorial males
setting up territories adjacent to each other, and females
moving from one to the next, while the males stay put. Other
males, or bachelors, rove freely in "gangs," sparring, play-
ing, and pestering the territorial owners and the females.
The females, however, are always bred by the territorial male.

Females produce young during the dry seasons and are
bred again within a few days of giving birth. With the
difficulty of keeping themselves fed during the dry time, and
with suckling the newborn, it would appear that to begin a
new pregnancy would be too much stress. To alleviate this,
the fertilized egg does not come down and implant in the
uterus for three months. By this time, the rains have come
and the fawn is almost weaned, allowing the mother to develop
a new pregnancy. Sometimes, the mechanism does not work,
and a new baby follows the last by three and a half months,
instead of the normal six and a half months, giving us a clue
to this process. This was the first time "delayed implantation"
had been observed in the Bovidae family.

The young gazelle is hidden in the grass. The mother
calls but never approaches it at feeding times. In this way,
the fawn is able to distinguish approaching predators. During
this period, the young coat is darker, adding to the camou-

flage. The baby drinks furiously at feeding times so as to be exposed to the keen eyes of predators as briefly as possible. Smell, an easy give-away, is dealt with by ingenious means. The young only defecates or urinates as a response to the licking of the mother at feeding times. In this way, she licks clean any smell that would otherwise attract predators.

In fascinating ways, nature fits each animal, plant, tree, bird, and insect to play its part symbiotically with the rest and to survive the harsh tests of life within each ecosystem. If the evolutionary path leads to the development of a feature or trait which becomes destructive, then that species dies out. We should take warning. It has happened countless times in the history of our planet.

ADAPTATION AND THE DEVELOPMENT
OF A NEW THINKING

Looking back at the work accomplished during the experiments, interpretations can be made on various levels. Quite clearly, the indigenous animal did not degrade the land, where cattle did. Those areas of land in dry zones of Africa which are still in healthy condition are those where nature still holds sway, and "livestock" have been kept out either by the tsetse fly, or by declaration of National Parks and Game Reserves. In livestock areas, the drier they are the more acute the problem - for livestock are not dry land animals. They come from the wetter, more temperate zones, and so require a lot of water. The gazelles used in the experiments did not drink water. The trough was eventually taken out of the enclosure, with no adverse effects. How was this possible? The secret was natural adaptation.

Over the millenia, animals have moved gradually from wetter zones where life began, to fill unclaimed positions, or "niches" in drier areas. They evolved physically and physiologically to be able to live in these harsher zones. How could they live without water? Surely this is impossible. We carried out a series of experiments and found that, indeed, it was very possible. These dry land animals have simply "closed" the avenues of moisture loss from the body. Their feces are so dry that the pellets are mucous-covered to ease passage. All the moisture is reabsorbed in the large intestine and recycled. Their kidneys are ultra-efficient, concentrating waste products in very small amounts of water, thus controlling moisture loss. Finally, sweating and panting, high moisture-loss areas, are controlled or eliminated by a specialized ingenious process. These animals allow body temperature to vary, like cold-blooded animals, following ambient temperature. On a hot day, when livestock are sweating to keep their heat levels down, dry land animals simply allow body temperature to rise, often to 106°F or more, thus eliminating the need to sweat, for sweating is only required as a cooling mechanism. Body temperatures of 107° or more have been recorded in the animals, enough to destroy brain enzymes. However, there is a protective mechanism at work. The blood from the heart, before reaching the brain, is dispersed, through nasal capillaries, or in some cases through capillaries in the horns, where it is cooled sufficiently to ensure there is no brain damage.

As a result of these factors, many dry land animals never drink. They can survive on metabolic water (a by-product of carbohydrate metabolism) and moisture from vegetation consumed. In some cases, these species have learned to eat hygroscopic species of vegetation (plants that absorb moisture from the atmosphere) at the hours of maximum water content. Living without additional water enables these animals to inhabit dry regions without the endless quest for water indulged in by man and his domestic stock. Here, then, is the key to the problem. Cattle must trek to water, trampling and compacting the land surface, causing water run-off and erosion. They trample vegetation which could otherwise be eaten and, to make matters worse, burn energy, to get to the water and back again to the grazing area. These treks get longer and longer as the grass around the water holes is eaten and trampled, until 20 to 30 miles becomes normal in dry periods. This problem became so acute in the Sahel that the destroyed areas enlarged to become one, and the cattle died of starvation. All this, to say nothing of the enormous costs of imported expertise and machinery required to construct these water holes and fuel required to operate the pumps to bring up the water. By continuing to use livestock, we are ignoring the advantages offered by nature through adaptation. The costs are enormous and the results catastrophic.

Adaptation also explains the higher level of efficiency of local animals within their home areas. There is less trampling of vegetation; and, with a variety of animals, all vegetation species are utilized, thus allowing higher stocking rates.

Table 12.4 provides data comparing stocking rates of dry areas under different land-use regimes, taken from Talbot and Talbot, working in East Africa.(1)

Higher stocking rates allowing more animals per acre mean increased meat production, and more hides available for sale.

Adaptation results in less energy being expended in walking, in panting, and in sweating. Less energy is lost at night, for as soon as cold sets in, body temperatures drop. Cattle must generate heat to keep their temperature levels constant. Adaptation also gives immunity to local diseases, resulting in great savings on veterinary, dipping, and inoculation costs.

Table 12.4.   Biomass per Square Mile (lbs.)

Cattle under traditional African stockraising methods. (Low rainfall)	12,000
Cattle on well-managed modern stock farms. (Low rainfall)	45, - 50,000
Plains game in marginal plains areas. (Low rainfall)	75, - 100,000
Plains game in natural higher rainfall areas.	100, - 140,000

Adaptation is clearly responsible for the success of local animals within these harsh environments. It accounts for the amazing wealth of animal and vegetational species found all across Africa in her native condition. We tend to forget that these animals are here in spite of us, whereas cattle are only here because of us.

CLINGING TO HUMAN TECHNOLOGY

Human tendency is to revere our own technology and forget natural systems, to the point that we are blind to natural technology. We realize that land is our primary resource but believe only in our own land-use systems, forgetting that long-tried and stable land-use systems have existed and evolved over the millenia. The vast lower rainfall grasslands, that today are in such peril, along with the uncounted herds of indigenous animals, which have been totally decimated, once formed an incalculable, self-perpetuating, natural resource. In Africa, in particular, this was by far the greatest of all resources, yet one which has gone unrecognized and, accordingly, has been neglected, abused, and almost entirely destroyed.

In worrying over desertification, and even acknowledging that it is a man-made problem, we continue to ignore the natural alternative. Instead, we talk of more expertise, better breeds of livestock, more water holes, and better management. In all these areas, nature is offering us a rich multicultural variety of plant and animal species, evolved and stabilized over the millenia. We know our livestock systems do not work in these areas, yet we are determined to make them work. "Human technology will prevail, even if we kill ourselves proving it!"

Why does modern man persist in this attitude? The Western world, through its major institutions, banks, and foundations, continues to pour money, expertise, time, and

energy into the livestock industry in Africa. Any amount of
money is available for "livestock development." All of the
scientific institutions and universities in 40 or more African
countries are studying cattle, sheep, and goats, but not
indigenous animals (most of which, ironically enough, belong to
the same family as our livestock - <u>Bovidae</u>).

The reasons I can only guess at. We have pushed and
developed the livestock industry. It is an area of our expertise and so "must be able to be exported." We have
developed secondary and tertiary industries surrounding "our
baby." We produce vaccines, medicines, and dips to keep the
stock alive. We produce or import pumps and engines, pipes
and water tanks, spray races and management equipment, and
finally oil to run the engines, all to keep the operation going.
We have fixed in our minds the continuum of land - ranching -
cattle, and staked our financial, scientific, and institutional
reputation on its success.

NATURAL TECHNOLOGY - A DEMONSTRATION

Following the results from the research described, and the
ideas and insights developed, I realized the only practical and
effective way of changing attitudes and land-use systems was
to demonstrate this natural land-use system on the ground. It
took five years of effort to obtain an official green light to
develop such a system. There was no governmental machinery
to cope with such an operation. This is true in most countries
of the world, where wild animals are treated as a curiosity and
perhaps a tourist attraction, but not to be used in any practical system. Funds had to be raised for land purchase.
Grants and loans had to be obtained for the set-up costs and
conversions needed for such an enterprise. Countless institutions were approached in the United States and Europe.
Finally, it was the Lilly Endowment of Indianapolis that agreed
to put up funds for the conversion/research aspect of the
project. They saw the far-reaching implications of such an
idea and, being involved already in attempts to alleviate the
plight of "desertification victims," saw that this must become
the future land-use system of Africa. And if such an operation was to be attempted, it had to be done properly, with
careful monitoring. The ranch is 25 miles from Nairobi in
Kenya.

The first thing to be done, once the land was secured,
was the construction of an 8-foot 6-inch high perimeter fence
around the 20,000 acres obtained for the operation. Seven
feet of this was to be chain link, with three strands of barbed
wire on top. The perimeter was 31 miles. With escalating
costs of material and transport, it was decided to construct

the chain link fence on the ranch. A home-made contraption was built from two old truck rear axles joined together by a shaft and driven by a single-cylinder diesel engine. The axles were used so that power could be switched on by braking one side or switched off by braking the other side, using a centrally mounted brake lever. A metal tube with precise grooves was mounted on one side of each axle, with a flat bar rotating inside the tube. Wire was fed in from one side and came out with the zig-zag chain link pattern. It was snipped into 7-foot lengths and then woven together by hand. Thus, 31 miles of fence was made, and then tied onto five line wires strung on posts placed every ten meters. The operation took 15 months.

The ranch still carries cattle to provide interim operating income. Over the last two years since its inception, the indigenous animals have been protected, encouraged, introduced, or attracted onto the ranch. There are now over 5,000 animals of 14 different species. Cropping of excess males will start very soon, thus avoiding any interference with the breeding stock. When full stocking rates are achieved, only the natural increase will be culled to provide the income for the ranch. Fresh and smoked game meat will be sold, as well as salted and dried meat or "jerky." This latter system used by man over hundreds of years alleviates the requirement of refrigeration and is of great importance where production areas are remote.

CONCLUSIONS

As we look to the future to try and find ways of stabilizing our world, both ecologically and socially, we must make a new and realistic assessment of our land-use systems. We are in need of more food to feed extra mouths each year. We are in need of recreational facilities to cope with increased leisure time in the West. We are in need of ideas to supplant the ones that have led to increasing land deterioration, causing erosion of our soils, our food supplies, and our human dignity.

A quote from President Roosevelt, on his safari in East Africa in January 1915, is perhaps relevant here. "When genuinely protected, birds and mammals increase so rapidly, it becomes imperative to cull them. The foolish sentimentalists who do not see this are the really efficient foes of wildlife and of sensible movements for its preservation."

The Natural system, or Nature's Technology, needs to be understood and embraced for the long-term solutions and secrets it holds. It is a technology of adaptation and evolutionary experience. It has worked over the millenia developing symbiotic and stable ecosystems that survive. These have proved, even in comparison to our modern land-use systems, to be highly productive and low in cost.   Ecological theory holds that these systems develop, over periods of uninterrupted time, the maximum energy flow possible within each area.   If this is true, and it is a cornerstone of ecological thinking, then man's systems cannot possibly be more productive, but can only tend toward lower levels of energy flow or productivity.   A second cornerstone of ecological theory holds that if one part of a system is changed, then all the rest is affected, changed, and degraded.   Thus, we should know better than to try and change the type of animals to be used within given ranges.

We must begin to think of living with nature rather than forever changing it.   We have in our culture, and even in our songs, developed the concept of conquering nature: "How the West was won"; "Taming the wild."   Our urgent need is not to conquer, but to understand and learn from nature.

Nearly 45 percent of the earth's land surface is now desert or faces imminent desertification.   At least half of the land surface is dry range land.   Here is an inexhaustible "bread basket" at present mainly inhabited by poorer nomadic or semi-nomadic peoples, hardly staying above the "bread line," following land-use systems that are leading area by area to disaster.   To advance to natural land-use systems in these areas would reinstate a healthy and wealthy alternative that could achieve our most cherished objectives, provide food and income, and reinstate national and social dignity.   This would also provide true recreational possibilities for man the traveler, attained so effectively when we are in natural surroundings with nature's own animals.

There are three basic guidelines which have come out of this work, and which I feel are crucial to the development of adequate and long-term land-use systems.

1.   We need to develop systems which are in line with the naturally evolved patterns.
2.   We need to move away from monocultures back to a multiculture, which, be it in plants or animals, is nature's way.
3.   We must work toward systems which do not require the quantities of imported energy that we use today.   We must work toward zero-energy import.   Only then will we achieve a stabilized entity.

The natural land-use system of game or wildlife ranching clearly fits in with the above guidelines.   It embraces nature's system, it is multicultural in terms of both plant and animal life (often 30 species of animals are found together), and it requires little energy importation.   In terms of our future, it is self-perpetuating and stable in terms of our food require-

ments, and it is, due to adaptation, far more productive than
the use of domestic stock. In terms of our environment, it is
our naturally evolved land system and is ecologically symbiotic
and sound. It is the first time that a conservation system has
been linked with production and profit. Thus, for the first
time, it has been shown that conservation can really work. It
is my hope that man will wake up and cooperate with nature in
the knowledge that only then will nature continue to support
life.

NOTES

(1)   L.M. Talbot and M.H. Talbot, "The High Biomass of Wild
      Ungulates on East African Savannah" (Paper presented at
      the 28th Wildlife and Natural Resources Conference, 1963).

SELECTED BIBLIOGRAPHY

Arman, P., and Hopcraft, D. "Nutritional Studies on East
   African Herbivores. 1. Digestibilities of Dry Matter,
   Crude Fibre, and Crude Protein in Antelope, Cattle and
   Sheep." Brit. Jour. Nutr. 33 (1975):255-64.

Bourliere, F. "The Vanishing Herds." UNESCO Courier 14
   (1961):4-7.

Darling, F. Fraser. "Wildlife Husbandry in Africa." Scientific
   American 203 (1960):123-28.

Dasmann, R. F., and Mossman, A. S. "Commercial Utilization
   of Game Mammals on a Rhodesian Ranch." National
   Affairs Association, Bulawayo, Rhodesia, 1961.

Harthoorn, A. M., and Hopcraft, D. "Adaptation to Solar
   Radiation by African Large Herbivores." Jour. South
   African Vet. Medical Assoc. 41 (1971):17-24.

Hopcraft, D. "Productivity Comparison Between Thomson's
   Gazelle and Cattle, and Their Relation to the Ecosystem in
   Kenya." Unpublished Ph.D. dissertation, Cornell Uni-
   versity, 1975.

Huxley, Elspeth. "Wildlife - Another African Tragedy." New
   York Times Magazine, October 1959, pp. 22-23.

Huxley, Julian. "Poaching - The Shocking Slaughter of
   Africa's Wildlife." UNESCO Courier 14 (1961):8-11.

Maloiy, G. M. O., and Hopcraft, D. "Thermoregulation and
   Water Relations of Two East African Antelopes - The

Hartebeest and Impala." Comp. Biochem. and Physiol. 38 (1971):525-34.

Phillips, John. Agriculture and Ecology in Africa. New York: Frederick A. Praeger, 1960.

Talbot, L. M., and Talbot, M. H. "The High Biomass of Wild Ungulates on East African Savannah." Paper presented at 28th Wildlife and Natural Resources Conference, 1963, pp. 465-76.

Treichel, George. "The Vanishing Herds." Atlantic Monthly 203 (1959):85-87.

13 Lessons from the Coastline of America: Management Strategies for a Sustainable Society
Kathryn Cousins

The coastline is the site of a complex interplay between finite natural resources and tremendous development pressures. In 1972, Congress established the Federal Coastal Zone Management Act to provide financial assistance to states wishing to prepare plans for preservation and development of their coastlines. In the process of managing the federal program, seven management strategies have been used which appear to be applicable to other governmental agencies trying to initiate a transition to managing a sustainable society. Although these strategies are not new to scholars of public administration, their practical application has proven their general efficacy. The seven strategies are: 1) prepare in advance to manage; 2) initiate action; 3) experiment with new analytical tools; 4) evaluate and adjust; 5) involve nongovernmental groups; 6) involve all levels of government; and 7) adopt an international perspective.

The concept for this chapter is well set in the following paragraph from Coastal Resources Management by Robert Ditton, John L. Seymour and Gerald C. Swanson:

> Coastal zone management is really the first attempt to control and administer resource conflict and use within a functional area of highly interdependent uses. The coastal zone is the world of Limits to Growth in a microcosm. All the problems raised by the limits proponents coexist in that finite area - population pressures, resources, industry, food production, and pollution. The area clearly has some carrying capacity that can be affected by one of these factors alone or as they interact. Coastal zone management as a solution to the problems raised by these interacting factors represents the attempt

to organize and bring science and technology - both physical and social - to bear on these problems. The efforts in this area may thus be prophetic for man's future as the test case is run in the coastal zone.(1)

Mark Twain once urged readers to invest in land because "they aren't making it anymore." Similarly, the ocean is a fixed resource, albeit less well understood. Where these two resources meet, the coastline, is subject to particularly intense, conflicting pressures. It is the thesis of this chapter that there are lessons to be learned from managing the American coastline that are applicable to managing a sustainable society.

The nation's seven largest cities are located on the American coastline, which includes the shores of the Great Lakes. Forty-two percent of Americans live within 50 miles of the coast. It is the location of the $145 billion annual foreign trade activities of ports, and of the $3.4 billion a year commercial fishing industry.(2) More than half of the nation's oil is either from offshore wells or is imported by ship.(3) Over 40 percent of the country's industrial employment is located in coastal counties.(4) Recreation is the largest coastal economic activity with 112 million people participating in 7.1 billion ocean-oriented events, spending approximately $14 billion annually in the process.(5) America's 36,900 mile coast (excluding Alaska) is approximately 41 percent developed and 59 percent rural or undeveloped.(6)

The coastline presents a challenge to government because of its complexity. It is not manageable in the usual governmental style of establishing single purpose agencies responsible for solving single problems such as providing recreation, increasing fishing, extracting oil and gas, or making shipping safe. In fact, coastal management encompasses all of these purposes and others. It is a tack "to manage unprecedented complexity," a situation that Harlan Cleveland and Thomas Wilson, in their essay "Humangrowth," assert is being handled by government with "apparent incapacity."(7) Eugene P. Odum wrote in Science, in March 1977, "at the national level, I believe, the current effort to mount a program of research and management for the coastal zone may be the first major test of whether we are yet ready to combine the best of reductionist and synthesis science as a basis for rational decisions."(8) While not proposing that the Federal Coastal Zone Management Program is a model, we will examine this program, which was specifically assigned in its enabling legislation to handle a complex problem. First, however, it is important to understand the dynamics of the American coast.

THE COAST - A PACKAGE OF LIMITED RESOURCES

The package of resources on the coastline consists of land, the estuarine environment, sandy beaches, and the sea. These resources are extremely interrelated, with impacts on one almost always affecting another.

Coastal land is subject to various natural processes that must be given consideration in managing the coast. Flooding, hurricanes, subsidence, and erosion make development somewhat more risky than at inland sites. While some damages can be reduced with design solutions (such as raising the level of the first floor above projected water levels), such precautions usually add to the initial cost of development in a way that would not be necessary away from the waterfront.

A serious problem occurs in highly urbanized areas when land uses not dependent on water location preempt waterfront land. The price a condominium developer is willing to pay for waterfront land in Boston greatly exceeds the amount many water-dependent users are able to pay, and yet water-dependent uses (ports, for example) have no alternative locations. Water-dependent uses include cargo facilities for international trade, fishing piers, oil and gas transfer points, marinas, beach recreation sites, waterview restaurants, and ferry slips. In a few areas, agriculture appears to be dependent on the salt air of a coastal location: for example, artichokes growing along the California coast. Land uses not water-dependent include housing, warehouses, highways, and airports.

The estuarine environment occurs where the salt water, fresh water and land meet in marshes, swamps, and wetlands. Acre for acre it is the most productive area on earth, producing in a year four times as much plant growth as an intensively fertilized corn field.(9) Of the ten most valuable fish and shellfish caught commercially, seven are dependent on the estuarine environment for breeding or obtaining food, some time in their life cycle. A wetland absorbs the velocity and desynchronizes the peaks of flooding, thus protecting dry lands. Some marsh plants and soil actually absorb water. Waterfowl dependent on the estuarine environment include the 10 to 12 million ducks that breed there as well as the visiting Canadian geese that winter in such areas. Wetlands act as a pollution filtration system with plants absorbing high levels of nitrogen and phosphorus. Under careful control, a marsh of 1,000 acres can purify the nitrogenous wastes from a town of 20,000 people.(10) This natural system is limited; if overburdened with pollution, the estuarine environment becomes less valuable for all the purposes it serves.

Beaches have been well defined as "fragile ribbons of sand that are frequently broken by acts of nature and man."(11) Their dynamic nature is little understood, but the fact that their source is from rivers and eroded cliffs should provide adequate indication of their variable nature. About one third of the American coastline contains sandy beaches, including spite, dunes, and barrier beaches.(12) Their value for recreation is well known. The value of dunes in protecting inland areas from wave action is beginning to be understood.

The sea was often considered an unlimited frontier in the past. Recent events, such as the periodic appearance of raw sewage on the shores of Long Island, have changed our thinking. Five-sixths of the total living matter in the world is in the sea, most of it in the 2 to 3 percent of the upper surface.(13) It is here that light penetrates and makes for a fertile environment. Microscopic plant plankton, the basic food for marine life, thrives in this surface water. Into this "living soup"(14) industrial society discharges its human and chemical wastes and heated water used to cool power plants and other machinery. While the sea has a capacity to dilute and disperse pollutants, it can be effective only for certain amounts. The pollution of water leads to the ironic situation – illustrating the need for coastal management – of public beaches where health officials will not allow swimming. The sea is also an important source of minerals including manganese nodules, which contain manganese, nickel, copper, and cobalt. Because they occur so far offshore, their extraction has been a catalyst in encouraging the search for a Law of the Sea agreement that will establish legal rights for mining them.(15)

PRESSURES ON THE COAST

There are growing pressures and demands for the use of these fixed resources. A brief synopsis of four of these demands will suggest the nature of the conflict:

- The average time spent in recreation on the coast is 10 days for every person in the United States.(16) The exponential rate of coastal recreation demand shows no sign of decreasing. Only 9 percent of the coastline, excluding Alaska, is publicly owned and available for public recreation.(17)
- The 200-mile fishing conservation zone, which gives priority to American fishermen off the American coast, has resulted in increased interest in building fishing boats and processing plants along the coastline.
- The trend toward containerized and specialized shipping can require greater storage space onshore and deeper channels with attendant environmental consequences. The average annual growth rate of U.S. seaborne trade in the 1970s was 7 percent.(18)

• America's attempt to achieve energy self-sufficiency has led to an accelerated effort to extract offshore oil and natural gas reserves. Over two-thirds of the nation's remaining oil and natural gas supply is on the outer continental shelf and in Alaska.(19)

MANAGING THE COASTLINE - THE PAST

It may be useful to understand how America managed its coastline until the 1970s. Colonial history was dominated by Americans living along the Atlantic coast using its rich fisheries resources and natural harbors for trade and commerce. The value of estuarine areas was not fully understood, but neither were they built upon because there was always inexpensive dry land nearby. Pioneers, except for tideland tobacco farmers, generally moved beyond the coastal area to develop agriculture. While the British monarch required the maintenance of port towns to encourage commerce, the principal form of coastal management involved private decisions of people when they moved and built homes and towns. Things remained essentially the same until the early twentieth century, when the federal government began to dredge coastal waterways to promote commerce. In the 1920s, after the rapid population increases which occurred in the early part of the century, large cities began to use zoning to control land uses. Until after World War II, these were the only major tools for managing development of the coastline.

With the continued increase of city density, both federal and state governments tended to focus on managing single purpose problems such as water pollution, dredging and filling, wetlands protection, recreation, and development of offshore oil and gas. It was in the late 1960s, in response to the diffuse and conflicting nature of these single purpose regulatory procedures, as well as because of a growing awareness of the principles of ecology, that a new solution was proposed, namely, the Coastal Zone Management Act of 1972.(20)

THE COASTAL ZONE MANAGEMENT ACT

The intellectual climate in the early 1970s reflected new-found attitudes toward natural resources. The pollution of air and water, and overcrowded, poorly-planned cities were popular issues in the press. It was a time of Earth Day; and terms such as "holistic," "ZPG," and "limits to growth" became topical even if only slightly understood. Key government reports, such as <u>The Natural Estuarine Pollution Study</u>, and

Our Nation and the Sea recommended the need to view and manage the coastline as an integrated system.(21) It was in this climate that the concept of coastal zone management developed and the Act was passed.

The Act reflects the fact that the then existing techniques of management in the coastal zone were inadequate. Congress found that unplanned and uncontrolled development in the coastal zone was destroying important ecological, cultural, historic, and aesthetic values. The Act established a voluntary grant-in-aid program for the states. In return for its participation, a state for four years receives 80 percent federal funds to prepare a management program. (In the 1976 amendments to the Act this limit was changed to six years.) If the program meets certain substantive and procedural requirements, it enables the participating states to receive annual grants to implement the program. States with approved coastal programs can require federal actions affecting the state coastline to be consistent with the program. Essentially, the Act requires states to establish certain resource and development policies to regulate significant land and water uses within the coastal zone. Although there is a provision for delegation of authority to local governments, the state must maintain an overview to assure that certain minimum policies will be carried out. Among the policies that must be implemented are wetlands protection, provision of beach access, water and air pollution control, protection of fisheries resources, and provision of land for water-dependent uses. After mandating the protection of critical resources, the Act requires the states to balance competing demands from among those who wish to develop and those who wish to conserve land. Thus, the Act has not been considered a perfect program by some environmentalists. On the other hand, it has been welcomed by some development interests who originally feared a solely environmental thrust.

The state programs have provided a more certain climate, a predictability of governmental decision making that some developers have long wanted. As of the summer of 1979, all 31 states, including the Great Lakes states, as well as territories eligible to participate, have been actively involved in the program. Two states are currently suspended from the program for failure to put together adequate legislative authority to implement their policies. The amount of funds received is based on population and miles of coastline and varies from $4 million a year for Alaska to $100,000 for American Samoa, with the average grant being about $750,000. The program is administered for the federal government by the Office of Coastal Zone Management within the National Oceanic and Atmospheric Administration in the Department of Commerce. There is a staff of about 50 federal employees to administer the program. Each state hires between 6 to 40 people to administer the program at the state level.

The common measures of success of a government program - increased staff and budget - cannot be considered appropriate in a sustainable society. Yet, until better measures are agreed upon, it may be helpful to note that the federal Office of Coastal Zone Management was given increased responsibilities by Congress in the 1976 amendments to the Act, and has received an increased budget and staff each year. The three cases of litigation in which the office was involved were decided in its favor. Another measure of success includes the fact that all elegible states have chosen to participate in this voluntary program, although it must be conceded that the provision for 80 percent federal funding has undoubtedly been a more important motivating factor than the existence of a well-managed federal agency.

Because a coastal management agency balances various points of view, it does not develop a vocal constituency as do single purpose government agencies. Nevertheless, evaluation by others is often an effective measure of success. The National Governors' Association passed a resolution in the summer of 1979 stating "it is pleased generally with the progress of the federal Coastal Zone Management Program."(22) William Reilly, President of the Conservation Foundation, said in March 1978, ". . . federal Coastal Zone Management has had a couple of unusual advantages since its inception. One, it has had the same leader through the terms of three Presidents, and he has been a very good leader . . . perhaps fulfilling some expectations even beyond what some of the congressional authors of this law intended."(23)

From the opposite end of the environmental spectrum, the American Petroleum Institute's National Coastal Zone Management Steering Committee ". . . recognizes that coastal zone management has become part of federal and state regulation, and that development and implementation of good state programs is in the best interests of the states, the nation and the petroleum industry."(24) Referring to the implementation of the Coastal Zone Management Act, former Secretary of Commerce Juanita M. Kreps said, "I rank it among the top accomplishments of the Department of Commerce during this decade."(25)

MANAGEMENT STRATEGIES IN A SUSTAINABLE SOCIETY

In "Humangrowth," Cleveland and Wilson said that the "main obstacle" to converting the new values necessary for managing a worldwide transition from indiscriminate economic growth to selective growth "is not limits to physical resources or limits to the human intelligence. It is the limits to government."(26) The remainder of this chapter will deal with how the coastal management program has used seven management strategies that have been responsible for its "success." It is important to note that none of these strategies is new to the scholar of public administration. What is unusual is that so many of them have been put into practice by a governmental agency. The practical application of these strategies has proven their general efficacy. Because they have been tested and are not only academic theories, they should be more acceptable to other governmental agencies who will be responsible for managing in a sustainable society.

Strategy I: Prepare in Advance to Manage

When it became apparent that a coastal management program would be enacted by Congress, the organization in which it was to be placed, the National Oceanic and Atmospheric Administration, assigned one of its young, bright administrators to a research ship to "get away from it all" to make plans for the new program. The assignment allowed him the time available only in such an environment to prepare to manage. As the responsibility was so complex, multidisciplinary, and uncharted, there were many optional ways to structure the program that he explored during this period before legislative enactment.(27) This willingness and opportunity to plan far ahead has been the basis for many of the sound management procedures of the agency. This is not to say that the results of planning ahead led to an inflexible attitude toward management procedures. If anything, the management style of the office can be characterized as "improvisation on a general sense of direction."(28) The opportunity to plan ahead provided the general sense of direction. Since that initial planning phase, the office has held periodic "retreats" to focus on continued planning for the future.

Strategy II: Initiate Action

Harlan Cleveland has aptly noted "that often the sum of specialized advice is to do nothing cautiously."(29) Congress guaranteed that the coastal program would move quickly into management activities by providing planning funds to the states for only four years. Congress clearly did not want another planning program which employed many bureaucrats and never made a difference on the ground. Because of the four-year time constraint, the federal agency and the states had to act before all research could be completed, before all evaluations were conducted, and even before there was universal public support for the programs. (It was recognized that these processes are never ending in real life, and that

too often they can be an excuse for excessive delays before
any action is undertaken.) Often the process of coastal
management has fit Herman Daly's description of the development of a steady-state economy:

> The development of a steady-state economy will
> be the product of an unpredictable but conscious
> social evolution in which many ideas will be tried
> out. However, just as the auctioneer must begin by
> calling out some specific price, so it seems we must
> begin by calling out some specific notions about a
> steady-state economy, even though we know that
> they are no more likely to be the final solution than
> the auctioneer's initial price is.(30)

Strategy III: Experiment With New Analytical Tools

Partly because coastal management is relatively new in government, there is an opportunity to use the latest tools in
decision making. Three of these tools are Capability and
Suitability Analysis, Environmental Impact Statements, and
Mitigation.

Capability and suitability analysis

The Coastal Zone Management Act requires states to define
"what shall constitute permissible land uses and water uses
within the coastal zone. . . ."(31) The Office of Coastal Zone
Management had flexibility in issuing regulations to determine
if this requirement was met. It chose to emphasize the need
for states to make this definition after an analysis of the
carrying capacity of land and water, especially determining
those fragile areas that could not sustain development as well
as areas that would be capable of handling development without
damage to natural resources.(32)

Although the states handled this requirement in different
ways, New Hampshire can be cited as an example. That state
identified 15 types of resources ranging from erosion-prone
areas to historic districts, and then prepared legislation that
would avoid inappropriate development in such areas.(33) Not
only does the New Hampshire program protect resources, but
it provides predictability to developers because they can locate
in areas where their proposals will be more acceptable. The
New Jersey program has identified over 60 types of resources
proposed for protection in the coastal area. That state requires a developer to submit a map of the proposed development site indicating if any of these threatened resources are
involved and, if so, how they will be protected.(34) This
concept of planning on the basis of land capability is closely

related to the theme Ian McHarg developed in his book, <u>Design</u> <u>with Nature</u>.(35) He pointed out the futility of fighting nature by building on barrier beaches or in flood plains. He dramatically demonstrated that, despite man's many engineering innovations, nature usually dominates in the long run. The classic example of this concept is in Miami Beach where groins built to "protect" the beach hastened erosion.(36) By being required to conduct a suitability and capability analysis, the states have been encouraged to design with nature. Partly for this reason, the programs approved to date have stressed nonstructural approaches to erosion and flood hazard problems. This means, for example, that the issuance of permits will be weighted in favor of developments that propose to set buildings back from the water rather than developments which propose to build groins or sea walls for protection.

Environmental impact statements

The National Environmental Policy Act of 1969 requires the preparation of an environmental impact statement for all federal activities significantly affecting the environment.(37) Although impact statements have been greatly misused by government, they do present the opportunity to evaluate alternatives under full public scrutiny. The federal approval of state programs did not clearly require the preparation of impact statements. A key management decision was made to adopt the impact statement procedure as a tool for focusing public attention on state programs. It is a format well understood by the public, business, and special interest groups, and one responsive to public input. In particular, because realistic alternatives must be described and explanations given as to why they were not selected, the consideration of alternatives in this aspect of decision making has been strengthened. Furthermore, the no-growth or the no-action alternative is always considered. The impact statement process also focuses attention on projects in the early stages when adjustments can still be easily made.

Mitigation

Mitigation as a management tool is newer than many others and is possible only because of recent advances in engineering. Mitigation comes into play when it appears that the wisest management decision is to allow the destruction of a resource, perhaps to save a larger resource elsewhere, or because of the overwhelming social and economic benefit that could occur as a result. Mitigation requires that, as a form of compensation, the developer recreate elsewhere the resource that must be destroyed. An example is a port authority recreating a new park if an existing park must be used for port expansion. It may mean that a marina developer would be required to rehabilitate a polluted wetland in order to gain approval to expand his operation into another wetland. The Oregon Coastal Program has been in the forefront in requiring mitigation. It specifically requires that dredging and filling activities in marshes must be mitigated by the creation or restoration of another area of similar importance in order to ensure that the integrity of the estuarine system is maintained. (38)

Strategy IV: Evaluate and Adjust

The key management tool in a situation where action is required is to evaluate the program frequently and be willing to change direction, despite the difficulties this may cause for those trying to implement ever-changing guidelines. After the Office of Coastal Zone Management was established, guidance papers offering examples of procedures and concepts that could be adopted were issued to the states to help them develop their programs. In 1975, the office evaluated its progress and found that these guidelines were almost impossible to implement in most states as there was an anti-environmental mood in the legislatures. It was recognized that the program could hardly be considered successful if 32 states participated in the program for four years but at the end of that period none met the federal approval criteria. The office once more reviewed the Act and its legislative history and issued new regulations that were more balanced between environmental and developmental issues yet were still within the guidance of Congressional intent. The wording of the federal Act easily allowed for this, as can be seen in the first Congressional finding statement, "The Congress finds (a) that there is a national interest in the effective management, beneficial use, protection, and development of the coastal zone." (39) New mid-level managers were brought into the program who understood the necessity of setting priorities and spending more time and money with the states that had the most likelihood of meeting the approval criteria.

    To assure effective evaluation, the Administrator established an Office of Evaluation that was given equal status with the program offices. That office reports directly to the Administrator. It conducts annual performance evaluations of the state programs reviewing extensive written reports prepared by the states as well as conducting three to four day on-site reviews. A public hearing is held at each of these reviews to receive citizen comments. Also arranged are special meetings with affected interest groups. For example, the site evaluation in Massachusetts included a meeting with the state's official citizen advisory group and smaller meetings with electric company representatives and environmental groups.

Strategy V: Involve Nongovernmental Groups

Although public participation in governmental programs was well underway when it was mandated in the Coastal Zone Management Act in 1972, it has been practiced under the program in the belief that outside participation results in better programs. Because the public participation process has often been manipulated by the federal government, it is important to distinguish between government rhetoric and practice. One criterion of valid public involvement is the percentage of time the top manager spends with outside interest groups. An agency trying to give an appearance of openness and yet is not serious about acting on public input will be more likely to have a deputy whose major function is to appear to be interested, but who is, in fact, outside the decision-making loop. The Associate Administrator for Coastal Zone Management estimates that 15 percent of his time over the last seven years has been spent meeting with nongovernmental groups.(40)   A percentage much higher than this would indicate the official's noninvolvement in key office decisions, and a figure much less would indicate that the function of maintaining outside contacts had been delegated.

Public participation necessitates holding meetings, giving speeches, and answering questions before a wide variety of groups ranging from the National Association of Home Builders to the Gloucester Fishermen's Wives Association. These groups often do not "trust" a government agency's interpretation of how the agency's responsibilities match their needs. To counteract this suspicion, the office of Coastal Zone Management has awarded small contracts to some of these groups to enable them to investigate and evaluate coastal management from their own point of view. These contracts have two functions: they explain to the government official the interest group's modus operandi and what its felt needs are. The second function is to describe the coastal zone program to the group's membership and suggest to them how they can best have an impact upon their state program. To date, the following groups have prepared such studies: The American Institute of Architects, the National Association of Conservation Districts, the National Ocean Industries Association, the League of Women Voters, and the Natural Resources Defense Council.

In addition to making intermittent contacts with diverse nongovernmental groups, the office has developed continuous day-to-day involvement with the American Petroleum Institute, the Natural Resources Defense Council (one of the most active conservation groups in the country), and, to a lesser extent, with the Edison Electric Institute. Their input is considerably more detailed and specific than that of other nongovernmental groups. While another agency with a more closed attitude could see the involvement of these groups as too burdensome, the Office of Coastal Zone Management has considered such contacts to be extremely advantageous to the determination of management decisions. While the involvement of only one of these groups might be inappropriate, their often conflicting views tend to lead to better reasoned decisions. A typical example of the involvement of these groups can be cited in the adoption of agency regulations regarding state program approval issued in March 1979. Extensive comments were received on the draft regulations from the three groups. In response to the comments on the draft regulations, the Coastal Management staff met with many groups to discuss ways their comments could be incorporated into the final regulations. Over 50 percent of the time spent on such meetings was devoted to the three major groups listed above.(41) The entire effort of public involvement has not only resulted in substantial changes to the program but has served to educate public groups about differing advice the office receives. It also helps these special interest groups to understand better the point of view other groups bring to coastal management issues.(42)

The third major involvement of nongovernmental participants in the program has been in the use of consultants. Although it has been a minor part of the office budget, averaging less than $500,000 a year, consultants have been used to evaluate how states are doing on certain issues, such as coastal mapping or providing beach access, and have provided suggested changes in office operating procedures.

In addition to the involvement of groups and their representatives, the office is aware of the need to create, in the average American, an understanding of the unique nature of our coastlines and of the need for their special management. President Carter's announcement on August 4, 1979, that 1980 would be the "The Year of the Coast" resulted from the Office of Coastal Zone Management's attempt to raise this issue in the public consciousness.(43) When the public better understands the limited nature of the resources involved and the need for certain water-dependent developments to have a coastal site, the job of managing in a sustainable environment will be much easier.

The discussion above has concentrated on the federal agency actions. In addition, each state has used methods of involving citizens in the development of their programs. For example, before federal approval of the Massachusetts coastal program, the state staff met with over 2,000 citizens to discuss program development.(44)

Strategy VI: Involve All Levels of Government

There are few problems today that can be addressed at only one level of government, whether local, state, or federal.

Managing the coastline is not one. Local governments make the majority of decisions affecting the coastline by controlling zoning. State governments become involved through creating state parks, building sewage treatment plants, regulating wetlands, etc. The federal government is involved in setting clean air and water standards, using military bases along the coast, and encouraging increased mining of offshore oil and gas.

James Sundquist, in his book Making Federalism Work, concluded that the "effectiveness of the execution of federal programs depends crucially upon the competence of community institutions to plan, initiate and coordinate."(45) The need to avoid centralizing power in the federal government has been seen as an important aspect of managing in a sustainable society.(46) Many federal programs established in the early 1970s were designed to do just that: to build competence at the state and local level. In fact, the grant-in-aid program is considered to have been "revolutionized" during this period in its effort to strengthen the capacity of state and local governments.(47) Programs such as Coastal Zone Management stressed the necessity for states to build in-house capacity and not to conduct all their work through consultants. In return for building management capacity, the coastal program has rewarded states and local governments by practicing one of Sundquist's major recommendations: namely, "defer increasingly to local judgments."(48) Coastal management has practiced a policy of deference toward states that allows them to work within their unique constraints and advantages. The programs appropriately respond to local issues - e.g., earthquake hazards in California, hurricanes in the Gulf, beach access in the Northeast. The Office of Coastal Zone Management has not wanted the option of second guessing the states so long as general mandates set in the legislation have been followed.

The Coastal Zone Management Act requires states to assume a leadership role in land-use decisions that they may have delegated to local governments in the past. Congress specifically stated that the existing way of doing business was not adequate; that too many land uses of regional or national importance were being locked out of the coastline by local government and private decisions. To be eligible for program approval, the states have had to give assurance that certain land uses and/or natural resource sites that are defined in the program as nationally or regionally significant are not unreasonably excluded from the coastal area. Examples of such uses include power plants, sewage treatment facilities, and state or federal parks. While state determination on the location of these facilities is customarily seen as infringement on local rights, most states have been able to get local government agreement because, by taking the heat at the state level on these normally controversial issues, the pressure is taken off the local politician. State overview is also accepted because the state's power is limited to a few, well-defined uses and areas. This cooperation of state and local governments has been a useful experiment and, although limited, shows a way to manage significant resources and land uses when more than the local point of view must be considered. Such a regional view is certainly a key element in managing land uses in a sustainable society.

Strategy VII: Adopt An International Perspective

The office has practiced a management strategy which is very important in managing in a sustainable society; namely, sharing information with, and learning from experiences in, other countries. Australia, Japan, and Indonesia are launching coastal resource management efforts based in part on the lessons of the United States experience. The development of the Mediterranean Action Plan through United Nations efforts is an even more complex undertaking than what is being done in the United States, although it parallels the American effort. To address water pollution and other coastal issues in 16 countries, in a variety of languages, when some countries are almost at war with each other is, to say the least, challenging. Yet preliminary monitoring of these efforts indicates positive, on-the-ground results.(49)   The Office of Coastal Zone Management evaluates such international efforts, not only so that it does not "reinvent the wheel," but so that it can better address our own international coastal issues. These efforts are undertaken while avoiding the too frequent accusations of "boondoggle" associated with international research and meetings.

Other Management Strategies

There are, of course, other management strategies the office has used. One has been to develop an interdisciplinary staff. The merits of such an approach need no repetition here. Other rather unique characteristics of the program include the recruitment of a vast majority of the personnel from outside the federal government, assignment of managers to geographical areas in which they have not lived, responsiveness to and attempted development of congressional interest in coastal issues, and establishment of an extremely efficient information center on coastal issues.

CONDUCTING BUSINESS IN THE COASTAL ZONE

It may be useful to note here some of the implications of conducting business in the coastal zone. The first one is that it may take longer to get development permits because of the more sophisticated analysis process. This lengthened time almost always adds expense. The Office of Coastal Zone Management has offered financial incentives to states that will reduce the time of the regulatory process or simplify the system. New Jersey, for example, handles all their coastal permits in 90 days. The positive side to the development interests is added predictability of government decision making. State coastal programs identify critical environmental areas as well as areas where development is encouraged. It will be very difficult for a state to argue that a site should not be developed after it has indicated otherwise in its program.

A second implication is that when the state coastal program office finds certain projects appropriate it may play the role of facilitator for such developments. For example, the Massachusetts Coastal Agency helped the Fall River Port Authority through the labyrinth of permits it needed to conduct maintenance dredging, including finding suitable sites for disposal of the dredged material. The Maine Coastal Program has assisted the state to identify suitable sites for heavy industries, including refineries.

The third implication is the advisability of early private business interaction with state and local authorities. Before a site is purchased or financing irretrievably committed, it would be advantageous to discuss certain opportunities and constraints with the stated coastal agency. New Jersey specifically encourages this by establishing a preapplication conference with major developers before the formal coastal development permit is submitted. At that time, the developer is advised of the various issues which must be faced in the state regulatory process. Tenneco Company worked with the Northeast Coastal Programs early in their efforts to identify a location for a natural gas pipeline from Saint John, Canada, to Albany, New York. Using the mapped ecological data, it was possible to plan the route to avoid critical natural resource areas. In addition, these state agencies were able to provide front-end guidance to facilitate planning to meet permit requirements, thus reducing costly delays and design and construction changes later.

Another implication is that government can be used by businesses that are interested in accommodating their plans to endangered resources while not losing a competitive position. George Steiner cites the example of industry requesting public officials to establish antipollution standards that will then apply equally to all industries.(50)

CONCLUSION

Management in a sustainable society is going to involve managing complexity; not only in the interrelatedness of things, but in terms of conflicting goals. Coastal Zone Management was mandated to protect the environment <u>and</u> to encourage development - a double challenge of the <u>sort</u> that more and more governmental managers must face.(51) The old ways to manage, based on straightforward assembly line techniques, are not adequate to meet this challenge. Other management principles must be applied, tested, and refined. The lesson to be learned from managing the American coastline is that management of a sustainable society appears possible. The seven management strategies described here can serve as a first step for other governmental agencies to apply as they also initiate the transition to a more stable society.

NOTES

(1) Robert B. Ditton, John L. Seymour, and Gerald C. Swanson, <u>Coastal Resources Management</u> (Lexington, Mass.: Lexington Books, 1977), p. 176.

(2) U.S. Department of Commerce, <u>U.S. Ocean Policy in the 1970's: Status and Issues</u> (Washington, D.C.: Government Printing Office, 1978), p. II-4.

(3) U.S. Council on Environmental Quality, <u>Oil and Gas in Coastal Lands and Waters</u> (Washington, D.C.: Government Printing Office, 1977), p. iii.

(4) American Petroleum Institute, "A Shore for All Purposes" (Washington, 1978) p. 1.

(5) U.S. Congress. Senate Committee on Commerce, <u>The Economic Value of Ocean Resources to the United States</u>, by Nathan Associates (Washington, D.C.: Government Printing Office, 1974), p. 63.

(6) U.S. Department of the Army, Corps of Engineers, <u>Report on the National Shoreline Study</u> (Washington, D.C.: Government Printing Office, 1971), p. 31.

(7) Harlan Cleveland and Thomas W. Wilson, Jr., "Humangrowth" (Princeton, N.J.: Aspen Institute for Humanistic Studies, 1978), p. 31.

(8) Eugene P. Odum, "The Emergence Of Ecology as a New Integrative Discipline," <u>Science</u> 195 (March 1977): 1291.

(9) Statistics in this paragraph, unless otherwise noted, are from Elinor Lander Horowitz, "Our Nation's Wetlands: An Interagency Task Force Report," U.S. Council on Environmental Quality (Washington, D.C.: Government Printing Office, 1978).

242   QUEST FOR A SUSTAINABLE SOCIETY

(10) John Clark, Coastal Ecosystems: Ecological Considerations for Management of the Coastal Zone (Washington,
D.C.: The Conservation Foundation, 1974), p. 69.
(11) Douglas L. Inman and Birchard M. Brush, "The Coastal
Challenge," Science 181 (July 6, 1973): 20.
(12) Report on the National Shoreline Study p. 31.
(13) John H. Ryther, "Photosynthesis and Fish Production in
the Sea," Science 166 (Oct. 3, 1969): 720.
(14) Anne W. Simon, The Thin Edge: Coast and Man in
Crisis (New York: Harper & Row, 1978), p. 26.
(15) Larry Booda, "The Oceans in Our Future," The Futurist
11 (4) (August 1977): 233.
(16) Natural Resources Defense Council, "Who's Minding the
Shore?" (Washington, D.C.: Office of Coastal Zone
Management, 1976), p. 1.
(17) Report of the National Shoreline Study, p. 31.
(18) National Academy of Sciences, National Research Council,
Maritime Transportation Research Board, Panel on Future
Port Requirements of the United States, Port Development
in the United States (Washington, D.C.: National Academy of Sciences, 1976), p. 128.
(19) Katherine Gillman, Oil and Gas in Coastal Lands and
Waters, U.S. Council on Environmental Quality (Washington, D.C.: Government Printing Office, 1977), p.
152.
(20) Public Law No. 92-583, 86 Stat. 1280.
(21) U.S. Department of the Interior, The National Estuarine
Pollution Study (Washington, D.C.: Government Printing
Office, 1969); Report of the Commission on Marine
Science, Engineering, and Resources to the President of
the United States and the U.S. Congress, Our Nation and
the Sea: A Plan for National Action (Washington, D.C.:
Government Printing Office, 1969).
(22) National Governor's Conference, "Resolutions" (July
1979).
(23) William I. Reilly, "Coastal Zone Management: A Bold
Experiment," Coastal Zone '78 (New York: American
Society of Civil Engineers, 1979), Vol. 4, p. 2445.
(24) J.R. Jackson, Jr., "Issues in Coastal Zone Management:
The Petroleum Industry View" (Remarks delivered to
Coastal States Organization Conference, Fredericksburg,
Va., Jan. 29, 1979).
(25) Letter dated July 10, 1979, from Juanita M. Kreps,
Secretary of Commerce, to Ingrid W. Reed.
(26) Cleveland and Wilson "Humangrowth," p. 31.
(27) Interview with Robert W. Knecht, Associate Administrator, Office of Coastal Zone Management, August 3,
1979.
(28) Harlan Cleveland, The Future Executive (New York:
Harper & Row, 1972), p. 29.

(29) Ibid., p. 85.
(30) Herman Daly, ed., Towards a Steady-State Economy (San Francisco: W.H. Freeman, 1973), p. vii.
(31) Subsection 305(b) (2).
(32) Ditton et al., in Coastal Resource Management, p. 176, pointed out that lack of specificity in such an analysis leads to negative results.
(33) New Hampshire Office of Comprehensive Planning, New Hampshire Coastal Resources Management Program (1968), Appendix 5.
(34) New Jersey Department of Environmental Protection, New Jersey Coastal Management Program: Bay and Ocean Shore Segment (August 1968), pp. 27-163.
(35) Ian McHarg, Design with Nature (Garden City, N.Y.: Natural History Press, 1969).
(36) "Costly Facelift for an Old Resort," Time (Aug. 13, 1979): 52.
(37) 42 U.S.C. #44321 et seq.
(38) Oregon Land Conservation and Development Commission, "Guidelines," Goal 16.
(39) Subsection 302.
(40) Knecht interview.
(41) Interview with Carol Sondheimer, Acting Chief, Policy and Program Evaluation, August 16, 1979.
(42) In a study of the U.S. Corps of Engineers entitled Can Organizations Change? (Washington, D.C.: The Brookings Institution, 1979), Daniel Mazmaniam and Jeanne Nienaber concluded that an open decision-making process is one of four factors indicating the ability of an organization to change (p. 6).
(43) U.S. Office of the President, "President's Environmental Message" (August 3, 1979).
(44) Massachusetts Executive Office of Environmental Affairs, Massachusetts Coastal Zone Management Program (1978), p. 123.
(45) James L. Sundquist, Making Federalism Work (Washington, D.C.: The Brookings Institution, 1969), p. 243.
(46) See Dennis L. Meadows's statement before the Subcommittee on Fisheries and Wildlife Conservation and the Environment of the Committee on Merchant Marine and Fisheries, U.S. House of Representatives, 93d Congress, in Growth and Its Implications for the Future, Part 1 (May 1, 1973), p. 8.
(47) Leigh E. Grosenick, ed., The Administration of the New Federalism (Washington, D.C.: American Society for Public Administration, 1973), p. 1. See also David B. Walker, "How Fares Federalism in the Mid-Seventies," American Academy of Political and Social Science, The Annals 416 (November 1974): 17.
(48) Sundquist, Making Federalism Work, p. 243.

(49) U.N. Environment Programme, Mediterranean Action Plan (Geneva, Switzerland: UNEP, 1978). See also Seyom Brown et al., New Regimes for the Ocean, Outer Space and Weather (Washington, D.C.: The Brookings Institutuion, 1978).

(50) George Steiner, "The Second Managerial Revolution," in Business and Environment (Washington, D.C.: The Conservation Foundation, 1977), p. 420.

(51) Robert Dorfman, "An Afterword: Humane Values and Environmental Decisions," in When Values Conflict, edited by Laurence H. Tribe, Corrine S. Schelling, and John Voss (Cambridge, Mass.: Ballinger, for the American Academy of Arts and Sciences, 1976), pp. 172-73, succinctly describes the difficulties of measuring and applying environmental values in decision making.

Index

ABSCAM, 5
Active research groups, 65
Adaptation, nature, 218-219
African tribes, ethnic identity, 23
Agrarian Era, 72, 75, 76
Agricultural Revolution of Europe, 72
Agriculture. See Food production
Alcohol-powered car, 5
Amazonia, 16
American Petroleum Institute, 231, 236
Animals, indigenous. See Gazelle
Antarctica, mineral wealth of, 83
Apocalypse, 85
Art as instrument of change, 98
Australian aborigines, 23
Automation, 76, 77
Authoritarianism, 7, 76, 146

Balance, concept of, 149-150
Bahr, H., 115
Bassham, J.A., 34, 35
Battlestar Galactica, 89
Biogeochemical cycles, 14, 16, 190-194
Bioresources, 4

Biotechnology, 4, 5, 6, 8
Biomass, 32, 34, 35, 37, 40, 42
  and by-products, 43
  energy market, 49
  fuels, 43-44, 47, 48, 50
  home-use, 46
  infrastructure, 46, 47
  production, 46, 49
  profitability of, 48
Bio-Solar Research and Development Corporation, 47
Black-box structure, 15
Black Power radicals, 23
Blake, Judith, 114
Bohrow, Davis, 24
Bolton, J.R., 34, 39
Boulding, Kenneth, 25
Brine, 82, 83
Britain. See Research Requirement Boards
British paradox, 55
British Post Office, 77
Bronfenbrenner, Urie, 108, 110, 115
Browning, J. A., 13
Budgeted Nonfinancial Objectives (BNFOS), 175
Bunyan, Paul, 93
Burris, Mary Ellen, 104, 105
Butterfly (Lycaena dispar), 26

Campbell, Angus, 106, 108, 109, 111

Campbell, Joseph, 96

Capital-intensive industries, 165

Capitalism, 20, 155, 203

Carbon dioxide, 41, 42, 50, 191-192

Carneiro, Robert, 72

Carter, President Jimmy, 237

Catch-22, 44

Cavalli-Sforza, L. L., 19

Central Policy Review Staff, 56

CERN (European nuclear family in Geneva), 61

Change, 1, 2, 8, 198
in economy, 79
environmental, 16
in political organization, 153
resistance to, in business, 165, 169
scientific, 64-65
social, 95
in society, rate of, 80
technological, 66, 71

Chemical engineering, origins of, in Germany, 65

Children, 103, 104, 108, 118-119
abuse of, 104-105, 116
basic needs of, 109
educating, 80
future of, 113, 120-121
quality of life, 115, 117, 118, 119

Christianity, 145, 157

China
and art, 98
Coca-Cola in, 19
and non-chemical pest controls, 134

Civilization, 128

Civilization, ancient, 75, 85

Cleveland, Harlan, 103, 104, 226, 231, 232

Coal, 42, 44, 82

Coal mines, automated, 83

Coastal Resources Management, 225

Coastal Zone Management Act of 1972, 229, 230, 231, 233, 236, 238

Communicative Era, 74-76, 84, 85

Communism, 20

Computer, 76, 77, 83
couples systems, 83
as metatechnology, 73
microprocessor, 76
revolution, 18

Concept Building Activities, 196

Consumers, 170-172, 175

Contextual map, 199

Corporate Energy Giants, 45

Counterculture, visible, 101

Credit-based economy, 78

Crops, 16-17, 33, 35, 134

Cultural centers, 93-97, 99, 100

Cultural variability, 16-19, 27

Culture, 148
diversity, 18-19, 25, 27
low saliency, 157
"poison", 111, 114
revolutionize, 95
sensate, 157-158, 159
vitalization of world, 160

Customer-contractor principle, 56-57, 62-63

Dahrendorf, R., 67

Daly, Herman, 25, 233

Dark Ages, 72

Decision making, cultural, 194, 200, 204-205

Decision-making process, 187, 188, 189

Deforestation, 40, 42, 127, 136

Department of Industry (Britain), 57, 58

Desert, 82, 83

Desertification, 211, 212, 219, 220, 222

Design With Nature, 234

Distribution of income, 202

Ditton, Robert 225

DNA, 17, 130

Doomsday Has Been Cancelled, 91
Double-bond, 155-156, 157, 159
Dow Chemical Company, 167
Drugs, origin of modern, 16
Durkheim, Emile, 160
Dust Bowl era, 131

Ecollage, 185-186, 196
Ecologic, 185-186, 200
Ecological diversity, 198
Ecological literacy, 185, 190, 195
Ecological Model, 190, 194, 195-196
Ecological world view, 184, 188
Economy, 148, 203
  dominant, 155
  growth of, 84
  high saliency of, 155
  interactions, 71
  nature's, 27
  reduction of, 159
  spaceship, 25
  of world, 154
Ecoresponse, 186, 204
Ecosystem, 8, 14, 15, 16
  definition of, 28 n. 1
  destruction of, 127-128
  education, 196, 199, 203, 206
  health indicators, 195-196
  preservation, 92
  recycling, 92
  values, 184
Education, 80-81, 161, 183-184
  higher and democracy, 75-76
  massive expansion of, 81
  overhaul in '80's, 84
  public, 27, 120
Einstein, Albert, 186
Eliot, T. S., 57
Emlen, Arthur, 104
Engineering Board, 61
ENIAC, 76
Electricity, production of, 40
Electromagnetic spectrum industries, 4
Electronics, 8
  data systems, home-based, 75
  polling techniques, 76
  Revolution, 73

Emission control devices, 42
Energy
  chemical, store, 32
  efficiency, 35, 37, 167, 168
  geothermal, 82, 125
  market, 32, 33, 42
  oceanic, 82
  problems of U.S., 20
  from recycled paper, 40
  solar, 32, 34
  storage, efficiency of, 34
  technologies, 20
Entropy, 79
Environment, deterioration of, 17
Environment, primary, 1, 2
Equilibrium, dynamic, 92
Equitable relationship, 1
Erickson, Erik, 115
Europe, business labor in, 176
Eutrophication, 133
Evolution
  battle of, 16
  cultural, 19, 71, 72
  ecological, 198
  mechanics of, 70
  speciation process, 26
Extinction of insects, 21

Family, 104, 105, 109, 110, 118
  decline of American, 113
  impact analysis concept, 120
  priorities, 121
  support systems, 112, 113, 117
Farmer, 49, 79, 138
  Amish, 132-133
  organic, 134
Farming, 131-132, 133
  bacteria, 5
  mechanized, 130
  traditional, 133, 137
Federal Coastal Zone Management Program, 226.
  See Also Coastal Zone Management Act of 1972
Feldman, M. W., 19
Fertilizers, 133, 137
Fisheries, world, 128
Fission process, 195

Food
  distribution, 91
  fermentation, 5
  needs of future, 136
  production, 126, 127, 128, 131, 138
  single-cell protein, 82
  supply, 125, 126, 130, 135-136
  system, present, 129
Forestland, 34, 40, 42
  conversion efficiency, 35
  decline of, 48
  owners and biomass, 45
  profitability of, 49
  U.S. and energy production of, 40
Fossel fuels, 41, 42, 48, 125, 130, 133, 195
Francophones, 23
Frankenstein monster, 74
Freud, Sigmund, 93, 118
Fuels for Biomass Programs, 45
Fuel,
  biomass, 32, 33, 34, 41
  generation reaction, 34
  oil, high-sulphur, 42
  utilization of, 50
Fusion energy, 82
Future shock, 80

Gazelle, experiments with, 213-218
General Motors, job structuring, 175
Genetics, 18
  diversity, 18, 22, 26
  engineering, future, 99
  mutation, random, 26
  variability, 16, 18, 125, 130, 135
Geographic mobility, 113
Gerontocracy of Soviet Union, 75
Global society, 81, 84
GNP, 4, 154
Good Life, 103, 105-106, 108, 110, 113-116
Good Society, 103
Gorilla mothers, 105

Grandmothers, computerized, 80
Grants, concentration of, 61
Great Depression, 203
Green Revolution, 17, 126, 137
Growth,
  of British industry, 53-54
  curve, 150, 152
  decline in Britain, 60
  excessive, 145-156, 160
  history of industrialized world, 50
  and human beings, 53-54
  human spirit, 102
  law of, 150, 152
  limitations of, 147, 158, 159
  macrocontrols on, 146
  of nation-states, 154
  natural, 90, 92
  policy debate, 119
  policies, U.S., 3
  as quantitative product, 103, 104
  rates of countries, 147
  reduction in West, 8
  unsustainable, 149, 150
  of world power, 155, 156

Hamilton, Alexander, 158, 159
Heat rejection, 42
Heirlooms, 7
Hellmers, Henry, 35
Hero-myths, 96, 97
Hildebrandt, A. F. 37
Holdren, John, 20
Hominids, 70
Homo sapiens, 17, 18, 23, 26, 27
Horizontal problems, 2
Howard, Jane, 112
Human, 93, 94, 111
  ancestors, 71
  beings, 7, 19, 90
  cultural diversity, 22
  culture, foundation of, 70
  development, 7
  diversity, fear of loss, 28
  experience, 107-108
  gene pool, 18
  needs, basic, 6, 8, 164, 108

Human, (continued)
  psyche, 71
  quality, 106
  resource, 101, 103, 104, 138,
    173
Hydrogen gas, 37
Hydrogen liquid, storage of,
  42
Hydrogen, production of, 39

Ideas, new order of, 98, 99,
  100
Industrial ethos, 67
Industrial research strategy,
  66-67
Industrial Revolution, 73, 75,
  85, 151, 155
Industrialized society, goals
  of, 53-54
Information
  communication growth, 6
  economy, 79
  and knowledge, 5
  operatives, 78
  organization of, 188
  Revolution, 73
  as resource, 4
  society, 5, 84
  technology and job displace-
    ment, 78
Infrastructures, 45-46, 47
Insolation, 37, 48
Integrated control, 134
International Paper Company,
  175
International Year of the Child,
  103
Iran, 23, 25
Islandia, 106, 107, 108, 110
Issues, nonmaterial, 7

Jefferson, Thomas, 158, 159
Johnston, W. D., Jr., 39
Justice, quality of, 6

Kahn, Alfred, 118
Kammerman, Sheila, 118
Knowledge, 79, 80.
  See also Information
Kondriatieff upswing, Fifth, 67

Kondratieffs, 156, 203
Kromkowski, J., 116
Kubrick, Stanley, 90
Kuhn, Thomas, 64
Kuznets cycles, 203

Labor, 76, 77, 78, 81
Lamarckian heresy, 71
Land ownership patterns, 48
Land-use system, 219, 220-
  221, 222-223
Language, 19, 70
Law of System Maintenance,
  202, 203
Law of the Sea Agreement, 228
Levi-Strauss, Claude, 148, 149
Life span, prolonged, 99
Life-support systems, 27
Locomotive, 73
Louisiana fuel farm, study of,
  47
Lovins, Armory, 20

Maine Coastal Program, 240
Making Federalism Work, 238
Malthusian nightmare, 75, 85
Manganese nodules, 82, 228
Marketing concept, 169-170,
  171, 173, 175
Maslow, Abe, 105, 204
Massachusetts Coastal Agency,
  240
Material goods, expendable, 7
Materialism, 103, 105, 110,
  119, 120, 121
Meadow, D. L., 146
Mechanical Era, 73, 74, 84, 85
Mechanical society, paradigm
  of, 76
Medical technology, 83
Medicine, modern, and Third
  World, 76
Medicine, shift to preventive,
  99
Mediterranean Action Plan, 239
Mercantilism, 74, 151
Metatechnology, 73, 78
Microbiological industry, 5
Microelectronics, 76, 77
Microwave power, 39

Middle Ages, 73
Military technology, 74
Mitigation, 234-235
MNCs (multinational corporations), 178
Model T Ford, 66
Morris, Desmond, 104
Moslems, 23, 152
Motivations of scientists and engineers, 63, 64, 68
Mumford, Lewis, 160

Nation-state, 74, 146-148, 153, 154, 155-159
National Engineering Laboratory, 57
National Environmental Policy Act of 1969, 234
National Oceanic and Atmospheric Administration, 232
National Physical Laboratory, 57
National Science Foundation, 213
Natural Estuarine Pollution Study, 229
Natural gas, 44, 45-46, 47
Neighborhoods, 116-117, 118, 119, 120
Neolithic Revolution, 71, 72
New England, plants using biomass, 47
New Hampshire Coastal Program, 233
New Jersey Coastal Research Program, 233, 240
New Mexico, Sandis Laboratory, 37
Niches, 14, 15, 198
Nippon Steel Company, 83
Nitrogen, 14, 130, 133
Northeast Coastal Program, 240
Nuclear,
 Armageddon, 23
 energy, 26, 42, 82
 fusion, 125
 missile technology, 74
 Physics Board in Britain, 61
 physics, dean of, 85
 war, 160
 weapons, 25, 74, 159

Ocean, fixed resource, 226
Ocean power, 124
Odum, Eugene, 226
Office of Coastal Zone Management, 230-233, 235, 237, 240
Office of Evaluation, 235
Oil
 crisis, Arab-induced, 82
 crude, 40
 drilling for, 82
 in North Sea, 82
 supply, America's, 229
Ophuls, William, 146
Optical fibers, 82
Organisms, 14
 microorganisms, 5
 sexually-reproducing, 17
 snail-darter, 27
Orbit, geosynchronous, 39
Oregon Coastal Program, 235
Orwell, George, 76
Ottoman conquest of Europe, 152
Our Nation and the Sea, 230

Paper products, recycling, 40
Paragenetics, 70
Park and wilderness in U.S., 24-25
Parsons, Talcott, 174
Peer-review system, 66
Pentagon papers, 5
People's Republic of China, 19
Perroux, Francois, 155
Pest control, 134, 135, 137
Petroleum, 131
Photoelectric system, 39, 40
Photosynthesis, 34, 35, 39, 41
 binding process, 14
 efficiency, 130
 enhancement, 5
 systems, 35
Photovoltaic cells, 39
Political systems, sustainable, 24
Politics, 148
 high saliency, 152, 153-154
 reduction of, 159
Pollution, water, 228, 239
Polymer chemistry, 61

Population
declines, 130
explosion and Third World, 76, 83
growth, 124, 126, 129, 136
resources outstripping, 75
shift in, 48
of solar system, 91
U. S., 2-3
Portugal, 154, 155, 157
Postindustrial society, 78-79, 80
Poverty, 109, 110, 111, 126
Power loom, 73
Preservation of biological diversity, 20-21
Preserves, biological, 21, 22
PRESTEL information-communications system, 77
Production, sustainable, 33
Products, resource-responsible, 170, 171, 172
Prometheus, 71
Proposition 13, world-wide, 159
Protein development, single-cell, 5
Public services, 13-14
Pulpwood, 49

Racial stereotyping, 7
Rain forest, Amazonian, 22
Raven, Peter H., 25
Reaction, fuel-generation, 34
Reaction, one-electron oxidation-reduction, 34
Recycling materials, 195
Redistribution of wealth, 24
Reductionist Model, 200
Reformation, 157
Refuse processing and biomass, 42-43
Reilly, William, 231
Religion, 160
Renaissance, 73, 101, 151
Research and development, 67, 81, 84, 156
Research Requirement Boards in Britain, 58-59, 60, 66, 69 n. 12
Research stations, cultural, 22

Resources
on coastline, 227, 228
conservation, 166, 167, 172-174, 176
consumption of, 2
control, 202
expandable, 4
metal, 178
nonrenewable, 81, 131
natural, exploitation of, 50
production of, 125
renewable, 111
Robegate concept, 77
Robot, 76-77
Rogers, Carl, 105
Roosevelt, Theodore, 221
Rostow, W. W., 67
Rothschild, Lord, 56, 57, 58, 60, 62
Regulations, government, 177-178, 179, 180, 202
Rural development, 136, 138
Rutherford, Lord, 85, n. 2

Sahel, 211
Sanger, Margaret, 110
School size, 118, 119
Schumpeter, J., 66
Science, 73, 145-146
Science Research Council (SRC) in Britain, 57, 60, 61, 62, 63
Selectivity and concentration, policy of, 60-61, 62
Sexes, equalization of, 161
Seymour, John L., 225
Silviculture, 34, 35, 44, 45, 48, 49
Sinclair, Sir John, 106
Social impoverishment, 109-110, 111, 113, 119
Slavery, 72, 74-75
Social pluralism, 113, 119
Social responsibility offices, 166, 167, 173
Societal System Model, 201
Society, idealized, 124-125
Soil protection, 131-132, 133
Solar energy, 5, 83
cost factors of fuel systems, 43

Solar energy, (continued)
  on farms, 32
  fuel conversion, 39
  Power Tower Concept, 37, 40
  space power system, 42
  system, 91
  thermal systems, 35-36
  in U.S., renewable power, 82
Sorokin, Pitirim, 157
Soviet Union, political changes
  in, 75
Soviet Union, child care, 111
Space, conquest of, 91, 92
Space operas, 89-90
Speciation process, 26
Species diversity, 14, 17, 21,
  26
Spurr, S. H., 34
Star Wars, 89
State as institution, 72
Statistical Account of Scotland,
  106
Steady-state, 24, 25, 27, 92,
  93, 98, 186, 233
Steam engine, 73
Steiner, George, 240
Strowgear, electromechanical,
  77
Structures, invariance of, 161
Sundquist, James, 238
Survival, 8, 13, 25, 72, 81
  and greed, 94
  human, 102
  of land and resources, 211
  and values, 206
Swanson, Gerald, C., 225
Sweetener, corn, 5
Systems
  biological, 32
  botanical, 32
  concrete, 198, 199, 203
  cultural, 203, 206
  Training Workshop, 189

Talbot, L. M., 218
Talbot, M. H., 218
Tassaday of Philippines, 19,
  27
Technocracy, modern, 100

Technology
  ambivilence about, 90
  beginnings of, 70
  benefits of, 106
  determinism, 67
  diversity, 19-20, 27
  innovation, 66
  shifts, 4
  world view of, 183, 187, 188
Television, manufacture of, 77
Tenneco Company, 240
Texas, wood products indus-
  tries in, 48
Thermonuclear pile, 85 n. 2
Thermonuclear war, 18, 125,
  159
Third World, 76, 83-84, 85, 98
Toffler, Alvin, 80
Transformation, inputs and
  outputs, 166-167, 169-170
Transportation, 26, 117
Tree-farming. See Silviculture
Trophic levels, 14-15
Tropical forests, source ma-
  terials in, 16
Tucker, Sophie, 110
Turkey, "miracle strain" in, 17
Twain, Mark, 226

United Auto Workers Union,
  175
United Kingdom, changes in,
  53-54
United Nations Conference of
  Desertification, 211
United Nations Food and Agriculture Organization, 126
United States
  business, 165, 168
  childlessness in, 114
  energy consumption, 40
  farming in, 131-132
  food resources, 127
  population, 2
  position in world, 148
  regionalism, 27
  regional tests for biomass, 47
  transport mix, 27
  wood source, major, 47

United States Census Bureau, 120
United States Department of Agriculture, 131
United States of Europe, 84

Vajk, J. Peter, 91
Values, 35, 97
 basic, 94
 changes, 8
 and future, 89, 90, 93, 94-95, 98
 hierarchy of, 206
 Model, 205-206
 sources of, 204
 shifts in industrialized countries, 7
 systems, ecological, 177
Vaux, H. J., 34, 35
Venice monopoly, 152
Vessels, cryonic, 37
Volkswagen, alcohol-powered, 5

Wagner's Law, 154
War
 global, 147, 153, 156, 159
 as institution, 72, 74
 technology of, 75
Waste wood, utilizing, 46, 47
Wastes, utilization of, 82
Water resources, 128
Welfare state, 53
Western
 civilization, fate of, 27
 Europe, island of peace, 74
 societies, 8, 78, 84
 thought, 89, 90
Westernization, rejection of, 23
Westernization of world, 19
Wind energy, 82
Whorf, Benjamin Lee, 19
Whorfian hypothesis, 19
Wilson, Thomas, 226, 231
Wood products industries, 45, 46, 48, 49
Work, trend toward, 7
Worker satisfaction, 173-176
Working mothers, 115, 117

World
 culture, 23, 160
 economy, 154
 politics, 147, 153-154, 161
 power, 155, 156
 system, 146, 147, 157-160
 view, one, 19
Wright, Austin Tappan, 106, 107-108, 110

Xenophobia, 28

·Year of the Coast, The, 237

Zigler, Edward, 110
Zoos, cultural, 21, 22

About the Editor

JAMES C. COOMER is an Associate Professor in Public Affairs and the former Chairman of the Studies of the Future program at the University of Houston/Clear Lake campus. He holds a B.A. degree from Carson-Newman College and a Ph.D. in political science from the University of Tennessee. His professional interests are the social and political consequences of rapid change in the society: where to look for them and how to plan for them. Since 1975, he has been closely associated with the biennial Woodlands Conferences on Growth Policy held in Houston, Texas. He has held workshops on the future of energy in the U.S.; the future of work and education in the U.S.; and he has edited a special edition of the Appalachian Business Review on the future of health care in the U.S. He has contributed to such journals as Futures, The Futurist, Long-Range Planning, and the Journal of Political Science.

255

About the Contributors

ROBERT CHIANESE is Professor of English at California State University, Northridge, and director of the NEH Liberal Arts Project there. His background includes study in engineering, art, and economics, with doctoral work on the relationships of British art of the nineteenth century to social change. He has published an anthology of utopian literature entitled <u>Peaceable Kingdoms</u> (Harcourt, Brace, Jovanovich, 1971). His current interests include the formulation of a new, emerging order of ideas, the revision and creation of mythologies for the future, and the development of teaching strategies and media to reach wide audiences.

EDWARD T. CLARK, JR. is Professor of Environmental Education and Associate Director of the Institute for Environmental Awareness at George Williams College, Downers Grove, Illinois. An academic generalist, his current work focuses on the development of holographic information systems based on an integration of ecological and cultural contexts; and the utilization of these information systems in economic, political, and social planning and decision making.

W. JOHN COLETTA is presently Program Coordinator for the Institute for Environmental Awareness, George Williams College, Downers Grove, Illinois. He is actively involved in designing curricula materials for teaching ecological and general systems theory to students, professionals, and the lay public. His activity is directed toward the goal of an ecologically literate citizenry. His present research interests include the identification of the nature and structure of cultural transformations and the underlying perceptual and philosophical foundations of such change.

KATHRYN COUSINS is the North Atlantic Regional Manager, Office of Coastal Zone Management, of the U.S. Department of Commerce. She holds an MPA degree in urban planning from The George Washington University and is a member of the American Institute of Certified Planners. Her present administrative and research interests are in the area of land use planning.

ANNE H. EHRLICH is a senior research associate in biology at Stanford University. For over twenty years she has been involved in both biological research and in policy research on the human predicament. She has published five books in collaboration with her husband Paul and others, as well as dozens of articles on both biological and policy topics. Among the books is the standard treatise on environmental problems, Ecoscience: Population, Resources, Environment, written with Paul Ehrlich and John P. Holdren of the University of California at Berkeley (Freeman and Co., 1977).

PAUL R. EHRLICH is Bing Professor of Population Studies and Professor of Biological Sciences at Stanford University. An evolutionist, he studies the genetics and ecology of natural populations of insects, plants, and fishes; and, with his wife Anne, does policy research on the population-resources-environment crises. Professor Ehrlich is author or coauthor of some 20 books and more than 200 scientific papers and popular articles. His most recent book, coauthored with Anne Ehrlich and historian Loy Bilderback, is The Golden Door: International Migration, Mexico and the United States (Ballantine, 1979).

ARTHUR A. FEW, JR. is an Associate Professor with a joint appointment in the Departments of Space Physics and Environmental Science at Rice University. His primary area of teaching is in atmospheric science and his research is in Thunderstorm Electricity. He has recently devoted an increasing amount of his research energies to solar energy conversion theory and biomass energy. His Mitchell Prize paper, "Social, Environmental, and Economic Implications of Widespread Conversion to Biomass-based Fuels" is the product of his new aspect of his research interests.

JAMES GARBARINO is currently Associate Professor of Human Development at The Pennsylvania State University, after having been a Fellow and Project Director at the Center for the Study of Youth Development at Boys Town. He received his Ph.D. in Human Development and Family Studies from Cornell University in 1973. Garbarino's major interest is the family support systems and social policy. His work has led to two books and more than forty published articles and book

chapters. In 1975 he was named a Spencer Fellow by the
National Academy of Education.

MICHAEL GIBBONS was born in Montreal, Quebec, where he
obtained degrees in science and engineering from Loyola
College and McGill University respectively. In 1967 he received a doctorate in theoretical physics from Manchester
University where he is now Professor and Head of Department
of Liberal Studies in Science. In 1974 he was appointed a
specialist advisor to the Parliamentary Select Committee on
Science and Technology when it was exploring problems of
scientific relations between the universities and industry. He
has published widely in the area of science and technology
policy and has written books in the fields of technology assessment and technological innovation.

DAVID HOPCRAFT is a third generation Kenyan who attended
London University and Berea College, with a U.S. Government
Scholarship, studying Animal Science and Agriculture. He
concentrated on Wildlife sciences in postgraduate studies at
Cornell University with a fellowship from the United Nations.
His research for a Ph.D. compared Natural and Human systems
of Land use, and was supported by the National Science
Foundation. The findings, published in various scientific
journals, form the basis for the on-going game ranch. Re-
search and demonstration aspects of this are supported by the
Lilly Endowment through Cornell University.

GEORGE MODELSKI is Professor of Political Science at the
University of Washington. He is the author of A Theory of
Foreign Policy (Praeger, 1962), and Principles of World Politics
(Free Press, 1972); and editor of Transnational Corporations
and World Order (W. H. Freeman, 1979).

TOM STONIER received his A.B. from Drew University and his
M.S. and Ph.D. from Yale University. He is presently Head,
the School of Science and Society at Bradford University in
England. The function of the School is to study the interaction of Science, Technology and Society. Professor Stonier
is the author of Nuclear Disaster, about 40 technical papers on
cell physiology, and several dozen general papers relating
primarily to the impact of science and technology on contemporary society.

DILLARD B. TINSLEY received an electrical engineering
degree from Southern Methodist University and spent ten years
in the aerospace industry with Ling-Tempco-Vaught and
Hughes Aircraft. After receiving a master's degree in economics from the University of Texas at Arlington, he earned
his Doctor of Business Administration from Texas Tech Uni-

versity. At the present time, he is Associate Professor in Management and Marketing at Stephen F. Austin University. He is widely published in professional magazines and in scholarly journals. Teaching courses in business policy and marketing management, Professor Tinsley is concerned with the interactions of business and society. His recent grants for research involve technological innovation, values in business, and business utilization of Mexican Americans.